THE UPPER ROO

Disciplines

2023

UPPER
ROOM BOOKS®
NASHVILLE

An Outline for Small-Group Use of *Disciplines*

Here is a simple plan for a one-hour, weekly group meeting based on reading *The Upper Room Disciplines*. One person may act as convener every week, or the role can rotate among group members. You may want to light a white Christ candle each week to signal the beginning of your time together.

Opening

Convener: Let us come into the presence of God.

Others: Lord Jesus Christ, thank you for being with us. Help us hear your word to us as we speak to one another.

Scripture

Convener reads the scripture suggested for that day in *Disciplines*. After a one- or two-minute silence, convener asks: What did you hear God saying to you in this passage? What response does this call for? (Group members respond in turn or as led.)

Reflection

- What scripture passage(s) and meditation(s) from this week was (were) particularly meaningful for you? Why? (Group members respond in turn or as led.)
- What actions were you nudged to take in response to the week's meditations? (Group members respond in turn or as led.)
- Where were you challenged in your discipleship this week? How did you respond to the challenge? (Group members respond in turn or as led.)

Praying together

Convener says: Based on today's discussion, what people and situations do you want us to pray for now and in the coming week? Convener or other volunteer then prays about the concerns named.

Departing

Convener says: Let us go in peace to serve God and our neighbors in all that we do.

Adapted from *The Upper Room* daily devotional guide, January–February 2001. © 2000 The Upper Room. Used by permission.

THE UPPER ROOM DISCIPLINES 2023

Upper Room Books® website: upperroombooks.com
Cover design: Left Coast Design, Portland, Oregon
Cover photo: Shutterstock.com

At the time of publication all websites referenced in this book were valid. However, due to the fluid nature of the internet some addresses may have changed, or the content may no longer be relevant.

Revised Common Lectionary copyright © 1992 Consultation on Common Texts. Used by permission.

Scripture quotations not otherwise identified are from the New Revised Standard Version Bible © 1989, Division of Christian Education of the National Council of the Churches of Christ in the United States of America. Used by permission. All rights reserved.

Scripture quotations marked CEB are from the Common English Bible. Copyright © 2010 Common English Bible. Used by permission.

Scripture quotations marked KJV are from the King James Version of the Bible.

Scripture quotations marked NIV are from the Holy Bible, New International Version®, NIV®. Copyright © 1973, 1978, 1984, 2011 by Biblica, Inc.™ Used by permission of Zondervan. All rights reserved worldwide. www.zondervan.com.

Scripture quotations marked TPT are from The Passion Translation. Copyright © 2017, 2018, 2020 by Passion and Fire Ministries, Inc. Used by permission. All rights reserved.

The weeks of April 10–16 and December 4–10 originally appeared in The Upper Room *Disciplines* 2014. Reprinted and used by permission.

Editorial note: The named contributors wrote the daily meditations and prayers. The editors supplied the scripture overviews and the questions and suggestions for reflection.

Writers of various books of the Bible may be disputed in certain circles; this volume uses the names of the biblically attributed authors.

978-0-8358-1986-2 (enlarged-print edition)
978-0-8358-1988-6 (epub)

Contents

Foreword

As I see retirement on the horizon, I find myself thinking that I should be an expert in prayer by now. After all, I've spent some three and a half decades writing and editing spiritual formation resources, leading worship, and engaging with colleagues as we attempt to live out what our resources proclaim to the world. But I know that rather than achieving some "expert" status, we are continually being formed through regular spiritual practice. I am encouraged by one of my favorite quotes: "A prayer practice is just that: practice" [Daniel Wolpert, *Creating a Life with God*]. Each day I practice being a Christian—through prayer, study, meditation, listening, and serving. And in these practices, I am shaped in the image and likeness of Christ by the Spirit.

As I reflect on the people and things that have formed me as a Christian, I remember my maternal grandparents in Norman, Oklahoma. *The Upper Room* daily devotional guide and a blue Bible sat on the side of their bathtub. The guide was fitted with a waterproof covering. (The Bible didn't get a protective cover!)

I remember my father, a Methodist preacher, leading the family in mealtime prayers and encouraging us as children to learn to pray over our meals. I remember Mom leading Sunday school and teaching us to show kindness and hospitality to guests. During the Advent season, my family gathered for devotional times. We lit the candles on the Advent wreath, read a scripture and a devotional, and sang a song. I recall Dad's practice of rising early before the rest of the house to have a quiet time of prayer and study.

I remember retreats with Upper Room staff at state parks and retreat centers. In Friday afternoon sessions with colleagues, I learned how to pray using *lectio divina*. I was shaped in liturgy by joining in our Wednesday morning worship services in the Upper Room Chapel. I remember the transformation I experienced at the Academy for Spiritual Formation where I was formed by liturgy and silence, by living together in community.

Over the years, I have tried various daily practices, but the one I have come back to over and over is *The Upper Room Disciplines.* There is a groundedness in this resource that continues to shape me as a Christ-follower. The daily meditations, written by spiritual leaders from around the world, invite me to reflect on the scripture and what God is saying to me through the Bible passages and through the feelings and thoughts I have when I read each meditation.

The Revised Common Lectionary is our guide for the journey. Beginning with the season of Advent (the beginning of the Christian year), we join in the journey of Jesus' birth, life, death, resurrection, and the ministry of Christ's church in the world. We read. We listen. We remember. We open ourselves to be shaped by the story of the One we call the Christ.

All of us reading this book together are part of the body of Christ, woven together in love. May we trust the Spirit to shape us through this collective practice as we are formed in the image and likeness of Christ for the sake of one another and the world.

BETH A. RICHARDSON
Dean Emeritus of the Upper Room Chapel

The Other Side of Christmas

JANUARY 1, 2023 • MARTHA C. HIGHSMITH

SCRIPTURE OVERVIEW: This week we celebrate the birth of Jesus! Isaiah reminds us that all that God does, including the sending of a Savior, flows from God's compassion and steadfast love. The psalmist declares that from the angels in heaven to the works of creation to all the kings and peoples of the earth, all should praise the exalted name of God. The "horn" is a metaphor used elsewhere in the Hebrew scriptures that is traditionally interpreted by Christians as a prophecy of the Messiah. The author of Hebrews emphasizes the humanity of Christ. Christ fully partakes of our human nature so that he would understand our weakness and fully execute his role as our high priest. Matthew interprets through prophecy the perilous early travels of the young Jesus.

QUESTIONS AND SUGGESTIONS FOR REFLECTION

- Read Isaiah 63:7-9. How has God's presence saved you?
- Read Psalm 148. How can you praise God for the glory of creation around you in your daily life?
- Read Hebrews 2:10-18. How does your relationship with God who is not only with us but like us help you understand yourself as related to all other human beings?
- Read Matthew 2:13-23. How has your church or faith community made the choice to act in the best interests of the institution rather than to follow God's way of humility?

PC(USA) pastor living close to the land on the family farm in North Carolina, keeping bees and chickens, growing food and flowers.

NEW YEAR'S DAY

It is a new year, a new chance to start fresh. Many of us have made resolutions about things we want to change in 2023. But in the clear light of this new day, the world seems to go on like it always has, and nothing is really new. Turning the calendar doesn't change anything. How quickly we can forget what we celebrated only last Sunday—God coming in Jesus to live among us! That event changed your life and mine—and has the power to transform the whole world.

But that first coming was thousands of years ago, and the Second Coming seems just as far in the future. And here we are in the meantime, in what too often seems exactly that—a "mean time," a terrible time. Rachel still weeps for her children, the children of God still suffer, and the fear of death is pervasive.

In this mean time, God's word comes to us as both promise and possibility: "I am making all things new." The One who dwelled among us (see John 1:14) promises to do so again. The One who created all that is promises to renew that creation. Rachel's tears will be wiped from her eyes. There will be no mourning, no crying, no pain. There will be no death, only life abundant and eternal. It will be heaven on earth.

The promise is indeed a possibility. In Jesus, the kingdom of heaven has come near (see Matthew 3:2, 4:17, 10:7). In him, we have seen the love of God incarnate. And because he is like us, it seems possible for us to be like him. So today let us resolve to make changes in ourselves and in our world, looking to the day when all things will be made new.

O God, your will be done on earth as it is in heaven. We want to be those who see the hidden kingdom among us and who work with you to make all things new. Amen.

What Do You See?

JANUARY 2–8, 2023 • F. DOUGLAS POWE JR.

SCRIPTURE OVERVIEW: As we celebrate the Baptism of the Lord, the readings draw our attention to the connection between baptism and the pouring out of the Spirit. The prophet points forward to the day when God's servant will come, empowered by the Spirit, and bring justice to all people, both Jew and Gentile. In the psalm, the same heavenly voice that will speak over Jesus at his baptism resounds on the earth with might and power. Peter realizes in Acts that he is witnessing the fulfillment of the promise in Isaiah, for through Jesus, God's favor is poured out on people from every nation. Matthew tells the story of Jesus' baptism and of the arrival of the Spirit, confirmed by the heavenly voice of affirmation.

QUESTIONS AND SUGGESTIONS FOR REFLECTION

- Read Isaiah 42:1-9. What does it mean for Jesus to be a Servant Messiah? In what ways does God suffer with or for you?
- Read Psalm 29. Consider the power of a thunderstorm and the danger of the ocean. What does it mean to hear thunder as God's voice? Why is baptism in water?
- Read Acts 10:34-43. Consider the author's proposal that those who fear God and do what is right may include people of other faiths. What would this mean for your faith and your relationships with those of other faiths?
- Read Matthew 3:13-17. Remember your baptism. Did you make the decision to be baptized or did someone else make the decision for you? How does remembering your baptism guide you to do what God wants?

Director of the Lewis Center for Church Leadership and the James C. Logan Professor of Evangelism at Wesley Theological Seminary, Washington, DC.

I like to think that I have it all together and that my role is to help others. I must confess that when I read "and a light to the Gentiles" (many translations say "and a light to the *nations*"), it sticks in my craw. Of course, this text is talking about me, and it is saying that I need someone else to help me see. I am simultaneously light and in need of light. I find that a hard pill to swallow. In my role as a professor or leader in the church, it is my job to help others to see. My job is to teach others how to draw closer to God and their neighbor.

This text is a wake-up call reminding me—and I imagine some of you—that we are light for others and also are in need of light ourselves, just as in a classroom one is simultaneously a teacher and a student. Titles and degrees do not exempt us from needing others and learning from them. We need others to be a light so that we can continue to grow and see things differently.

When we vow as a community of faith in the baptism liturgy to journey with others, it should be a commitment to be light for others and to allow them to be light for us. No matter where we are on our journey, there will be times when we need to be released from external or self-imposed dungeons. One of the things that should make a Christian community different from other communities is that there are Christians journeying with you who can be that light when you need it, even if you (like me) want to think you have it all together.

Lord, open my eyes so that I may see those people you have placed in my life to be a guiding light. Amen.

We have all heard the phrase "Talk the talk and walk the walk." What we say cannot stand alone, but we must back it up with what we do. I love these verses in Isaiah because God is saying, "Look, I talk the talk, but I also walk the walk. All you need for proof of my faithfulness in the future is to look at my faithfulness in the past."

What do people see when they look at the former actions by our denominations, congregations, or those representing Christianity? Do they see us simply talking a good game, or are we walking the walk?

I am not naive, and I do not expect us to exist in a utopia. I do believe that if we are honest, we will admit that we do a better job of talking the talk than walking the walk. It is easy for us to point out the faults and misgivings of others while ignoring the ways we are not living into our own discipleship.

It is my dream to live in a way that makes this text come alive. I pray that when I talk, others will be willing to listen because they know the former things I have done. This does not mean I will get it right every time, but I will strive for that and hope I succeed enough times to establish a body of work. Michael Jordan did not hit every last-second shot he took as a pro, but his body of work for winning every NBA final he played in speaks for itself.

What would others see if our body of work truly backed up what we said in terms of mercy, justice, and love? I think they would see heaven here on earth.

All-seeing God, may our words and our actions help others to see you. May we talk the talk and walk the walk as Christians. Amen.

I do not like the water. I do not swim. I remember taking swimming lessons when I was young, and I did not enjoy going under water. I always felt disoriented when I came up into the air, probably because I was just looking for how to get out of the pool. My son, who did much better with his swimming lessons, likes going under the water and popping back up. He is comfortable in the water and enjoys the change in perspective between water and air.

When Jesus is baptized and comes out of the water, he doesn't just come back into the air; he sees the Spirit of God descending on him and hears a voice from heaven. Jesus reminds us in this text that the transforming impact of baptism should start in us. Baptism is not simply a rite of passage or life insurance for salvation. Baptism should help us to see with new eyes and hear with new ears the working of the Spirit.

Many reading this text were baptized as babies and will not remember that day. When those baptized as babies later confirm their baptism, this is a confession of living into seeing things differently. The same is true for those baptized as children or adults.

Baptism orients us to see and live differently. We cheapen baptism when we do not open ourselves to its transforming power. Although baptism is typically performed on an individual, all of us who are a part of the Christian community commit to journeying with newly baptized people to help them experience and see the Spirit. We also are having our eyes opened to seeing things differently on this journey.

Take a minute to ask yourself whether you are still living into your baptism or are in a season of disorientation.

Holy God, help us to live into our baptism and help others to do the same. Amen.

Is there anyone who does not like to hear that they have done well? Can you imagine an elementary schoolteacher going an entire year and never telling any of the students "good job"? Can you imagine a parent never telling their child "good job" their entire life? Both scenarios seem very sad. Almost every elementary schoolteacher tells each child in the class "good job" over and over again. Almost every parent praises their children.

God too is pleased with Jesus, God's beloved Son. Why is God pleased? It is because Jesus models for others the importance of baptism; but it is something else too. God is pleased because Jesus shows us true humility by being baptized by John the Baptist, the prophet tasked with preparing the way for him.

Jesus submits to being baptized in the presence of others by one whom he should be baptizing. Jesus leads by example and not by relying on his high position. I am sure this caught the people off guard and possibly made them ponder the meaning of what John and Jesus were modeling.

Am I modeling God's grace and love, or am I modeling envy and greed? I know my parents praised me when I modeled grace and love. My parents encouraged me to do better when I did not do well. They wanted me to be a model for my brother and others who were watching. God is pleased because Jesus is showing all of us an aspect of true servant leadership. As Jesus' disciples, we are called to do the same every day.

Lord, may I model for others the true meaning of servant leadership so that they can see you. Amen.

EPIPHANY

Have you ever looked for a sign that something was right? You wanted evidence that you were making the right move or doing the right thing. Maybe you had been offered a new job that would have required your family to move, and you were looking for that sign from God that you should go. In today's text, the Magi see a star and take it as a sign. The Bible says they are "overjoyed." The star guides them in finding Mary and Jesus. The star is clear and visible evidence that the Magi trust and follow.

When we are seeking insight from God, we do not always get clear and visible evidence. It can be frustrating because we are uncertain about what to do. Honestly, there are times when we may not receive a visible sign no matter how hard we look and pray. I do believe, however, that a closer look at this text reveals why the Magi receive an epiphany. The Magi are seeking Jesus because they believe him to be the king who will fulfill the prophesies in scripture. Herod, on the other hand, seeks Jesus because he sees Jesus as a competitor.

The reason we have for seeking a sign is important. If it is for selfish reasons, we may not see it. We cannot just make a sign appear—and if we do, we should question its validity. I find I often receive epiphanies from God when I least expect them, when I am not focused on myself and am truly seeking to draw closer to God.

I often read this text from the perspective of the Magi, but if I am honest, I need to read it through the eyes of Herod. Herod is a reminder that we cannot control what God reveals and to whom God reveals it.

Gracious God, may we seek to draw closer to you. Amen.

James Earl Jones's voice is one of the greatest I have ever heard. He has a voice you can listen to all day long. I often think it would be great to have his voice. Of course, we all do the same thing listening to a singer or sports broadcaster. When we find something compelling about the way a particular person sounds, we wish we had that voice.

In our text the author describes God's voice, and the description is so vivid we can almost experience it. The Lord's voice is a sound so powerful that it breaks the magnificent cedar trees of Lebanon like twigs. What a powerful voice! While the text helps us to comprehend the voice of God, we also know that we cannot literally see or hear God. Why use such dramatic imagery to describe God's voice if we cannot hear God? I believe it is because there are times when we need to feel that we can touch God. I have heard lightning crackling, so comparing God's voice to lightning makes God more real to me. The imagery used in the text is reassuring because it helps me to know God is acting all around me.

Like any journey, the Christian journey has its challenges. Getting baptized and entering a community of believers does not mean all problems will go away. All of us are still susceptible to illness, depression, anger—the list goes on and on. When we are going through these experiences and searching for God, it can be hard to sense God's presence. This psalm helps us to know God is in our world. It lets us know the voice of God can be heard and felt, and it reassures us that God is near.

Merciful God, thank you for reminding us that you are closer than we imagine. Amen.

BAPTISM OF THE LORD

Have you ever been caught off guard and seen something unexpected? One time my family and I went far away on vacation. As we walked into our hotel, the first person we saw was a member of my church. It caught me off guard because we were many miles away from home, and I was used to seeing the person at church. It threw me to see this individual in a different context.

Today's text is about Jesus being seen after being raised from the dead. The image of being raised reminds us of Jesus' baptism and Jesus coming out of the water. I imagine those witnessing Jesus' baptism were thrown for a loop the way those witnessing the resurrected Christ were. We all develop expectations about how things should be in our lives and in our congregations. It unsettles us when something unexpected—like someone sitting in our spot in the pew—happens.

Being a disciple gives us a rich tradition that helps us shape and order our lives, our weeks, and our days. We participate in baptism, Communion, and worship. The part we sometimes forget is that being a disciple also means having an openness to the unexpected. Jesus went against expectations by being baptized by John. The expectation is that the teacher baptizes the student, not the other way around. This catches most people by surprise—even Jesus' followers.

I believe Jesus prepares us to be disciples by teaching us to be open to the unexpected. Jesus prepares us to see the world differently if we are open and not so stuck on things remaining the same.

Majestic God, may we continue to be witnesses for the baptized Lord who disrupts our expectations. Amen.

The Good Stuff

JANUARY 9–15, 2023 • MATTHEW R. SCHLIMM

SCRIPTURE OVERVIEW: These readings contain the common theme of the power of spoken testimony. Isaiah begins by telling his audience, "Listen to me!" He then recounts not only his own story but also the promises of restoration given to him by God. The psalmist testifies about his experience. Although he has been in a difficult place, God has called him out and has given him a new song of praise to proclaim. Paul and Sosthenes write to the Corinthians to remind them of the powerful testimony that they had given them in person, which was confirmed by God. John the Baptist cries out that Jesus is the Lamb of God and bears testimony to the miraculous signs at the baptism. Our testimony as believers today can be just as powerful.

QUESTIONS AND SUGGESTIONS FOR REFLECTION

- Read Isaiah 49:1-7. What does it mean to be God's servant? How does this Servant Song speak of your experiences of serving God?
- Read Psalm 40:1-11. When has scripture sustained you? What words have become a real presence to you?
- Read 1 Corinthians 1:1-9. When have you turned your gifts inward as a sign of spiritual or social status? How can gratitude help you use your gifts in service to God and others?
- Read John 1:29-42. How have you experienced Jesus' saying to you, "Come and see"?

Professor of Old Testament at the University of Dubuque Theological Seminary; ordained pastor in The United Methodist Church; author of *This Strange and Sacred Scripture* and *70 Hebrew Words Every Christian Should Know*.

Life is hard and so is faith. Most of the time, most of us struggle just to make it. Anxiety looms large, and we grow tired. The demands of living give rise to an infectious weariness that's difficult to shake.

Relief comes when we remember all that's good about the life of faith. We get new wind in our sails with reminders of the blessings God showers upon us. Our scriptures this week overflow with the good stuff: the reasons why the life of faith is worth living.

Isaiah 49 comes out of Israel's darkest moments, a time when Jerusalem was in ruins, conquered by the superpower Babylon. In the agonizing wake of defeat, Jerusalem's inhabitants became homeless refugees. The person speaking here talks on behalf of all Israel, saying, "I have wearied myself in vain. I have used up my strength for nothing" (CEB).

Yet amid the sheer exhaustion of such trauma, the speaker goes on to talk about how God provides justice, rewards, honor, and strength. In the end, this scripture assures us that even the harshest realities of the time will not win out: War-torn refugees will find their way home again. God's salvation will go out to the ends of the earth. Those who are despised, rejected, and reduced to slavery shall instead receive honor.

The God who sustained Israel through exile will also see us faithfully through our hardships. We do not face them alone. In our weariness and weakness, God's hope shines. The pressures and stresses of this present moment fade in comparison to what God has in store.

God of Israel, we confess our deep need for you. Shine light in our darkness. Give hope that outweighs our anxieties. Bring us to places of peace and rest in you. Amen.

Recently I went backpacking for the first time in twenty years. More than anything, the mud surprised me. I didn't mind getting dirty, but trudging through gooey ground in sneakers presented unforeseen challenges. My ankles constantly readjusted to the unpredictable ways that my feet sank into the earth. Soon they ached. The pain combined with weariness made me unstable, and I fell over while on uneven, muddy terrain. I didn't get hurt, but I realized how quickly injuries could happen.

The terrain in Israel is notoriously uneven. In a span of about fifty miles, the land moves from sea level at the Mediterranean coast to 2,400 feet (730 m) above sea level at Jerusalem to 1,200 feet (370 m) below sea level at the Dead Sea. People in biblical times didn't have hiking boots, and they usually traveled everywhere by foot. The rugged terrain could quickly present a host of problems. When seasonal rains struck hard, people could have found themselves facing exhaustion, pain, danger, and even death.

The text today proclaims good news: God lifts people "out of the slimy pit, out of the mud and mire" (NIV). Rather than let them continue amid such hardship, God sets their "feet on a rock," giving them "a firm place to stand" (NIV). While facing traveling dangers, ancient readers would have thought of these words in a literal sense. At other times, they would have found in them a rich metaphor that applies to countless aspects of life: Whatever causes danger, exhaustion, pain, and death is just a passing thing. God rescues us from the worst that life has to throw at us. God works to set things right. God wants us to walk on solid ground. God's rescuing acts are the cause for deep blessing and happiness.

Saving God, you have rescued us more times than we can count. Help us sing your praises. Amen.

In college I attended a church that would open the microphone every Sunday morning to those who wanted to share what God was doing in their lives. Week after week, I heard how God was walking with people through the storms of life.

Worship in the Bible looked similar to this testimony service. The Psalms were Israel's hymnal, filled with songs, prayers, and other worshipful moments. In it, the psalmists share their personal stories of what God has done in their lives. Our reading today talks of spreading good news in a large congregation and not holding back. It insists on the importance of imparting—rather than hiding—God's righteousness, faithfulness, salvation, and truth.

Why is it important to share what God has done in our lives? It's often said that when people of faith gather together, they're like a mighty bonfire. But when they're by themselves, they're like lone embers that cool and go out. When we share the good stuff of faith with others, at least two important things take place. First, we reflect on what God has done for us—something we should be doing weekly if not daily. Second, we encourage others in their faith. We open others' eyes to how God will work in their own lives. We bring into the open all the goodness God has accomplished in our lives.

Our cultures teach the importance of self-sufficiency, but self-sufficiency is a lie. We need each other. We need other Christ-followers, and they need us. On our own, the light of our faith can dim. With others, it can light up the dark night all around.

Righteous, faithful, saving, and truthful God, show us people with whom we can share the good stuff of our faith. Amen.

One of my favorite pastimes is playing video games with my kids. A common feature that brings us instant excitement is a power-up. A power-up is a special ability or upgrade that your character receives in the course of the game. Suddenly, you are able to do things you could not do before.

In the classic *Pac-Man* game, players worked their way through mazes, trying to avoid ghosts. However, each corner held a "power pellet." Once Pac-Man ate a power pellet, he became temporarily invincible. Instead of ghosts eating him, he gobbled up the ghosts.

In another classic game, *Super Mario Brothers*, if Mario or Luigi touched a super mushroom, he would instantly double in size and become able to take damage without dying.

In racing games, players gain access to new vehicles and abilities. In sports games, players can become "on fire" and able to do things they never could do before.

In Paul's letters, Christians receive grace from Christ Jesus. For Paul, grace is Christians' power-up. It allows them to do things they couldn't otherwise.

So our reading talks about spiritual gifts and how God provides strength to the end. Elsewhere in Paul's letters to the Corinthians, he talks about God's grace giving people the ability to be generous (see 2 Corinthians 8:1–7). In Romans 5:20–21, he says that grace gives believers power over sin and even death. It leads to eternal life.

When we learn of God's grace and love, we become more gracious and loving. When we learn that Jesus died for our sins, we become more ready to sacrifice ourselves for others. When we see that God forgives us, we're more ready to forgive those who wrong us. God's grace gives us power to act like Jesus in the world.

God, help us use the power you give to reflect your love, sacrifice, and forgiveness. Amen.

While growing up in the 1980s, my sister and I watched a popular television show called "Lifestyles of the Rich and Famous." We tuned in to see the incredible mansions of the world's wealthiest people. Each show ended with the catchphrase, "champagne wishes and caviar dreams."

In our scripture reading, Paul talks about how Christians have become rich, but he doesn't say we're rich in money. He says we're rich "in speech and knowledge of every kind." What does he mean?

As Christians, we have special knowledge of who God is and how God is at work in the world (see Romans 11:33; 2 Corinthians 4:6). We have the scriptures, which contain countless insights into what God has been doing since the creation of the world. When we use our speech to share our knowledge, it's like we're releasing a sweet-smelling aroma into the world (see 2 Corinthians 2:14). Our knowledge of God is powerful, able to overcome prideful thoughts (see 2 Corinthians 10:5).

As with monetary riches, there's a danger in the rich knowledge we have from faith. The danger is that we could become more focused on what we know than on how we love. We slip into this temptation when we think it's more important to be right than compassionate. As Paul will later say in 1 Corinthians, "Knowledge puffs up, but love builds up" (8:1). Our knowledge can lead others to stumble (see 1 Corinthians 8:11). So, Paul writes, "If I . . . understand all mysteries and all knowledge . . . but do not have love, I am nothing" (1 Cor. 13:2). Even our knowledge will pass away (see 1 Corinthians 13:8).

When we interact with others—through social media or in person—our goal should never be to lord our rich knowledge over others. Our aim should be to love.

Gracious God, help us to use our knowledge with humility, placing love first. Amen.

The Gospel of John loves rushing in to big ideas. John lets loose with the good news of Jesus from the get-go. In today's reading, John the Baptist sees Jesus and says, "Look! The Lamb of God who takes away the sin of the world!" (CEB).

It's quite an introduction, but what does it mean? We often think of Jesus or God as a Good Shepherd and ourselves as sheep (see Psalm 23; John 10:11-16). But here things are reversed: Jesus is not the shepherd but a sheep—and a baby one at that, a little lamb. What's that image supposed to mean?

In biblical Israel, barbecues were special opportunities for fellowship with God. People would take an animal to the Temple. There, a portion of the animal would be placed over a fire and offered to God. The rest of the roasted meat would go to the priests and the people making the offering. People could bring all sorts of food for these barbecues: cows, poultry, even grains and wine. On special occasions, they brought pure and spotless lambs. They were used when the priesthood started (see Leviticus 9:3), when Hezekiah brought people back to God (see 2 Chronicles 29:21), and when the exile to Babylon ended (see Ezra 6:17; 8:35).

When John the Baptist calls Jesus "the Lamb of God," he's suggesting that Jesus is pure and spotless. He's suggesting that God is doing something new and momentous. He's suggesting that Jesus will be a sacrifice offered to God.

The result, we learn, is the removal of the sin of the entire world! Jesus not only forgives the sins that each one of us has personally committed; he takes away all the evil in our world that causes harm to ourselves and others.

Savior, come and take away the sin and evil that breed care-lessness, hatred, and hopelessness. Help us to make way for the new things you plan to do among us. Amen.

I lose stuff a lot. Car keys. My cell phone. I spent one entire afternoon of my honeymoon trying to find my wallet.

It's one thing for me to miss something for a few hours or even a day. But imagine a whole people looking for something for centuries. Israel's deepest longing was for a leader who would set everything right. For a thousand years, they looked for someone who would make society function the way it's supposed to: without inequality, poverty, violence, or oppression. They tried to find a king who would level the playing field and give everyone a fair shot. The books of Samuel and Kings tell how Jerusalem's kings failed, failed, and failed some more. None of them managed to be the ruler that Israel searched for. This ruler they wanted so much came to be known as the *Messiah* or *Christ*—the two words mean the same thing. This one would be anointed by God to set the world right once again.

In the Gospel of John, the good news can't be contained: In the very first chapter, we learn that the one whom people have spent centuries looking for is now—finally—among us. When Andrew tells Simon Peter, "We have found the Messiah," he's saying that now at long last after centuries of waiting and searching and looking, God has shown up. The One we've always needed is now among us. John will spend the rest of his Gospel explaining who this Messiah is and how he will set the world right again. But it is the most promising of beginnings. *Eureka!* God is now among us, present in the Anointed One who works to undo the suffering and pain and oppression that haunt us. Thanks be to God!

God, open our eyes to how the Messiah is now among us, rescuing us from the evils of this world. Amen.

The Courage to Change

JANUARY 16–22, 2023 • HANNAH ADAIR BONNER

SCRIPTURE OVERVIEW: Sometimes we struggle with the challenges we face. If God is good and God is for us, then why do we experience pain and loss? Isaiah feels the sting of darkness and despair, and the psalmist has experienced days of distress. Yet both encourage themselves with the promise that God has not forgotten them. The light will come, as will the shouts of joy. The New Testament readings warn against following human leaders to the extent that we take our eyes off Christ. The Corinthian church has divided into factions that identify primarily with Paul or Peter, not Christ! The Gospel reading shows that Peter, like all other human leaders, is merely a disciple himself. Jesus is the one we should seek to follow.

QUESTIONS AND SUGGESTIONS FOR REFLECTION

- Read Isaiah 9:1-4. How has God's love freed you to find your calling?
- Read Psalm 27:1, 4-9. When have you called out to God? How has God helped you turn your cries to praise?
- Read 1 Corinthians 1:10-18. How have you experienced division within the body of Christ? How might a focus on Christ rather than particular faith leaders or denominations help you to repair division and work through differences?
- Read Matthew 4:12-23. How have significant changes in your life (like a loved one's death or a career change) allowed your ministry to grow?

Committed to God's vision of justice; ordained United Methodist elder, speaker, and author; currently pastoring students at the University of Arizona.

Today is Martin Luther King Day in the United States, so it is appropriate that we begin this week with words from the psalmist that have been a source of courage for those facing opposition and prejudice.

In his final sermon, Martin Luther King Jr. closed with words that echo the psalmist: "I'm not worried about anything. I'm not fearing any man. Mine eyes have seen the glory of the coming of the Lord."

It was not that he had no cause for fear. Like many before him who have clung to God's promises in moments of difficulty, he had every reason to think that harm would come his way. What made the difference in his life—and can make the difference in our lives—is refusing to let fear make the decisions.

There are worse things to lose than our lives. It is possible to lose our whole selves by bargaining with fear. Yet fear loses its hold over us when we refuse to let it choose our path. It cannot control us anymore.

The scriptures say, "Perfect love casts out fear" (1 John 4:18). Perfect love is the embrace of God, for no one can love us perfectly but God. We can rest then—in whatever hardships, trials, and terrors we may face—knowing that this life is meant to make a difference. This life is meant to serve the goodness, justice, love, and compassion of God.

Today as we remember the life and ministry of the Rev. Dr. Martin Luther King Jr., may we choose love over fear, courage over cowardice, and compassion over self-interest.

Lord, help me choose love over fear. May my courage help change the world to reflect your plan of justice and mercy. Amen.

My favorite image of God is the description of Jesus' wanting to gather and shelter the people of Jerusalem like a mother hen (Matt. 23:37). If you have ever seen a bird nesting, you know how hidden those chicks can be under her wings. Outside my kitchen window, I have a mourning dove who consistently lays multiple sets of eggs throughout the year. She raises them in pairs, and unless an egg falls from the nest, I never know they are there until the chicks are almost big enough to fly.

I like to think that is how God wants to take care of us. Concealing and sheltering us when we feel the most vulnerable, and then revealing us to the elements when we are ready to face them. It does not work that way all the time, however. Some of us have to face things long before we are ready.

What then does it mean to make our home with God? Is there one place, or is it a way of living? Perhaps the psalmist meant for it to be a particular place, but we know that God is everywhere. Anywhere that we are—in whatever nation or city—God is there. Therefore, we can cultivate a way of living in all of those spaces that sees God's beauty and notices God's presence.

Even when change and challenge come to us, when it feels as if we are being thrust out of the nest, we can remember that God is with us in all places and circumstances. We never have to face something without God. The world around us is God's dwelling, the home we share.

Mothering God, help me face this world unafraid, knowing that wherever I dwell is your dwelling; wherever I go, you are with me. Hold me close. Amen.

Everything changed for me as a kid the first time I experienced a harvest. I vividly recall riding the bus home in second grade, carefully cradling a tiny sprout. I began to understand the world and my role in it in a whole new way. I began to see that with patience and care, I could be a part of God's plan to bring good things into the world.

Perhaps you have your own memories, whether from childhood or adulthood, of getting to hold and share something you have nurtured. What a joy it is to share! In fact, the scriptures describe sharing as essential. In Leviticus, God is clear that the harvest is not to be hoarded, and what overflows onto the ground must be left for widows, orphans, and immigrants (see 19:9-10). Together the community is to burst out in celebration.

Likewise, when God's presence comes to us, it overflows onto the whole community. Something begins to change. Like a flame passed at a Christmas Eve service, it illuminates us all.

In order to see the harvest and change that God wants to bring into our lives, we need to pay attention to what is around us. We make it dark during a Christmas Eve service to make the light more visible in the darkness and connect with the "people who walked in darkness." The darkness and the light work together, compelling us to adjust and focus.

The light is seen because of the darkness, the seedling is possible because of the dirt, the baby emerges from the darkness of the womb, God brings new life to those who are in darkness, and joy grows out of our willingness to see and celebrate the wholeness and interconnectedness of it all.

God who created the light and the darkness, help me to recognize you in all things, in the dirt and in the harvest it produces. Grow good things in me. Amen.

The change God wants to bring into our world and lives has a consistent rhythm. When Jesus spoke in his home synagogue for the first time, he announced that he had come to bring "good news to the poor" and to "let the oppressed go free" (see Luke 4:16-19). Wherever oppression and suffering appear in the scriptures, God sets about to end them or to send the prophets to denounce them.

What would it mean for us to view the world the way God does? To notice where the areas of oppression are and seek to end them?

If you have ever tried to carry too many grocery bags at once, you know the relief it is to reach your destination. Even greater is the relief when someone comes along and helps, removing from your shoulders the burden that may be more than you can bear. Could you have made it, or would the bags have fallen? You will never know the answer to that question, but isn't it better not to have to find out?

Unfortunately, the burdens that feel too great on the shoulders of so many are much more complicated than groceries. Whenever we look at hunger and do nothing, whenever we turn away from our unhoused neighbors, whenever we stay silent when cruel words are spoken, it grieves God's heart.

God does more than lift the yoke; God breaks it. God destroys, dismantles, and even demolishes the means of oppression. Perhaps we will find the opportunity in our own journeys not only to share or lift the burden but to break some rods of oppression as well.

God who frees us, may we use the strength and wisdom you give us to spread that freedom. Help us break the systems that hurt your children. Amen.

Earlier this week, we remembered the ministry of the Rev. Dr. Martin Luther King Jr. We also remembered the sermon he preached in Memphis, Tennessee, just before he was assassinated. He had come to support the Memphis Sanitation Workers' strike and spoke on the necessity of unity. He reminded his listeners that when the Pharaoh wanted to keep people from pursuing change and freedom, he would keep them fighting with one another. Unity, King stated, was the only way that the community would be able to resist these tricks and break free.

When we are arguing, we are not getting anywhere fast. Growing up as one of five energetic siblings, I learned this only too well. When the racket from the back seat got too loud, my parents would simply pull the car over and wait until we calmed down. In our passage today, Paul is telling the early Christians in Corinth to calm down and quit fighting. Quarrels and divisions are keeping them from moving forward and living into being the church.

Sometimes the goal is right in front of us, but we do not notice it because we are too focused on sticking our finger in our neighbor's face. We run the risk of missing the whole point of being a community. Bickering is certainly not the point of community and only diminishes our ability to do good. That's why vested interests like Pharaoh and union busters promote conflict and division.

In order to find our unity, we need to want to be a community. That commitment should drive us to listen to one another and to Jesus. We need to discern together what would honor a God who cares for the vulnerable and the outcast and pursues one lost sheep.

Trinitarian God, you who contain community within yourself, may we learn from your example. Amen.

We live in a world where platform and audience equal power and profit. It is an era when people are tempted to gauge their worth by how many people listen to them or wear their name. Consultants teach people to develop their personal brand, and public personas are shaped and airbrushed to hide all imperfections.

Similar temptations of self-aggrandizement were present in Paul's day. It would have been difficult for him to resist—with his citizenship in the Roman Empire, his credentials, and his history of being a movement leader—if he had not been a changed man. He had given his life to a man without citizenship, credentials, or earthly power.

Despite that, people were still grasping on to his name, his brand, his platform and wanting to claim a connection to him and the power he represented. Paul knew the task he had been sent to do. He had not been sent to take the focus away from Christ. He had been sent to proclaim the good news to those who would hear it.

Have you ever been tempted to make yourself the center of the story? Have you ever felt tempted to make someone other than Christ your savior? To follow their voice and wear their brand as if it were the thing that would save you?

Paul is grateful that he has given the people no real excuse to claim his brand. He recognizes that the change the world needs will not come through his name or the name of Apollos. In not wanting to be a distraction from Jesus, he shows that he is a changed man.

Loving God, may I hold no name higher than I hold yours, cherish no task more greatly than to share your story. Keep me centered on you. Amen.

Fishing involves a whole lot of waiting, waiting, and more waiting. And even after all that waiting, sometimes nothing happens. The disciples knew that as well as any fisherman today does.

Yet there is a moment when the word *immediately* comes into play. When you feel that nibble on the hook or tug on the net, you know you must move immediately. Up comes the pole, down comes the spear, in comes the net. Immediately.

Sometimes life can feel like an awful lot of waiting, but when the moment comes to reel, to shift, to change, to move—we have to be ready. If we are not ready and willing to grasp the calling and change our path, we miss the opportunity altogether.

So, yes, Peter and Andrew and James and John knew an awful lot about waiting, but they also knew an awful lot about moving immediately when the moment comes. Those disciples left their jobs, their families, and their belongings because they did not want to miss their moment. They did not want all that waiting to be in vain.

We too need to stay alert so that when our savior calls, we can respond, act, and change what we need to change immediately. Like a fisherman waiting by the water, we can never allow the waiting seasons of our lives to cause us to forget that the waiting is preparation for the change that is to come.

Dear God, help me to stay alert in this season. Help me to notice your callings and give me courage to change. Amen.

What God Requires

JANUARY 23–29, 2023 • JOEL BENGBENG

SCRIPTURE OVERVIEW: We must beware counterfeit gospels. According to one current counterfeit gospel, we deserve God's favor based on our deeds or intellect or status. The readings for this week remind us that this is false. Yes, the Israelites offer sacrifices, but they are first and foremost called to show mercy because they have received divine mercy. The psalmist asks who can stand in God's holy dwelling and so provides a list of ways to live morally. Ultimately no one can stand before God on merit alone. Paul reminds the Corinthians that human wisdom is foolishness compared to the wisdom of God, and thus we should not puff ourselves up based on our intellect. Jesus teaches that those who may seem insignificant in the eyes of the world are great in the kingdom of heaven.

QUESTIONS AND SUGGESTIONS FOR REFLECTION

- Read Micah 6:1-8. How have you let down God? What changes can you make to recommit to your relationship with God?
- Read Psalm 15. Consider the notion that the requirements for dwelling with God are in how we treat our friends and neighbors. How does this change the ways you seek God?
- Read 1 Corinthians 1:18-31. When have you seen God's work in the world in a way that is antithetical to human standards?
- Read Matthew 5:1-12. How do you maintain a poverty of spirit in your relationship with God? How does this help you to serve God and others?

Elder in the Northwest Philippines Annual Conference of The United Methodist Church, serving as district superintendent of Ilocos South District; editor of *Siled ti Kararag*, one of the editions of *The Upper Room* daily devotional guide in the Philippines; member of the Order of Saint Luke (OSL); interested in the intersection of liturgy, spirituality, and social justice.

Remembrance is central in the divine-human covenantal relationship. Our journey is largely shaped by past events of God's encounter with God's people. Today's reading begins with God's rebuke against Judah for the latter's failure to uphold its covenant with God. Every time it falls into the trap of sin, God's community is invited to remember God's liberating acts in the past. Israel will find its way back only when it remembers. In the words of the prophet Micah, remembering is necessary "that you may know the saving acts of the LORD."

Closely linked with Israel's liberation from Egypt are the Passover meal and the Passover lamb. Interestingly, Christian liturgy is shaped by the same event. In the sacrament of the Lord's Supper, our holy meal, we celebrate our freedom from the power of sin and death through the self-giving love of Christ, our Passover Lamb. We remember God's gift of life and creation. We celebrate God's presence in the present. We look forward to the new day when God will restore creation. At Christ's Table, the past, present, and future come together. Remembering is not mere recollection. When we remember, the transforming power of a past event becomes an ever-new experience in the present.

Along our journey, we often drift away from God's path. Remembering God's saving acts enables us to see ourselves where we are right now. Remembering helps us confront our state of brokenness in the light of what God has already done in the past with the hope for God's redirection in the future.

What memories in your faith journey always bring you back to the path of God?

In remembrance of these your mighty acts in Jesus Christ, we offer ourselves in praise and thanksgiving as a holy and living sacrifice, in union with Christ's offering for us. Amen. (UM Book of Worship, Service of Word and Table 1)

Micah deplored the wealthy who were oppressing the poor, and he warned that Judah was doomed to fall because of its failure to do justice. When we reject justice, we reject Godself. Justice is when everyone has a place at the table with full access to the abundance of life.

God does not condemn the Jewish sacrificial system. God rather abhors liturgy detached from justice, prayer devoid of compassion, ritual not translated into mercy, and offerings not coupled with sacrificial love for others.

I live in a developing country where a large percentage of the population lives in poverty. There is a growing gap between the rich and the poor, worsened by the current political system that perpetrates and perpetuates social injustice. Our country purports to be the only Christian country in Asia, with a big majority of the population professing the Christian faith.

Following Christ is not a choice between worship and work, contemplation and action, sacrificial worship and sacrificial living. The total embodiment of worship is doing the will and work of God in the world. We join Christ when we worship, but we must follow that by joining in God's ongoing work in the world. Passion for God ought to be translated into compassion for people.

Our faith should enable us to see the world as it is, with all its brokenness and pain. To see the world with God's eyes is to face reality with the divine vision of a new reality. Worship makes us courageous enough to transform the world according to God's will.

God of justice, teach us to incorporate our worship with works of justice, our liturgy with love and humility. May our prayers be full of compassion, our rituals translated to mercy, and our offering coupled with sacrificial love for others. Amen.

When I was a child, my parents farmed land we did not own for a living. Every planting season, we had to take loans from wealthy businessmen so we could buy the necessities of farming. In our country, big business owners lend money to farmers and then force them to sell their products to them at a below-market price.

Micah asked, "What shall I give to the LORD?" In today's reading, the psalmist asks, "LORD, who may enter your Temple? Who may worship on Zion, your sacred hill?" Like Micah, the psalmist highlights the link between worship and daily life. Genuine worship is intertwined with good words and good works, a right relationship with neighbors, and compassion for the needy. The demand of worship includes all spheres of personal and social life, including our economic and legal dealings.

Jesus embodies an integral spirituality that links prayer and compassion. He healed the sick, lived with the poor, fed the hungry, and ate with sinners. It is disturbing to see Christians who spend Sunday professing their love for Jesus Christ who commanded us to love the least, but use the rest of their week taking advantage of the powerless.

Much of the world today, including the church, has ignored the pain and suffering of the least and the poor. There is a troubling gap between how we pray and how we act, how we praise God and how we treat others. Righteous living is deeply rooted in an intimate relationship with God but must be expressed in genuine love for others. Either we change our prayers and hymns, or we change our way of life.

Gracious Lord, help us realize that economic issues are genuinely spiritual issues. Forgive us for prioritizing our pleasures above our neighbor's basic necessities. Enable us to do justice, love mercy, and walk humbly with you. Amen.

Paul was writing to a congregation beset with disunity, immorality, infidelity, and other problems. In many ways, the Corinthian church was a microcosm of Corinth itself. Corinth was a major Greek city known for its commerce, culture, immorality, and plurality of religions. The apostle had to remind the Corinthian believers that their identity is in Christ and his cross. The death of Jesus on the cross did not convince the Greeks and the Jews who saw preaching the cross of Christ as foolish. But for the followers of Christ, it meant new life.

For some, a cross is religious architecture. For others, it is fashionable jewelry. But for the early Christians, the cross was a sign of their daily walk with the crucified Redeemer.

The cross helps us remember the death of Christ and its saving power. But we must also remember that his death was murder. It was political assassination. He was a threat to the Temple authorities. He was a threat to the Roman Empire. At the cross, God in Jesus Christ identified himself with the sinners, the weak and downtrodden. So in remembering how and why he was murdered, we become the sacrament to the world, inspired by the courage and grace Jesus showed in his life and in his death.

Identifying ourselves with the cross of Christ means yielding our lives to the way of Christ and the death-defying power of the gospel. As we follow Christ, death is inevitable but so is new life.

Crucified Redeemer, may your cross remind us to stand against powers that silence and tyrannize and to see the light of resurrection in the face of death. Amen.

I belong to an indigenous community that inhabits the mountains and hills in the northern part of the Philippines. Our ancestors were labeled as barbaric, demonic, ignorant, and foolish by Spanish and American colonizers and missionaries. Many of our people still suffer discrimination from the lowlanders. But even in our struggle for inclusion, our community has often experienced the grace of God through the ministry of the church. Pastors, deaconesses, civic leaders, and good citizens have come among us, embodying the truth that God's Table is a celebration of grace for all. God invites all because God is love and transcends all.

This reminds me of brother Cosme Haban, a member of a United Methodist congregation in our area. After an intense discussion in his congregation about the possible split in the denomination, Cosme offered this closing prayer: "Almighty God, bind us closer in the midst of our differences. We pray that no child of yours will be discriminated against because of who they are. Give us a bigger vision and a wider embrace, lest we oppress others. Create in us hearts wide enough to accept and love without discrimination as shown by your Son Jesus Christ. In his name we pray. Amen."

The invitation to be God's sacrament to the world—to share the grace we have received—demands inclusion. It would be truly unfortunate if we claim to be sharing the good news of God's grace through the Eucharist but continue to practice forms of discrimination. Some arrogantly claim the right to declare who gets to sit and eat at God's banquet. But God's amazing grace demands inclusion because every person has within them the inextinguishable divine mark.

Almighty God, create in us hearts wide enough to accept and love without discrimination as shown by your Son Jesus Christ. In his name we pray. Amen.

Too often we read the Beatitudes as passive statements or promises of future rewards, but they are an active proclamation of God's reign amid human misery, a prophetic reversal of the status quo, a call to build a just and humane society. True blessedness is not meek or submissive but rather subversive. It is an invitation to rise up and act righteously. True blessedness starts with holy anger and divine discontent, followed by a burning desire to change the world to conform with the righteousness of God. True holiness begins with a transformed heart and seeks God's righteousness in all spheres of human life. Kingdom values must penetrate not only individuals but also the family, economy, culture, and politics. Holiness devoid of social justice is a caricature of the gospel of Christ.

The late United Methodist Bishop La Verne D. Mercado was the head of our country's ecumenical council during an authoritarian rule in the 1970s. He guided the council during the dark days of martial law. He firmly stood against abuses and was himself imprisoned in 1974. After his own release, he worked for the release of those imprisoned with him and of other political prisoners. He showed that faith communities should take a stand on the side of the oppressed and marginalized. By his dedication to the cause of peace and justice, he exemplified servanthood—a quality so badly missed in our days. Despite overwhelming admirations and compliments, Bishop La Verne remained humble. When the Council honored him, he stated: "I think I haven't really done anything. I only tried my best to be of service to God, to the church and to his people."

In your blessedness, what prompts you to get up, go ahead, do something, and move toward social justice?

O God, "give us the freedom and power . . . to resist evil, injustice and oppression in whatever forms they present themselves." Amen. (UM Hymnal, Baptismal Covenant IV)

The Beatitudes are both a promise and demand. They promise God's action breaking into the affairs of this world. They demand that Christ's followers manifest kingdom values in their daily life. The Beatitudes do not disregard or downplay present suffering in exchange for a future life of joy in heaven. Jesus is not glorifying or legitimizing poverty, suffering, pain, misery, grief, or persecution. He is proclaiming the present inbreaking of God's power in all aspects of life.

While serving a large congregation in a predominantly United Methodist town in northern Philippines, we learned that the government planned to build a large dam that would inundate at least five villages, displace communities, and endanger at least three towns. Our church was at the forefront in campaigns opposing the dam. But the church and its clergy, including me, were tagged as subversives and enemies of the state. We have experienced harassment and intimidation.

Around fifty years earlier, a man named Macli-ing Dulag was the tribal leader during an authoritarian rule in our country. Driven by hunger for righteousness and love for his people, he led the resistance against the construction of a megadam that would have submerged ancestral lands and displaced many communities. Despite threats and intimidation from the state, he organized communities in opposing the destructive dam. He was killed by the state forces. He was silenced, but the movement he started continued and succeeded.

A faithful proclamation of the gospel requires readiness to be confronted by dehumanizing powers. But even in the face of hostility and rejection, we are assured of God's abiding presence. Christ walks with us in the narrow way.

Almighty God, you created us in your own image. Grant us grace fearlessly to contest against evil and make no peace with oppression. Amen.

A Call to Integrity

JANUARY 30–FEBRUARY 5, 2023 • ERIC A. HERNÁNDEZ LÓPEZ

SCRIPTURE OVERVIEW: According to another counterfeit gospel, our inward convictions about God are enough, so our actions do not really matter. Isaiah chastises his audience for being half-hearted in their religious observance. They ignore the plight of the oppressed and the poor, and by doing so they reveal that they do not grasp the heart of God. The psalmist argues that the true faithful are steadfast and generous, and as a result God establishes them and their cause. The understanding of God's view of the world, Paul writes, must be spiritually discerned, for it opposes the normal thinking of the world. In Matthew, Jesus tells his followers that living faith is shown by bringing flavor and light to the world. Otherwise, our faith is useless to those around us.

QUESTIONS AND SUGGESTIONS FOR REFLECTION

- Read Isaiah 58:1-12. What can you do to be a foundation of many generations, the repairer of the breach for your community?
- Read Psalm 112:1-10. How have you seen God's blessings abound from your faithfulness? How do you remain faithful when God's blessings seem absent?
- Read 1 Corinthians 2:1-16. Consider the many ways wisdom comes. How do you seek to understand God's wisdom?
- Read Matthew 5:13-20. When does your faith community resist the call to be the salt of the earth and light of the world? How can you transform yourself or those around you to fulfill God's commandments?

Author, psychologist, teacher, and elder in the Methodist Church of Puerto Rico; born in Guatemala, raised in Puerto Rico, married to Heidy Soam, and father of Aurora Isabel; chair of the board of directors of the Evangelical Seminary of Puerto Rico.

Integrity can be defined as the congruence between our inner and outer world, between who we are and what we do. Matthew 5 is precisely a call to integrity. In the first twelve verses of this chapter, Jesus reveals through the Beatitudes the identity of those who choose to follow him. Then in the following thirteen verses, he makes sure they understand that identity is not merely a theoretical matter but rather a lifestyle characterized by good works. So why does Jesus emphasize good works?

The times in which Jesus developed his ministry were characterized by corrupt religious leaders who sought to serve themselves rather than others. Their teachings were clearly contrary to their actions. They lived according to falsehoods and not by the truth. In psychology, this is known as *cognitive dissonance.* That is why Jesus warned his followers, "Let your light shine before people, so they can see the good things you do" (CEB).

Perhaps the religious leaders couldn't shine before people because they had not undergone an internal transformation. They could not give what they didn't possess. Shining before others means that we allow the light of Christ to transform the darkest and secret areas of our lives, even those that cause us shame. Our good works reflect the light of Christ acting in and through us.

My young daughter reminds me that the call to integrity begins at home, as her actions reflect what she sees me do more than what she hears me say. Aurora Isabel invites me to a continual self-reflection that exposes me to the transforming light of Christ. My light must shine in her sight, since her mother and I are the light that illuminates her house.

God, illuminate our lives today with your light, and help us be more like you. May we be the light of the world, beginning in our own home. Amen.

In a postmodern context in which almost everything is being deconstructed and in which people increasingly lose faith in institutions, there is no better way to evangelize than with the witness of good works. Religious institutions, just like individuals, are not bad in and of themselves but lose credibility when they lack integrity. They are corrupted from the inside out for many reasons, among them being the absence of spiritual disciplines that allow the transforming light of Christ to bring their darkness to light. There can be times when churches sin by paying too little attention to the collective disciplines that can place us before sanctifying grace: confession, covenant groups, and mentoring.

Attending to these disciplines as an institution or an individual is easier said than done. It can be a great challenge to build safe spaces where we can confess our sins. Because of our fear of being judged, we build our lives in secret. However, sin loses its power over us when we confess it, sustained by a community full of grace and forgiveness.

On a wall of our church sanctuary, there was a sign that said that we are a hospital for sinners not a club for saints. We all share the same humanity; we all have the potential to sin. Therefore, it is important to practice compassion, the "ability to suffer with people." Our churches need to take steps toward compassion, vulnerability, transparency, and grace. If we do not practice community life, our justice will not surpass that of the teachers of religious law in Jesus' time on earth. Without these disciplines, we will lose our capacity to shine.

God, help us accompany each other on our journey to be more like you. May grace be stronger than judgment. May compassion be stronger than competition. Amen.

A Call to Integrity   49

Our word *religion* derives from the Latin word *religio*, which means "encounter, reverence, or devotion to the divine." *Christian spirituality* in turn is defined as "the practices that allow us to be transformed to be more like Jesus." Christianity, then, should be an encounter with God that transforms us to be more like Jesus, the one who chose to serve and not to be served.

Fasting is one of the disciplines that transform us to be more like Jesus. By fasting, we affirm that, more than on any food or activity, we depend on God. During a time of fasting, we remember that everything revolves around God; we are only servants. Jesus himself fasted as he began his ministry of compassion, peace, and justice.

As were people in Isaiah's time, we can be tempted to put ourselves instead of God at the center and twist the spiritual discipline of fasting until we use it to gain power, recognition, or control. There are many examples today—on religious television, in political movements, at local churches—of people using fasting and other visible religious disciplines to build religious authority and political factions. This kind of selfish fasting does not transform us to serve like Jesus.

These verses remind me of the time when the church used the fear of purgatory to sell indulgences to pay for the building of St. Peter's Basilica in Rome. The Protestant Reformation and Martin Luther remind us how religious systems can become corrupt and lose their essence of serving. Just as Isaiah was God's instrument to speak to the people regarding their sins, today we must ask ourselves if our religious systems are serving the people or just ourselves. Are we truly growing closer to God or merely pretending?

God, help us remember that you are the center, and we are only servants. Amen.

Isaiah's call was not only to point out the collective sin of corruption but also to show the people that the way forward is through justice. Isaiah described the path of integrity and the good deeds that will make our light shine in the darkness. Verses six and seven explain how to be the light of the world and salt of the earth by setting free those who are unjustly imprisoned, easing the burden of those who work for us, liberating the oppressed, sharing food with the hungry, sheltering the unhoused, giving clothes to those who need them, and not hiding from relatives who need us.

It is not enough to develop a process of introspection that brings out our individual and collective darkness; it is necessary to align our priorities to the will of God. That is precisely the purpose of fasting: to empty ourselves of our own will and fill ourselves with the love of God that enables us to be instruments of justice. Fasting reminds us that there must be congruence between worship and justice, as the prophet Micah taught: "He has told you, human one, what is good and what the LORD requires from you: to do justice, embrace faithful love, and walk humbly with your God" (Mic. 6:8, CEB).

Our internal spiritual disciplines must lead to external spiritual disciplines. Individual piety does not replace justice. The blessing is that those who practice this balanced lifestyle and seek to integrate the internal with the external enjoy the continuous presence of God: "I'm here" (CEB). God's presence implies justice. Do our priorities as a church reflect God's will as expressed in Isaiah 58:6-7?

God, align our will with yours. May justice, peace, and compassion spring from our hearts as a result of our love for you. Amen.

The Greek word *sophia* appears twenty-six times in the first three chapters of First Corinthians. It was a word widely used to refer to wisdom. In the context of this letter, Paul uses the term to contrast a gospel based on human wisdom with the gospel based on the cross of Christ. Many rejected Paul because they believed that human wisdom was the basis of power and authority. Paul emphasized his dependence on God and not on his own wisdom or intelligence. For him, human ability was not enough; divine power was necessary.

Paul had a rigorous religious and academic background. He had studied in Tarsus where he was exposed to the philosophical currents of his time. And his membership with the Pharisees ensured that he knew the scriptures thoroughly. Rather than using his knowledge and persuasive words to impress or intimidate his hearers, however, Paul focused on the simplicity and truth of his content. Just like Jesus, he used the Cross to shame the strong and wise.

It has been said that talking a lot may be a sign of a desire to control things, and silence can be a sign of vulnerability and dependence on God. Although silence is not always the appropriate discipline, particularly in the face of injustice, the spiritual discipline of silence can help us discern whether our faith is based on our own wisdom or divine wisdom. Silence can be an instrument for the Spirit to search us thoroughly and reveal to us the "depths of God" (CEB). It can help us allow ourselves to be controlled by God.

God . . . (just repeat that word several times and be silent).

The Quaker tradition is a model for discernment. These brothers and sisters have over the years developed detailed instructions for collective discernment. When a member of the community needs to make a crucial decision, all form a circle of clarity. Group members can ask the person a series of questions for hours without making any kind of judgment. The goal is to gain clarity on the motivations behind the decision and its potential consequences.

Integrity is not a gift that we receive once and for all from the Spirit. Rather, it is a journey in which we intentionally listen to God's voice in our own silence and in the collective voices of our brothers and sisters. Our community can observe things that we cannot see on our own. It is in the community that we can know the "mind of the Lord" (1 Cor. 10:16, CEB).

It is ironic that the people we tend to consider incapable of having the mind of Christ—because of our prejudices about their nationality, sexual orientation, skin color, profession, age, family of origin, or lack of formal education—are frequently the spiritual people who can "discern all things."

That has been my experience as a pastor. Despite my academic background, there have been times when I have been unable to discern God's voice. Then, people I least expected to be spiritual have helped me find congruence between my teachings and actions, between my inner and outer worlds.

Who has been the mind of Christ for you in your journey of faith? Remember them and give thanks.

God, help us hear your voice in the community around us. Help us to be humble and allow ourselves to be guided by those you are guiding. Reveal to us that which we cannot know for ourselves. Amen.

Much of the Old Testament literature reflects a way of thinking that affirms that suffering results from sin, and prosperity results from doing God's will. The book of Job challenges this thought and reveals that not everything in life can be seen through the lens of cause and effect. Jesus himself affirmed that we will have affliction even when following him (see John 16:33).

Although many of the psalms present this theology of retribution, they also contain great truths. One of these truths is that whoever fears the Lord will be blessed. The fear of the Lord, however, has nothing to do with *fear* but rather with the respect, recognition, and reverence with which we approach God. When we listen for God's voice guiding us in our desire to live in integrity, we are blessed.

The incongruity between our private and public lives often leads to suffering. Lack of integrity brings pathological behavior. The soul cannot remain at peace when it lives in darkness and lies. Lies always lead to more lies. When we seek to serve ourselves by using religion to gain recognition, power, and control, our souls will never be satisfied.

We are created in the image and likeness of God. Just as the essence of God is love, compassion, generosity, justice, and peace, our souls will be satisfied as we imitate our Creator. We can never feel complete until our inner life produces external good works that shine and invite people to praise the Lord.

Integrity will bring fulfillment because our good deeds "will be remembered forever!" (CEB). That is true happiness.

God, thank you for satisfying our soul. Help us live in integrity so our good deeds will be remembered forever, allowing us to experience true happiness. Amen.

Proclaiming the Law

FEBRUARY 6–12, 2023 • CAMERON BARR

SCRIPTURE OVERVIEW: This week we continue to explore the importance of Christian morality. We do not earn God's grace by our actions; rather, our obedience is a response to God's grace. In Deuteronomy, we read that the choice of life will bring prosperity and is the proper response from a heart of gratitude. The psalmist echoes this sentiment, for blessed are those who follow the Lord not just with words but also with actions. The Corinthians have not understood this, so they continue to act like those in the world around them, living by the flesh instead of by the Spirit. Jesus pushes us even further. God sees not only what we do on the outside but who we are on the inside. A true life of obedience begins on the inside and flows outward.

QUESTIONS AND SUGGESTIONS FOR REFLECTION

- Read Deuteronomy 30:15-20. When have you experienced the choice God sets before us of life or death, prosperity or adversity, blessings or curses? How have you discerned how to obey God?
- Read Psalm 119:1-8. How does following God's commandments bring you joy?
- Read 1 Corinthians 3:1-9. What affiliations of yours or of people you know could you insert in place of "Paul" or "Apollos" in the scripture?
- Read Matthew 5:21-37. When have you experienced legalistic interpretations of scripture? How do you get to the heart of scripture?

Senior Pastor of United Church of Chapel Hill, Chapel Hill, NC.

Scholars identify much of the book of Deuteronomy with an ancient collection of laws called the Covenant Code. The first five books of the Bible are full of legal artifacts that give us clues to how ancient Hebrews lived and worshiped. The Ten Commandments recorded in Exodus and Deuteronomy are the most famous collection of biblical laws. The Priestly Code in Leviticus governing purity and cleanliness also comes readily to mind—these laws are most memorable because they are occasionally deeply objectionable to contemporary readers. They address what to eat, what to wear, and how to use one's body to be ready for worship. Justice-minded Christians will also be familiar with biblical laws concerning how to relate to immigrants, resident aliens, orphans, and widows. There are laws about property ownership, livestock, charging interest on debt, and the rights of workers. All these laws offer us a glimpse into the history of daily life in Israel.

Among all the law codes held in the Bible, the Covenant Code is distinguished by the principles it establishes for Israel's relationship with God. Frequently repeated throughout the code is this familiar formulation: "If you obey the commandments of the LORD your God . . . the LORD your God will bless you in the land that you are entering to possess." The covenant frames the choice for Israel: life or death, blessing or curse, prosperity or adversity. Obedience to God's law is the path to keeping in relationship with God. Or, to put it another way, there is no life outside this covenant. The only way of life is within the relationship God has established with us.

Gracious God, you have given us the law to accompany and instruct us. Grant that in keeping faith with you we will be responsible to one another so that grace may abound in the life we have with you. Amen.

The legal codes of Deuteronomy describe Israel's life in the context of God's covenant and offer us a window into ancient history. They show what conflicts arose out of daily life, what the community valued, how the nation treated the poor, and how its leaders executed justice. But the law codes themselves are not always easy reading. The legal information enclosed in the otherwise gripping narratives of Exodus and Deuteronomy is taxing for most readers. And even the most devoted scripture readers usually skip over the dense codes of Leviticus and Numbers.

The psalmist takes a different approach. Here the law is poetry, reminding us that scripture is a great library that presents God's word to us in many different ways so that we have every opportunity to hear it.

Notice the psalmist's fixation on what God has said and the strong nouns used to intensify "the law of the LORD." *Decrees. Precepts. Statutes. Commandments. Ordinances.* And what are the feelings associated with obedience to God's law? They are *happiness, gratitude,* and *praise.* You might say that the psalmist takes a milder approach than the Deuteronomist. Rather than describing the if/then paradigm—life or death, blessing or curse—the poet gives his energy to the positive goods associated with life in God's law, leaving the negative consequences of disobedience to fall into the silence. The poet describes the light and leaves the darkness to our imagination.

Poets and historians have different vocations, but here we see them working together to the same end. The poet elevates the historian's work. They carry the same message by different means: *We have true life only inside God's covenant.*

Praise, thanksgiving, and glory to you, O God, for the happiness we share in your covenant. Grant that in living with justice and mercy we may experience the joy of your creation. Amen.

Proclaiming the Law

Law codes mentioned in the New Testament are also a revealing window into the past. The authors of the Gospels appeal to Jesus as a source of authority. None do so more than Matthew, who reports Jesus' comments on Hebrew law codes concerning murder, making oaths, and marriage. The attention Jesus gives to these laws in particular suggests that Jewish and early Christian communities had special interest in these topics.

The Sermon on the Mount intensifies the Hebrew law and demands perfection of Christ-followers in our outward action and the inward thoughts of our hearts. Where the law says "Thou shalt not murder," Jesus forbids anger. Where the law forbids adultery, Jesus prohibits desire. Where the law condemns the making of dishonest oaths, Jesus says we should live our lives so that no oaths are necessary at all.

Jesus' words raise the expectations for Christian character and require of us virtue that exceeds the letter of the law. But another consequence of this sermon is that we are all confronted with our personal shortcomings. Who among us has never been angry? How could we avoid attraction and still be human? Of course none of us is absolutely blameless. So by raising the bar well above the heads of even the most virtuous people, Jesus shows how we all fall short of God's perfect love.

And by mentioning these particular subjects in the law—murder, marriage and divorce, the making of contracts—Jesus comments on subjects where we must exercise moral judgment. That leaves us wondering: Is the greater sin to violate the law or to walk self-righteously within it?

God, when we give, remind us of our poverty. When we counsel, awaken in us our grieving. When we feed others, strike us with our hunger. When we pass judgment, afflict us with the mercy we have received. Amen.

Any preacher braving the narrow ridge this week between the law on one hand and grace on the other may want to rethink their route. Few will navigate it without falling into anti-Jewish habits or even supersessionist ideologies. Nowhere is the journey more perilous than when traveling with Paul.

The images suggestive of maturation—of children fed milk before solid food, of seeds watered and cultivated—require careful treatment in the context of other readings that address the meaning of Hebrew law. Any assertion that Jesus' treatment of the law is an improvement over Jewish practice is to be strictly avoided. Versions of this harmful predilection include unnecessary distinctions between the *Old* Testament and the *New* Testament, portrayals of the Hebrew law as especially vengeful or graceless, and presenting first-century Jewish people as rejecting Jesus as a well-meaning but unwelcome savior.

Paul gives us more than enough room to use these images properly with reference to our own experiences and our own communities. Asking, "Are you not merely human?" Paul questions the spirit of division that reigns in the Corinthian church and points to the human condition that we all share (see 1 Corinthians 3:4). We know that Paul's communities were riven with disputes over circumcision, marriage, sexuality, untrustworthy leaders, structure, and organization. Against the backdrop of these quarrels and jealousies, Paul's message has an equalizing effect similar to Jesus' use of the Hebrew law in the Sermon on the Mount. He reminds us of our humanity. We use these images—the milk, the growing garden—not to suggest that our faith is more advanced than someone else's but to describe our own dependence on God's grace.

Mothering One, we are still learning and growing. Teach us to respect and honor our neighbors so we may not puff ourselves up by shaming those who are different. Amen.

Proclaiming the Law

We can often take our preaching cues from the form of the text itself. If the text tells a story, we might preach in a narrative form. When preaching from a parable, we might try to model the mystery or irony in Jesus' teaching. Or if the scripture is a direct teaching, perhaps the sermon could be didactic. The form of the sermon often follows the form of the text.

But it would be a good idea to think carefully about following the form of the text when we dare to preach on law and grace. Do we really want to follow the Deuteronomist and present the law as an ultimatum? "But if your heart turns away and you do not hear . . . I declare to you that you shall perish." Or do we really want to recite Jesus' harsh judgments on adultery and divorce in the Sermon on the Mount without adding a measure of pastoral sensitivity?

Biblical law is more than a guide to what's right and wrong. It's a record of our humanity—where we fall short, how we've struggled, and how God has interceded for us. So when my sermons are sounding a little preachy, or when the form of the text tempts me toward finger-wagging and harsh judgments, I find it helpful to reconsider how I'm preaching the gospel in the first place. Maybe tell a different story. Or ask a question. Or—for the sake of all God's people—just lighten up!

Let Jesus say, "Be perfect, as your heavenly father is perfect." The rest of us should make room for grace.

Creator God, through Christ Jesus you have taught us how to pray. Guide us also in our speaking and our teaching, that proclaiming the law among your people may lead us into renewed life with you. Amen.

Most of us can recall a teacher or mentor who profoundly shaped how we understand ourselves and the world. I often think with gratitude about my high-school English teacher. Most teachers used ballpoint pens to comment on student work, and many used blue ink as a signal of gentleness and mercy; but not my English teacher. He kept on his desk a fat-tipped red Sharpie. He would cross out entire paragraphs and write blunt notes in the margins. Though he was harsh in his judgment, there's no denying he was an effective instructor. The skills he taught me with so little delicacy prepared me for college and sustained me when I found expectations suddenly raised.

Analogously, the psalmist relates to God's law with the gratitude of a student who has been shaped by its instruction. Whereas the law is often presented as a litany of negative prohibitions—"Thou shalt not"—the psalmist shows us the benefits of studying and obeying God's law. Like the needful critique of a teacher, the instructions are a sign of God's care. And like a student who is seeking assistance, the psalmist looks to the law for help in living up to it. Keeping the law faithfully becomes a gratifying and enjoyable discipline, as writing has become for me. Hence the odes of thanksgiving and praise: "Happy are those who keep God's decrees."

Psalm 119 is both a hymn of praise for the help that God has rendered and a prayer for God's help. It is praise and plea in the same breath: *Thank you for showing me the way; help me to stay on the path.*

You know the material, O God, and you know the student. You know us better than we know ourselves. Reveal the truth we need to know, and speak to us in the way that we need to hear. Amen.

To close a week of reflection on the law—the Hebrew law, an ode to it in the Psalms, and Jesus' radical ethic—we hear a final word of grace from Paul, who is having some trouble with the Corinthian Christians. One of his problems is that members of the church are loyal to different sources of authority. Some are listening to him; others follow Apollos. We can't tell from the letters we have what the exact differences are, but we do know that the congregation is divided.

Rather than argue for his own position (there is plenty of that in other passages!), Paul refers to the original purpose of the congregation as a place of Christian community. He sees the "jealousy and quarrels" reported from Corinth as signs of our humanity. His teaching carries the conviction that Christ will soon return. In Paul's mind, the kingdom of God is soon to be at hand. He hopes this expectation will motivate the communities of faith in his care to live peaceably and righteously. So Paul is pleading for humility—and doing his best to set a good example—that we may look to God and not to ourselves as the promise of salvation.

Ecclesial disagreements and political turmoil in the church are the surest sign that we continue to await the fulfillment of Christ's promises. The community aspiring to be Christlike is the very place we continue to find unChristian behavior. It's a humbling irony known to every Christian.

Merciful God, we trust you know we are doing our best. Thank you for renewing your covenant with us day by day. Bless the community of the church with faithful hearts so that when we fall short of Christlike love, we may recall your love for our humanity and turn once more in hope toward you. Amen.

Come Up and Be Free

FEBRUARY 13–19, 2023 • JUANITA C. RASMUS

SCRIPTURE OVERVIEW: The Transfiguration is a striking manifestation of the union of humanity and divinity in Christ. In Exodus, Moses goes up the mountain to meet with God, and the divine presence on the mountain is like a consuming fire. The psalmist says that all who take refuge in the Lord are happy. In Second Peter the author declares that the truth of Christ's message is affirmed by the glory that surrounds Jesus on the mountain and the voice from heaven that confirms his authority. In Matthew's account, the revelation of the glory of the divine son of God on top of a mountain causes the disciples to fall down in fear. Moses and Elijah are present, demonstrating the continuity of Christ with the prophets and the always overwhelming splendor of God's presence.

QUESTIONS AND SUGGESTIONS FOR REFLECTION

- Read Exodus 24:12-18. When have you experienced God's cleansing and transforming fire?
- Read Psalm 2. How have you taken refuge in God?
- Read 2 Peter 1:16-21. How can you be attentive to the light of God in the world around you?
- Read Matthew 17:1-9. When have you experienced God's love shining through you?

Spiritual director; co-pastor of St. John's United Methodist Church in Houston, TX; author of *Learning to Be: Finding Your Center After the Bottom Falls Out.*

Yahweh invites Moses to come up higher where he will receive instructions to guide the children of Israel. Moses reminds us all of the necessity of obedience. God called only him, and he followed Yahweh's instructions to the letter. How often do we sense the presence of God calling us into silence and solitude—into seclusion with God alone—and instead we invite family and friends? Moses' obedience encourages us to be mindful that some tasks are ours alone to fulfill.

"Come up, come close." We are always being invited to come up. Ours is a movement upward, an invitation to enter into the presence of Divine being. This world's invitation is always to "do" first, to "have," and then ultimately to "be." God is always inviting us first and foremost to "be." Come be present to the God guiding your footsteps. "Come be with me so I may prepare you," says our gracious God, calling each of us into our most expansive self.

The benefit of obedience to the grand invitation is access to knowing something more of God. We are transfigured, changed by coming into contact with Yahweh. The invitation may be offered at odd times—when we are weary and indecisive, when our plates are way too full, when our plans are set and seem unchangeable. Still the Spirit says, "Come, get away with me to learn."

Eugene Peterson wrote in *The Message* version of Matthew 11:29 about "the unforced rhythms of grace." The gift of being alone with God is walking away with Divine influence upon us and guidance within us. Nothing is forced; rather it is a way of being that gives us life and empowers us to lead and serve well.

Gracious God, help me be immediately obedient to your guidance so I receive all you have for me and for those whom I am called to lead and serve. Amen.

Even though Jesus just miraculously fed 4,000 people, not counting women and children—with leftovers to prove it—the Pharisees still seek a sign (see Matthew 15:32–16:4). Jesus declares that no sign shall be given to that generation and later says, "There are some standing here who will not taste death before they see the Son of Man coming in his kingdom" (Matt. 16:28). Some people perpetually seek signs and some simply want to see; it is the latter who are rewarded. Jesus invited Peter, James, and John to come up and see.

Six days later, Jesus took his companions with him. It was a time for them and Jesus to be alone together. Jesus took them to a space of intimacy and invited them to see more of the kingdom of God, more of its dazzling power and glory. Upon the high mountain, they were separated from the distractions of the noisy crowd who were demanding signs of what was already present.

Not all who clamor for signs are interested in seeing. Peter, James, and John were invited to see what the crowd soon would only blaspheme, ridicule, and deny. Like the disciples, we are invited to see the radiance of the kingdom of God made visible before our very eyes. Separated from the crowd of doubters, haters, naysayers, and spectators, Jesus longs to take us up higher, to draw us closer.

The question is whether we are the "show me" generation, the "prove it to me" cynics, or are genuinely interested in being in a relationship with God.

Deliver me, Jesus, from the desire to be entertained by the kingdom of God. Help me see the kingdom that calls me to climb higher and see better. Amen.

What happens while we pray? Would that we, like Jesus, could experience the power of being transfigured!

How often we approach prayer scowling, smirking, or rolling our eyes from a day filled with too much doing. Too often we come to prayer without the slightest sense that we are entering the presence of God. Too often we forget that in God's presence things can be changed—*we* can be changed—made more like God, transformed. Would that we could see ourselves as entering into the infinite mystery that is God! How might we be moved beyond our limited vision of our capabilities? Jesus was changed beyond anything the disciples could have imagined of him.

Imagine what it must have been like to watch as Jesus' face changed while in prayer. What if we remember that others are watching the effect our praying has on our lives?

Times of prayer always hold the possibility that we too may be called, invited to enter into the Holy of Holies to stand in God's presence. Scripture encourages us to imagine that we are with Jesus experiencing what the disciples felt in the presence of his transfiguration.

Take a moment to reread the passage slowly and allow your mind and spirit to embrace the words. Sit up tall and straight. Breathe in deeply and exhale slowly. See yourself along with Jesus and the disciples together in prayer. Allow yourself to enter this text.

Light of God, I ask that you flow freely through me. Change me so that I radiate your love in my day and my world. Amen.

Jesus invites his inner circle to come up the high mountain to experience an exalted state of consciousness, a higher state of spiritual reality. As Jesus is transfigured before their eyes, their lives are transformed. They encounter the grandeur of God's love for his Son. Peter is so moved he feels they need to commemorate the moment. When have you known a moment so rich, so pure, so love-filled that it became like a high mountain?

Sitting in front of a grand fireplace near the Rockies one winter, I simply allowed myself to be with the fire, to tune in to its warm glow. When I finally walked away, I realized I had become the warmth I had been present to; it radiated throughout my body. I was now living the warmth of the fire—which was an image of transfiguration. We are invited to know God in the way I came to know the warmth from the hearth. We are invited to return frequently as we notice our old ways, biases, judgments, and unhealthy thinking starting to resurface. We are invited to linger with God, who warms us from the inside.

Spiritual practices like meditation can help us be with God deeply, and in the process we can find ourselves changing, warming up from the divine presence.

I have found being with any of the natural elements can offer this deep being with God. Mountains, streams, beaches, gardens, the woods, even golf course greens can become places of transfiguration. These are all places where we can experience God's presence.

Gracious Creator, oh how you love us! Help me today to stay open to your invitation to go higher and know you more deeply. Amen.

At first, Psalm 2 throws you headfirst into conflict, with nations competing for power, conspiring and plotting in vain, pushing and jockeying for position. It can all too easily be read as "their problem back then." It is simply too easy to see this as an obsolete, historical issue even though we see this kind of wrangling for power all around the world today: tribes, homeowners' associations, governments, coworkers—no one is immune from the pandemic of people plotting for power and position. So after reading this text, I put it down, then came back and used *lectio divina* to let the text inform me and transform my assumptions.

A deep listening to this text reminds us that it is not solely an "out there" matter but rather a projection of what happens all too often in each of us. We human beings want our own way. Our opportunity for growth is when we notice how often we find ourselves striving to have our way over God's way.

Even though God invites us to forgive, we dig in and declare that we will forgive *once we get our apology* and not one second earlier. It is impressed upon our heart to call a friend we haven't heard from, but we put it off. We feel a longing that simply will not be satisfied, a longing that could serve others, but we ignore it because it would require effort or inconvenience or sacrifice.

The Spirit speaks in all these longings, urgings, and promptings, and our delays disregard God as sovereign—just as clearly as did the conspiring nations in our text. How are you being invited to settle the power question? What word or phrase is speaking to you after rereading and listening to this text? What needs to be settled in you today?

Gracious God, I am open and willing to surrender to the way you offer to lead me. Amen.

Peter affirms that his message came from his personal experience with Jesus Christ. His energy and enthusiasm almost leap from the printed page. What about your story? What have you come to know as the reality of your life with God? What have you seen? What have you heard? How often do you remember your history with God when you need comfort or support in times of difficulty or disorientation?

Our capacity to remember is a transformational tool. When we recall moments of great joy, great revelation, or even great sadness, our brains release the chemicals in our bodies that we felt when the memory was impressed upon us. We have the ability to relive and reengage our moments by returning to them over and over again, especially those that served us well. We can imagine Peter and the crew gathered at meals, each telling the timeless story of the moment when the Creator entered into time and space and spoke life to them.

Recall a moment that was transformative, a moment you will always remember. Perhaps it was a time when it seemed that your back was against the wall financially, emotionally, relationally, vocationally, or a bit of them all. Then remember a time when you couldn't have been more certain about what you saw and heard from the Spirit. How might such a spiritual practice serve you as you routinely remember God's love for you being declared and manifested over your lifetime? Take a moment to select a memory of a particular time where the presence, power, or word of God was alive for you. Take the memory in fully, then think about the life of God made known to you.

Gracious God, you declare that we are your children. Help me recall a moment where you declared your love for me. Amen.

TRANSFIGURATION SUNDAY

God provides Moses with instructions for guiding the people of Israel. The law and commandments invite the freed children of former slaves into life with God. God is building a new kingdom among people whose DNA was rooted in another kingdom order.

I recall a time when I was leaving the United States for Africa to attend a United Nations World Conference on Racism. We attended an orientation session to be briefed on African laws and how to conduct ourselves there. We were told about daily check-ins for debriefing our activities and for planning our week. Our experience was strongly affected by the quality of our orientation.

God invited Moses to come up to meet him on the mountain to receive the tablets of stone designed to orient the Israelites into a new way of being. This provided the Israelites with a means to orient and guide themselves into their new life. They were in essence pledging allegiance to a set of governing principles designed to work the old ways out of their system and to facilitate living in the kingdom of the everlasting God.

It was God's idea that these followers would have the benefit of a guidance system in their hearts and minds. They were being invited to experience the transformational effects of God's word being hidden in their hearts so that they would not sin against one another or against God. These laws and commandments were established to cultivate responses of thought, feeling, emotion, and action. The result of the law would be that the followers would begin to live freely and abundantly in the flow of God's love.

Gracious God, orient me by the power of your word so that I think, believe, and behave differently and come to know all the freedoms you have for me. Amen.

The Practices of Hard Days

FEBRUARY 20–26, 2023 • TEX SAMPLE

SCRIPTURE OVERVIEW: In this first week of Lent, we prepare our hearts for a period of reflection. We think about areas of our lives in which we might be falling short of God's desires. The problem of sin enters the human story at the very beginning when Adam and Eve choose to follow their own wisdom rather than guidance from God. The psalmist highlights the importance of recognizing our sin and asking for forgiveness, which God is quick to give. In Romans, Paul argues that we all partake in the broken human condition because we all have sinned as Adam did. The teachings from the Sermon on the Mount warn us against misplaced desires and selfishness.

QUESTIONS AND SUGGESTIONS FOR REFLECTION

- Read Genesis 2:15-17; 3:1-7. How might this story help you turn to humility throughout your Lenten journey?
- Read Psalm 32. What seeming dichotomies comprise the full picture of your life of faith?
- Read Romans 5:12-19. How do you sense the differences Paul draws between Adam and Christ prompting you to turn toward God?
- Read Matthew 6:1-6,16-21. How do you practice your piety? What is your treasure, and where is it?

A specialist in church and society, a storyteller, author, and the Robert B. and Kathleen Rogers Professor Emeritus of Church and Society at the Saint Paul School of Theology, a United Methodist seminary in Kansas City, MO.

Three teenaged buddies and I were on a camping trip when we discovered a watermelon patch on a farm on the other side of a barbed-wire fence. The watermelon patch was dried up, and only one melon, about the size of a football, remained. As we crawled through the fence, we knew we were stealing, but after all, it was just one small watermelon. We could've quoted Satan: "You will not die" or "This is not a big deal."

I was about to cut open that watermelon with my big Boy Scout knife, when the farmer who owned the land suddenly appeared at the top of a hill about one hundred yards away. He knew, though we did not, that the birdshot shells in his 12-gauge shotgun, would not hurt us from that distance. But when he fired, those birdshot hitting dried up watermelon vines around us sounded like the world was coming to an end. I jammed that football-sized watermelon under my right arm and hurdled a three-strand, barbed-wire fence to escape. Deep in the woods, a half mile away, we gorged down that watermelon—the worst I ever ate.

How could such a sorry watermelon "be a delight to the eyes" and be so desired? The Genesis story of the forbidden fruit seems exactly right. Saint Augustine tells the story of stealing pears that he didn't want and which he finally dumped to the hogs. He even says that he had no real inducement beyond that of just doing the evil itself. He says he took the pears simply to disobey.

Once we have knowledge of good and evil, there seems to be a dynamic that makes the forbidden desirable. With that comes a craving to cross the barbed-wire fences of our lives.

Dear God, help us ultimately to desire only you and to cast off cravings that lead to our diminishment and death. Amen.

The day's work had ended at a church conference on urban ministry, and a group of us were seated around a hotel room reviewing the day. Suddenly, one of the clergy said, "I guess I need help. My wife committed suicide a few weeks ago, and I am having a terrible time. The day she died I felt strange leaving home. After an hour at the church office and still feeling very unsettled, I called home. No answer. I drove back home and ran through every room, not finding her. Then I went back to our bedroom and thought to look under our bed. She was there, lying face up, dead from an overdose. She had struggled with depression for a long time. Now I feel such a deep guilt about her death that I cannot get free of it."

We were at a loss for words. We sat there for moments that seemed like hours. Suddenly, my friend, Jimmy Hope Smith, who was sitting on the bed beside the pastor, turned sideways to address him and said:

"By the grace of God, I am ordained to declare people forgiven of their sins. Tonight I declare to you that you are forgiven of all your sins. You are forgiven of those things for which you are guilty and for a false guilt that holds you captive. From this day on you are free to live and you are free to die."

It stopped everything, and shortly thereafter the meeting broke up. Sometime later, I checked with people who knew the grieving pastor. They reported to me that that evening had turned his life around. Apparently, he had been released from his captivity to guilt and, indeed, was free to live again.

God of mercy, forgive us for the wrongs we have done. Set us free from false guilt that controls our lives so that we can live in freedom before you. Amen.

The Practices of Hard Days

ASH WEDNESDAY

I can remember times in my life when I have been wrong. In those times I had difficulty with guilt. What frustrated me was not the absence of forgiveness; I knew I was forgiven. But I was captive to guilt. My issue was not so much forgiveness as it was deliverance and release from the powers of guilt that had me in bondage. I found new direction in Paul's writings. I discovered that I must be freed from my sense of guilt in order to receive forgiveness.

It is interesting that forgiveness is hardly mentioned at all in the authentic writings of the apostle. And in those few times when Paul does write of forgiveness, it is in terms of the people of the *ecclesia,* the church, forgiving each other.

The big issue for Paul is not forgiveness but *deliverance* from powers that enslave us: death, sin, the flesh, the law, and other cosmic powers. These are the problems we face. The human condition for Paul is one of human captivity. This is very clear in our biblical passage today where death exercises dominion over our lives. But Christ on the cross takes on this enslaving power; that is, as Christ is obedient to God, he becomes subject to the power of death. But then in his resurrection he has victory over death. In these acts of Crucifixion and Resurrection are our deliverance and our hope.

Dear God in Christ, set us free from the captivities that enslave us, and enable us to live in the freedom of your Spirit. May we be your people doing your work in the world. Amen.

I played catcher in baseball and softball for thirty-five years. The most difficult thing about catching is holding on to the ball when you are run over by a runner trying to score. A crucial practice, it requires training. One way to train a catcher is for someone to make a soft throw (which is harder to catch) to the catcher and for a second person to slam the catcher with a big pillow just as he catches the ball. This action is repeated over and over again. The natural tendency is to release your grip when you are hit. This practice reverses that tendency.

I thought about this while reading our lesson from Joel. Sure, he is speaking of a much more serious situation, a Day of the Lord, one of darkness and gloom. But I am intrigued by the great range of practices he suggests for facing this hard time. Calling us to return to God, to rely on God's grace, mercy, and steadfast love, to gather, and to blow the trumpet. He even calls the bride and groom to leave the wedding and come to the event. And he calls on ministers and priests to weep and ask God to spare the people. Meanwhile, we are not to make a mockery of our tradition or to question God's presence and power.

These are sound practices for our own times of pandemics, climate change, and grave social inequality. It is a time to rely on God, to assemble, to call people to the urgency of the moment, indeed, to spare the people and not make a mockery of our heritage of love, justice, righteousness, and peace.

Loving God, be with us through these difficult days, and prepare us through practices of faithfulness to love, do justice, and be a righteous people. Amen.

This psalm is tough. David has had what can at best be called an adulterous dalliance with Bathsheba and has gotten her pregnant. He then tries to cover up his actions by placing her husband, Uriah, in combat to get him killed. This leads to Nathan's confrontation of David: "Thou art the man!" (See 2 Samuel 12:1-10.)

This psalm is one of the most powerful confessions of sin in scripture. People reading this devotion may not ever have engaged in the violations and violence of David, but there have been times when each of us has needed a prayer of repentance as powerful as this one.

I once taught a first-year class with students whose names I did not know well. One of the students was blowing off assignments and doing failing work. When the class turned in a required paper, I wrote a note at the end of what I thought was the unmotivated student's paper that she should either get serious or consider withdrawing from the school. The paper, however, was that of a student who was working and needed my support, not my negative appraisal of her motivation.

Seeing my comment, the second student came to see me to let me know she was withdrawing from class and from seminary. When I realized what I had done, I felt guilt I have seldom known in my entire life. I apologized profusely.

She was generous of spirit and felt she was not ready for seminary and that she needed to withdraw—and she did. She later returned and did fine work. But I shall never forget my sin against her. Thanks to her forgiving character we remain friends to this day.

Dear God of grace and mercy, we repent of our violations of you and of others. Grant us, O God, the presence and power of your Holy Spirit that we may live more faithfully to you and to our neighbors near and far. Amen.

My uncle was a bootlegger in my hometown in the late 1940s and 50s. He wore $300 suits, a ten-gallon Stetson hat, and Italian shoes. The roll of money in the front right pocket of his pants was so big he had his pockets custom made to accompany this excess of greenbacks.

When he infrequently attended church, he sat up front, placed his cowboy hat with the label up on the pew next to him, and eagerly awaited the offering. During the collection, he pulled out that big roll of money and, holding it shoulder high, drew out a $20 bill. He would then, in full view of the congregation, ceremoniously fold it lengthwise and spear the collection plate with it. It was an impressive performance.

Some people were critical of my uncle, but I remember one saint in the church who thought he fit in rather well with the pretensions of any number of other members of the congregation. It seemed to her that the distinction between authentic piety and just plain showing off exposed plenty of blame to go around. She seemed to think that the main difference between my uncle and some others in the congregation was that they just hid it better.

Today's passage in Matthew lists three practices meant to be authentic in faithfulness, but they are easily corrupted. These are dangers of showing off: giving alms so that people will think you're generous, praying so that you can be seen, and fasting to look so bad that people will think you are a saint. There is probably enough there for all of us to work on.

Great God, help us to love you authentically, to be compassionate toward others, and to fall so much in love with reality that we may no longer be captive to pretense. Amen.

First Sunday in Lent

Invited to interview for the deanship at the Boston University School of Theology, I pursued the job for all the wrong reasons. I wanted to succeed my great teacher, Dean Walter Muelder. I sought the status and authority of that office and its affirmation of my life at thirty-six years of age. It didn't occur to me that I wouldn't enjoy the job itself, or that I was called to be a full-time teacher.

The first interview with the faculty went well; they wanted me. The interview with the president of the university was the final hurdle. We were into that interview not ten minutes when the president and I got into a heated argument. He walked out. I was crushed. It was over.

I went to see Harold Beck, a wonderful professor of Old Testament at the school. There I broke down and wept like a child. Providing an empathic silence, Beck canceled his afternoon appointments, offered to take me to supper and then to the airport. He participated with me in my grief and pain.

I remembered Beck when I read Paul's comment: "For our sake [God] made [Christ] to be sin who knew no sin." I do not equate Beck's actions with Christ on the cross. Rather, Beck's actions were an implication of what Christ had done. Paul's comment does not mean that Christ's character became sinful but rather that God placed Christ in a relationship of participation with us and thereby became subject to the powers of torture, sin, and death. That day Beck entered into my life in a sensitive and participational way. He became Christ to me. His actions began a transformation of my life that was healing and finally redemptive.

God of love, we thank you for the participational love of Christ and for all those who have loved us into life and hope. Amen.

Stepping Out, Delving Deep

FEBRUARY 27–MARCH 5, 2023 • ELIZABETH W. CORRIE

SCRIPTURE OVERVIEW: The readings for this week provide an overview of the history of God's people. Genesis recounts the story of Abraham, who because of his great faith leaves his home and goes to a land that God has promised to show him. The psalmist speaks for the descendants of Abraham, who trust the Lord to watch over them and be their helper. Paul in Romans argues against those who believe that God's grace is a result of correctly following religious law. It is Abraham's faith (for there is no law in Abraham's time) that prompts him to follow God, and for this he is commended. John emphasizes that the story of Jesus is the continuation of a relationship with God's faithful people that began with Abraham and continued through Moses.

QUESTIONS AND SUGGESTIONS FOR REFLECTION

- Read Genesis 12:1-4a. Recall a major and a minor crossroads in your life. How did you listen for God's call during each time?
- Read Psalm 121. Reflect on the times in your life when this psalm has most strongly resonated with you. How do your strongest emotions point you to God's presence?
- Read Romans 4:1-5, 13-17. What motivates you to do good works? How do you balance "faith alone" and the action to which God calls you?
- Read John 3:1-17. How do you hear again the powerful words of verses so familiar that they permeate culture? What makes these words fresh for you?

Professor in the Practice of Youth Education and Peacebuilding and Director of the Program in Religious Education at Candler School of Theology, Emory University, in Atlanta, GA; General Editor of the *CEB Student Bible* and author of *Youth Ministry as Peace Education: Overcoming Silence, Transforming Violence.*

The Psalms are the songs and prayers of the Israelites, and this psalm, part of the Songs of Ascent (see Psalms 120–134), most likely functioned as a pilgrimage song for people journeying toward Jerusalem to the Temple for religious festivals. Likewise, we can begin this second week of our Lenten journey imagining ourselves as pilgrims stepping away from our daily distractions to move intentionally toward a deeper awareness of the God who creates, keeps, and redeems us every moment of our lives.

Imagine yourself as the psalmist. If you look up toward a mountain, across a large lake, or up at the stars on a clear night, you can feel what the writer experienced—amazement and wonder at how vulnerable and fleeting your existence is compared to the vastness of the earth and the universe in which it sits.

This is a humbling moment, that moment of realizing how utterly dependent you are upon your Creator for your very existence. It is not a terrifying moment, unlike moments when you might feel vulnerable during extreme weather, global pandemics, societal turmoil, or broken relationships. No, this is a moment of assurance, a moment when you realize that you are utterly dependent on a Creator who is also your keeper and your redeemer. Our God "keeps" us—the Hebrew word used here is *shamar*, which can be translated as "keep," "guard," "watch over," or "preserve." Our God never slumbers, keeping each one of us "from now until forever from now."

What would it mean to trust that the One upon whom you are utterly dependent truly is keeping you as you step out into your Lenten journey? What might this free you to do?

Lord, teach me to embrace my vulnerability and trust that my help comes from you, the maker of heaven and earth, the keeper who never slumbers. Amen.

Abram who becomes Abraham is our forefather in faith. Why? Because he stepped out into an unknown future to an unknown land, trusting fully in God's promise that he would be a blessing to the nations. Before this moment, we know very little about Abram other than that he is the son of Terah, who had migrated from Ur to Haran with his extended family, and that Abram's wife Sarai was unable to have children (see Genesis 11:30-31). We also know that God commanded him to leave his land, his family, and his father's household—and that he apparently did this without any questions or conversation.

Pause here to consider the risk Abram was taking. Leaving behind his land, family, and household, taking only Sarai and Lot with him, to journey to an unknown place left him vulnerable to violence, hunger, disease, and even loneliness. He also had to carry the responsibility of exposing his wife and nephew to these risks, even though they had not heard directly from God as he had. We know nothing about Abram's relationship with God before this moment. Did he, like the psalmist, lift his eyes to the hills around Haran and realize that he was created by a God who will never slumber and who would protect him from all evil?

Rooting himself deeply in his vulnerability as a creature utterly dependent on God for his existence, Abram becomes free to trust that his Creator is also his keeper—the protector and the keeper of promises. This is the blessing that Abram becomes: He blesses us by showing us how to take risks that will move us closer to God's promises. We bless Abram when we follow his example—embracing our vulnerability by trusting in God our Creator and keeper.

God of Abraham, free me to trust you enough to take risks that bring me closer to your promises for me and for all of your creation. Amen.

Abraham is central for Paul in his letter to the Romans because Paul sees Abraham as the common ancestor for Jews and Gentiles, showing both peoples how faith works. While we might imagine Abram lifting his eyes to the hills and embracing the vulnerability of his createdness in trusting the God who never slumbers, we also have no reason to believe he did anything special leading up to the moment God spoke to him to deliver the divine promise. This is how Paul wants us to understand grace through faith: Just as Abraham did nothing to earn the divine promise, so we can do nothing to earn our salvation. And just as Abraham nonetheless became a blessing to all nations, so all Christ-followers can become adopted into the family tree that begins with Abram.

As simple as the concept of grace is—we cannot work our way to salvation because salvation is a gift—living into this concept daily is challenging. Western culture in particular promotes the idea that we are only as valuable as our last accomplishment, that we should be measured by what we produce, consume, or display. This is why practices of fasting and rest are radical forms of discipleship.

If you are not already doing so, consider deepening your Lenten journey by fasting from a habit or practice that ties you too closely to human economies that rely on overwork and over-consumption. Find moments this season to rest in the assurance that you are God's precious child, loved unconditionally, chosen, like Abram, before you did anything to earn it.

Gracious God, thank you for adopting me as your child. Allow me to rest, knowing you never rest. Allow me to know—deep down—the gift of grace you have offered me. Amen.

When considering the conversation between Jesus and Nicodemus, it is important to note that Nicodemus shows up again later in two places in John's Gospel—when he challenges his fellow Pharisees to refrain from judging Jesus' teaching without first listening to and learning from him (see 7:50) and when he works with Joseph of Arimathea to care for Jesus' body after the Crucifixion (see 19:39). Nicodemus, in his own way, shows up for Jesus and arguably does a better job of it than those disciples who scatter after Jesus' arrest.

We can thus appreciate Nicodemus' faith journey. Coming to Jesus at night, perhaps out of fear or embarrassment, Nicodemus confesses that Jesus is a teacher from God from whom he wants to learn. He stumbles, however, over Jesus' metaphorical language. Though well educated in Jewish law, Nicodemus fixates on the literal interpretation of "born again" or "born from above" and cannot grasp that Jesus is calling for an entirely different kind of "rebirth." But his confusion and persistence in asking questions prompt Jesus to give a speech clearly intended not just for Nicodemus but for all of us: "God so loved the world that he gave his only Son."

We don't know if Nicodemus found clarity in this moment, but we do know that he continued his faith journey and showed up for Jesus to defend and care for him. Nicodemus is a very different model for us than Abraham, but he is a model nonetheless: He shows us the value in asking questions and wrestling with Jesus' teachings, moving beyond literalistic interpretations that fixate on the "how to" of getting into the kingdom toward a deeper understanding of the mission of Jesus that shows up in acts of ongoing learning and care for Christ's body.

O Lord, my keeper, give me the courage to listen to and wrestle with your word, that I, too, may understand what it means to be "born from above." Amen.

Stepping Out, Delving Deep

Jesus responds to Nicodemus's questions with a reference to a curious part of the Israelite story: Moses' creation of a bronze serpent statue to protect the Israelites from dying from snake bites in the wilderness (see Numbers 21:4-9), a statue that later had to be destroyed because it had become a source of idol worship (see 2 Kings 18:4). What do we make of this?

Moses "lifts up" the snake so that Israelites can be saved from death by gazing on this image. Now the Son of Man—Jesus—must be "lifted up" from the grave so that we can be saved from spiritual death and gain eternal life. God now comes to us in the flesh, giving us something upon which to gaze so that we can be saved.

But just as the bronze snake changed from being an image that saves to an idol that kills, Christians sometimes make their particular images of Jesus into idols, creating stumbling blocks to others growing in faith. Consider the images of Jesus in artwork around your church or in your home. Consider the stories of Jesus lifted up most in your context. Do they ever create stumbling blocks for others seeking to know Jesus? Are they ever used to exclude Christians with whom you disagree? How would it change your spiritual life if you lifted up images of Jesus from other parts of the world and considered Jesus from other perspectives?

Perhaps stepping out in trust is not always the risky journey Abraham made. Perhaps it is examining our images that have become idols and naming ideas and positions we need to hold looser if we want to share what we love most about Jesus with those who have been hurt by Christians in the past.

Lord, my protector and keeper, you have lifted up your Son for my salvation. Give me courage to step out from my own comfort zone so that my images of you never become idols. Amen.

God promises Abram that all families of the earth will be blessed because of him. This is important to remember, particularly in light of the covenant God made with Noah and every living creature on behalf of every future generation prior to God's promise to Abram (see Genesis 9:12-17). God has a plan to redeem all the earth, but to do so, God must begin with a particular man and a particular family whose descendants will later fill the earth. This is crucial for Paul, who seeks to overcome divisions between Jews and Gentiles by reminding them of their common ancestry through Abraham.

Jews, Muslims, and Christians are often divided over politics and land, as well as over how to live their faith in the world. These groups are also divided within themselves for many of the same reasons. As Christians, we know that much divides Christians from each other, as well as Christians from other children of Abraham. But as Paul reminds us, Abraham stepped out in trust of God's promise long before the Mosaic Law existed. Abraham is our ancestor and role model because of his deep and immediate trust in God, not because of his works under the law.

Abram lifted his eyes to the hills around Haran and knew that God was his keeper, and this empowered him to take a risky journey toward a blessed future for all. The deep trust in God that propelled the psalmist toward Jerusalem and Abram toward Canaan is the same deep trust we need to reach out to people of faith across political, theological, cultural, or economic divisions. While it is unrealistic to expect everyone to "just get along" in our divided world, we find more common ground than we might expect when we step into the chasm dividing us with trust that God is our keeper.

God of Abraham, unite me with my siblings, honoring our shared heritage. Inspire us to bless one another and so bless Abraham, fulfilling your promise. Amen.

Stepping Out, Delving Deep   85

SECOND SUNDAY IN LENT

It is worth re-reading and even memorizing Psalm 121. In its brevity and simplicity, it takes us straight to the heart of what it means to embark on a journey of faith and trust. Notice as you read that the voice of the speaker changes. In verses one and two, we hear the voice of the lone pilgrim: "I lift my eyes" and recall that "my help comes from the LORD." But as we move through the rest of the verses, we find that the words of the first speaker elicit a refrain from elsewhere, affirming that "God won't let your foot slip" and "the LORD will protect you." Visualize this pilgrimage song as a call and response, with the leader beginning and the rest of the community of pilgrims singing out in unison as they step out together toward Jerusalem.

This can be your Lenten journey and your journey of growing in faith beyond Lent. You begin with the moment of centering, the moment of remembering with humility that you are God's precious creation. You trust God to keep and protect you as you take risks—to resist forces that evaluate humans based on their productivity rather than on their inherent worth as children of God; to ask deeper questions that might open up new insights about how God is working in the world; to wrestle with the images of who God is; to step into the gap between people of faith who are in conflict. And when you proclaim this intention to step out in trust to take these risks, know that you are not stepping out alone. The community of God's people, stretching from our ancestor Abraham through all the peoples of the earth, journeys with you.

Gracious, protecting, loving God, bind me with all your people, and give us the humility, wisdom, and courage to step out in trust into your promise for all your creatures. Amen.

Thirsty for God

MARCH 6–12, 2023 • L. ROGER OWENS

SCRIPTURE OVERVIEW: Three of the passages this week connect water and faith. In Exodus and the psalm, we read about the Israelites grumbling in the desert. Although they have seen God's mighty deeds in Egypt, they have begun to question God's provision for them. God provides water through Moses, but the place is remembered (and named) as a site where the faith of the people fails. In John, however, a place to draw water becomes a site of salvation for the Samaritan woman and eventually for the people in her village through her faith. The reading in Romans goes a different direction. Paul emphasizes the importance of faith in the face of trials and the fact that God brings salvation through Christ when fallen humanity has no other hope.

QUESTIONS AND SUGGESTIONS FOR REFLECTION

- Read Exodus 17:1-7. How do your memories of God's provision sustain you through tough stages of your spiritual journey?
- Read Psalm 95. What object, image, or memory serves for you as a symbol of God's faithfulness?
- Read Romans 5:1-11. How have you found hope in stages of life when God is forming your character through suffering and endurance?
- Read John 4:5-42. When has letting go of your expectations or rules allowed God to work freely in your life or in the lives of others around you?

Professor of Christian Spirituality and Ministry, Pittsburgh Theological Seminary; author of *Everyday Contemplative: The Way of Prayerful Living* (Upper Room Books, 2022).

I teach preaching at a theological seminary, and each year my colleagues and I assign this passage as a sermon text to a number of students. I'm accustomed to hearing sermons that berate the Israelites for their grumblings and lack of faith.

I remember one sermon that bucked this trend. The student had lived in a desert region and had experienced drought; she knew what it meant to thirst. She invited her hearers to consider what it's like to be parched, saying the word *parched* slowly so we could hear how dry and gritty it sounds. By the time the sermon ended, we felt sympathy for the Israelites. Any judgment we might have harbored had turned to compassion.

I took the invitation to discover compassion for the Israelites as an invitation to practice compassion for our own suffering. There are real conditions of need in the world. In some cities children thirst for lead-free water. People live in urban food deserts, where it's nearly impossible to find fresh, affordable food. Immigrants traverse dangerous deserts to find hope in a new country. People who complain in these conditions, who call for justice and for change, do not lack faith. Rather, their pain deserves acknowledgment; their cries should be heard.

We thirst in other ways as well. The lonely thirst for community, the weak for strength. The tired thirst for rest, the sick for healing. We all thirst for God when God seems distant. In these situations, we can turn to our own thirst with compassion and acceptance.

When I'm parched, I remember that sermon and put the brakes on berating myself. Rather, I turn to the One who knows our pain and carries our sorrows, who from the cross cried out, "I am thirsty" (John 19:28, CEB).

God, help me to have compassion for my thirst and the thirst of others, knowing that longing and thirst are not foreign to you. Amen.

Sometimes when we read a passage of scripture, we have to fill in the gaps, noticing what's not said. In this passage, I think something is missing: a celebration.

After the Israelites complained of their thirst, accusing Moses of bringing them to the desert to kill them, Moses himself complained to God. So God told Moses to hit a rock with his rod, and water would come out. "Moses did so while Israel's elders watched. He called the place Massah and Meribah" (CEB). Do you see what's missing? The passage never specifies that the Israelites drank.

When I close my eyes to imagine the scene, I see a throng of people—men and women, old and young—running toward the fountain, pushing at first (they're parched, after all). But their jostling turns to celebration when they realize there's enough for everyone. I see kids playing in the water and adults acting like kids, splashing one another. I see relief and joy on their faces. I see a people refreshed. Surely between Moses' striking the rock and his naming the place, the people drank with joy.

The season of Lent is somber. We journey through a metaphorical wilderness. Like the Israelites in their forty-year journey, we stumble and struggle on the way to learning our own identities as we grow closer to the God who journeys with us. Some of us worship in churches that stop saying *Alleluia* during Lent as a way to emphasize the penitential nature of the season.

Yet the God who listened to the Israelites and refreshed them with water goes with us as well. There's no season in which God isn't attentive to our needs, so we shouldn't be surprised to find ourselves refreshed by divine goodness during the journey of Lent. And when we are, why not let an *Alleluia* or two slip from our lips?

God, thank you for the gift of your refreshing presence in every season of our lives. Amen.

Thirsty for God   89

Most mornings when I was in graduate school, I joined the Episcopal campus minister and a few other students in a small chapel for morning prayer. I fell in love with the prayers in the *Book of Common Prayer*, especially a canticle comprising the first seven verses of Psalm 95. I carried the last line of the canticle in my heart throughout the day: "O that today you would hearken to [God's] voice!" (*Book of Common Prayer*).

Those words reminded me that God can and does speak to us at any time. God's voice can whisper to us while we're stuck in traffic, washing the dishes, or playing with our children. I appreciated the command to listen to God while I was grading student papers, preparing to teach a class, or reading a dense volume of theology.

Though God can speak to us at any time, we are more likely to recognize the divine voice if we give God our fullest attention: in other words, *pray*. I no longer attend morning prayer with a group, but I still pray most mornings. I scribble in a journal for a few minutes, meditate on a short passage of scripture, and sit with God in silence for a while—nothing elaborate or complicated. But I do believe the habit of taking intentional time to open myself to God allows me to be more available to God when I'm occupied in other ways.

I've started to think of my daily habit of prayer as unlocking the back door for God so that God can sneak into the house of my heart any time during the day and speak to me. Sometimes God does just that, and the divine voice surprises me when I least expect it.

God, I know you want to communicate with me. Help me be attentive to your voice today and always. Amen.

When I read the second half of Psalm 95, which reports God's reaction to the Israelites' complaining of thirst in the wilderness, I find myself asking whether God really said these words. Did God really announce that he "loathed" the Israelites who begged for water in the wilderness?

We are thirsty to hear from God, and we know that Christians primarily listen for the voice of God by attending to the words of scripture. But we also know that scripture is complicated, crafted by human beings in particular situations who were grappling with painful memories and fragile hopes. Is it possible that the writer of this psalm engaged in what psychologists call "projection," ascribing to God their own thoughts and feelings? Maybe they were ashamed of the way their ancestors tested God and assumed God felt the same.

We still have to test the voices we hear and take time to discern whether what we are sensing is God's voice or some other voice—the internalized voice of our parents or peers for instance, or the voice of our own subconscious speaking its deep longings and fears. It gets even more complicated when we remember that God can speak to us through these other voices as well.

So we have to ask ourselves whether the voices we hear are leading us to love, compassion, self-acceptance, and joy or whether they are drawing us into negative thoughts and feelings. When I pay attention to Jesus, though he sometimes has harsh things to say, his words typically lead to abundant life, greater joy, and genuine community. I have found these to be helpful guidelines as I discern the voice of God, even in the words of scripture.

God, I am thirsty to hear your voice but know how easy it is to confuse your voice with the voices of others. Help me hear you and respond in love. Amen.

Thirsty for God 91

A few years ago, I returned to the home I grew up in to clean out my childhood bedroom. The closet was still crammed with trophies, certificates, and medals I'd accumulated as a teenager. These artifacts reminded me of many of my accomplishments early in life and signaled that I'd had some achievements to boast about.

We usually associate the word *boast* with accomplishment or achievement; we earn the right to boast. But in this passage Paul turns the word on its head, using *boast* in a nearly unrecognizable way. Paul says that because we are people of faith, "we boast in our hope of sharing the glory of God." This hope of sharing life with God now and forever is not something we have acquired through effort or accomplishment; it is a gift that comes through faith, a result of Jesus Christ's accomplishment on the cross. The hope that comes through relationship with God is not a trophy we can add to our collection.

Paul also says that we can "boast in our suffering." Far from being an accomplishment, suffering is a trophy most of us would want to return. Though there is no reason to seek suffering or to believe that suffering is God's will, Paul contends that when suffering does come, we can receive it graciously, knowing that through it God can shape us into people capable of hope.

Western culture is obsessed with achievement. We thirst for accomplishment and recognition. In the midst of that, Paul offers a challenge: Can we imagine letting go of pride in our accomplishments to find instead pride in the gift of hope God gives us through Christ?

> *God, help me discover in you that my deepest gladness will not come through my own achievements but through the gift of hope I discover in faith. Amen.*

During those years in high school while I was thirsting for accomplishment, someone gave me a small book that discusses the verse from this passage that says, "But God proves his love for us in that while we still were sinners Christ died for us." At seventeen, I'd never thought of myself as a sinner, but I sensed that something wasn't right with my life. I was stressed and anxious, burning the candle at both ends. Was it possible that being a sinner didn't mean that I did a lot of bad things but that I was thirsting after trophies and accolades that drew me away from God?

For Paul, being "ungodly" or a "sinner" doesn't mean that we spend all of our time committing sinful, shameful acts. It refers to the more fundamental direction of our lives. Are our lives oriented toward God or away from God? Are we searching for our deepest satisfaction in relationship with God or in other things, however good those other things might be? In high school, I was a good kid. I practiced my music, got good grades, and went to church. But I had no sense of what it meant to love and serve God until I read that book.

I read late into the night and found myself weeping and praying to God. I don't remember exactly what I prayed, but I knew at that point my life would be different. When I woke the next morning, there were no bad habits I needed to give up so I wouldn't be a "sinner" anymore; nor were there particularly religious things I needed to start doing. But my life had an undeniably new direction—I was now thirsting for God, and I knew it.

God, help me discover in you the ultimate direction for my life, you who are the source of my life and its truest end. Amen.

Thirsty for God

THIRD SUNDAY IN LENT

The woman who meets Jesus at the well in the middle of the day has gotten a bad rap in history. She's been maligned for her sinful lifestyle, evidenced it is said by her many marriages and her living with someone out of wedlock. But it's possible that her first five marriages were to brothers, each of whom had died, so that she'd been passed through the family like property. Perhaps her current relationship is one in which she is loved, respected, and freed from feeling owned.

Jesus certainly doesn't judge her. His statement indicating he knows the history of her relationships is often read as if he were trying to shame her. But this woman, obviously sensitive to shame since she's fetching water alone in the middle of the day, doesn't react to Jesus out of embarrassment. Rather, his statement suggests to her that he might be able to answer a question about her own life of faith, which she boldly asks. Her question about where to worship God reveals that she is thirsting for a relationship with the Creator.

What if we could see something of ourselves in this woman, if we could look past the layers of judgment that have been heaped on her over the years and see in her longing for God a mirror of our own? She is a person who feels some shame and yet thirsts for God—as, at some level, we all do.

And Jesus meets her right there, at the intersection of her shame and longing, her embarrassment and thirst. He speaks to her directly, dispelling her shame and revealing that he is the one who can fulfill her longing.

He can meet us in the same place, unafraid of any baggage we carry, and satisfy our deepest thirst.

God, thank you for coming to me in Jesus and revealing your-self as the only one who can satisfy my spirit's deepest thirst. Amen.

In a Different Light

MARCH 13–19, 2023 • MANDY SAYERS

SCRIPTURE OVERVIEW: The two readings from the Hebrew scriptures focus on the life of David. In First Samuel, the prophet is sent to anoint the next king of Israel. God chooses David not because of outward appearance but because of his heart. David is not perfect, nor is his life always easy. Psalm 23 declares David's trust in God in good times and bad times. Just as Samuel has anointed David with oil, so does the Lord anoint him. The New Testament readings both employ images of light and darkness. Ephesians instructs us to live as children of light, not darkness. In John, Jesus heals a blind man and brings him from darkness into light. Some religious leaders protest because although their physical eyes can see, their spiritual vision is darkened.

QUESTIONS AND SUGGESTIONS FOR REFLECTION

- Read 1 Samuel 16:1-13. How often do you judge others by outward appearances or worldly successes? How can you "look upon the heart" to judge leaders in your community?
- Read Psalm 23. When have you experienced Jesus' presence with you in the wilderness?
- Read Ephesians 5:8-14. How does God's light help you persist through struggles within yourself or in the world around you?
- Read John 9:1-41. What questions does Jesus ask you? How do your questions of Jesus help you understand him?

Lead Pastor of Glen Mar United Methodist Church in Ellicott City, MD; likes to read great books, watch baseball games, and laugh at her children's jokes.

Samuel is sure he knows what God is looking for in Israel's next king. Now that God has sent him to Jesse's house, Samuel's confidence grows: *Don't worry, God, it will be clear which one is the best choice. I'll take it from here.* Promising candidate after promising candidate comes forward only to be rejected. What seems clear on the surface—that God would choose the oldest, tallest, or strongest to be king—doesn't turn out to be true at all. Instead, God chooses the runt of Jesse's litter of sons, the one who has a talent for shepherding, which is a clue that he has the gifts and graces God is looking for. Good kings are often described in "good shepherd" terms in scripture, whereas bad kings hurt or scatter their flocks. David has all the ingredients—hidden though they were—to be Saul's successor.

Samuel looks at surface characteristics to find the person he thinks God will choose. God sees things in a different light, looking at the heart, at promise and potential that Samuel cannot see at first. In the same way, we are tempted to leap to conclusions based on how things appear to us, overlooking what God can see. We write off people based on what we think we know about them, or we think situations are beyond God's redemptive power.

One of the beautiful things about Lent is that it allows us to slow down and take a second look at the people and circumstances of our lives. We can begin to see where God is working and what God is calling us to do.

Lord, help me slow down and see people and circumstances as you see them. Give me eyes to see and a heart to love all the people you put in my path. Amen.

This psalm is so familiar in our churches and in our culture that it is hard to read it without bringing considerable baggage. It is the sort of biblical excerpt that has found its way onto needlepoint pillows, T-shirts, and wall hangings sold at greeting card shops. If we aren't careful, it becomes a nursery rhyme like "Mary Had a Little Lamb."

However, this psalm is far from the saccharine simplicity we have attached to it. God's provisions have power. We read that the Lord is our shepherd in a world where distractions in every form try to lead us astray and so many other people vie for the job of being our "shepherd." God, our true shepherd, is powerful and makes things happen.

The verbs are not conditional. We are not invited to lie down in green pastures; instead, our shepherd makes us lie down. He leads us, and he restores us, and we shall not want. It doesn't sound optional. Also, the places we are led are not easy places to be, green pastures and still waters notwithstanding. This shepherd also leads us through the valley of the shadow of death and sets a picnic next to our enemies. This is a powerful shepherd for our real life, not our needlepoint pillows.

This Lent we shall not fear because this Good Shepherd is with us. We can walk through the valley of self-examination, self-denial, and sacrificial living and giving. Whatever the journey brings, we are not alone—this mighty, powerful Good Shepherd is with us.

Give thanks to God for all the times your Good Shepherd has led and guided and fed and provided for you. What is God calling you to know and do in response to this powerful passage?

One part of this psalm that has always made me pause is the part about preparing "a table before me in the presence of my enemies." I picture the shepherd as a restaurant server, leading me to a table with fancy tablecloths and candles and bringing baskets of fresh bread and pitchers of water and wine. I imagine my "enemies" up against the walls of my fine dining establishment, glaring resentfully as I feast in front of them.

In the midst of my reveries about this, the image of Jesus, our Good Shepherd, inevitably comes before me. What kind of table does he set? I recall how he ate with tax collectors, sinners, and people on the fringes of society. At his table, we might find ruffians and royalty, sinners and saints. Jesus gives living water and bread of life to all who will have it, so that none shall want and there is always enough.

Perhaps setting a table in the presence of my enemies means the table includes them. If all of us have sinned and fallen short of God's glory, then I might even be an "enemy" for another lamb of Jesus' flock, and there is a table for them that our Lord sets also. In Christ, "enemy" and "friend" are redefined and our notions of "us and them" fall away.

The Lord's table is large enough for all, a banquet table where enemies can become friends, and strangers can become family. The abundance of grace described here, with overflowing cups and oil flowing, means that all the sheep are welcome, and all can be fed at the Good Shepherd's table.

Lord, help me know that I need not be afraid and that you will provide for me. And help me to use that courage and provision to extend your table even to my enemies. Amen.

When I was little, I was afraid of the dark. I imagined my bedroom was full of monsters just beyond the range of my vision. To make matters worse, there was a streetlight outside my window that would cast a light on my bedpost, creating the perfect image of a scary monster to my vivid imagination.

The writer of Ephesians uses the image of darkness and light to contrast life before and after being "in the Lord." It turns out that if we stay in a dark environment long enough, our eyes begin to adjust to it. Maybe our expectations of ourselves slip a little. We more often miss the mark of God's call to love God and neighbor, and we tell ourselves that it's OK. Maybe we hide behind the notion that "it is what it is" because we cannot see anything more.

But those who are in the Lord are called to turn on the light and to live in the light of God's love and truth. Even more than that, it says that in the Lord, we are light and are called to live as children of that light. The works of darkness that we thought were so satisfying are "unfruitful" and turn out to be mere shadows. Instead, those who live as light have fruit that is good and right and true. In this we hear echoes of the fruit of the Spirit, like the list found in Galatians 5:22-23.

Lent is the time when we throw open the curtains and let Christ's light in. When we become believers, we are called to live in the light and to be light. At first, the light might hurt our eyes a bit, but our faults and failures and bedpost monsters disappear in its glow.

God, help me live in the light of Christ's love. Amen.

In a Different Light

"Wake up, sleepyhead! Rise and shine!" My mom awakened me this way for years. If I had something fun to do that day, I was excited to wake up. If not, I'd have preferred to pull the covers over my head and keep snoring.

The end of this passage reminds me of Advent because of its language about shining, and it reminds me of Easter with its resurrection language. And here we are in the middle of Lent. It is like a liturgical calendar in just a few sentences. Jesus admonishes us to wake up, to rise from the dead and let the light of Christ shine on us. The writer of Ephesians has been contrasting the unfruitful and gray life in "darkness" with the fruitful, bright, truthful, and good life in the light of Christ. And here at the end, we learn that entering the light of Christ is like waking from sleep, like rising and shining.

Jesus' crucifixion was an attempt to put out his light, to extinguish the light of the world in Christ. It is one of the ironies of our faith that through the darkness of Calvary, the forces of darkness were defeated, a sort of divine "flipping the script" on the forces of evil. When Jesus rose from the dead, his light was shared with the world, and in believing in him, we too "rise from the dead," not just in the world to come but in the here and now. That is why this passage talks about life in the Lord in the present tense and urges us to "awake" and "rise."

Lent is the time to rise from the dead places of our lives and awaken to the new life Christ offers.

Jesus who is light of the world, shine on me, shine in me, and shine through me. Amen.

Here we have Jesus, the Light of the world, healing a man born blind. The Pharisees want to know who sinned—this man or his parents—to cause this punishment of blindness. It's still a common thought today. Despite all the experiential evidence to the contrary, on some deep level we believe that bad things should not happen to good people. So whenever we face a calamity, we might be tempted to wonder what we did to deserve this. A beloved pastor of mine once admitted that when he gets a cold, he wonders what he did wrong morally to deserve it, even though that isn't how viruses operate.

Thankfully, Jesus rejects this way of viewing suffering. He says no one has sinned to cause this man's blindness. God is using this man's life for God's glory.

Jesus' work in healing the man is important, but the man is empowered to participate too. He is told to go wash in the pool of Siloam, which we are told means "sent." Jesus is sent from God to be the light of the world, and to love, save, heal, and free. And Jesus in turn sends the man to complete the process of restoration. Far from being a victim of fate, the man born blind is enlisted in the work of sharing the good news of Jesus and the good news of his own healing. He shares what he knows from his experience and comes to faith in Christ and worships him.

Almighty God, forgive me for asking "Who sinned?" in the face of suffering. Use me to show and share your love, presence, and peace with all I meet, especially those who do not yet know you. Amen.

Fourth Sunday in Lent

This story appears to be about a man born blind and the Pharisees who can see just fine. However, we discover that the man who physically cannot see has more insight than these scholars who could perfectly read an eye chart.

The Pharisees believe the man's infirmity is caused by someone's sin, the man's or his parents', which Jesus dismisses as a misunderstanding of how God works. The Pharisees believe that making mud on the sabbath day makes Jesus a sinner, but the newly sighted man reminds them that God listens to Jesus, so he must not be a sinner.

The Pharisees cannot see who Jesus really is or appreciate his mission. They are the blind ones. The man born blind can see just fine, both physically and spiritually, after his healing. He testifies to Jesus' identity and comes to faith. His responses in the debate with the Pharisees show he has more insight about Jesus than they do. Jesus tells the Pharisees that being sure you are not a sinner may be evidence that you are one. "Now that you say, 'We see,' your sin remains."

This Lent, we have the opportunity to give our spiritual blindness to Christ, to ask him to heal it, and to participate in that healing through our spiritual disciplines, our obedience, and our faith in who Christ is. What are some blind spots you need Jesus to heal?

Lord, forgive us for the times we think our vision is better than yours. Touch our hearts and lives today to help us see more clearly who you are. Help us see one another more clearly as brothers and sisters. Send us to the world's broken and blind places and situations with your loving light and a testimony about Jesus, the Light of the world. Amen.

The Hope for New Life

MARCH 20–26, 2023 • ROBERT BREWER

SCRIPTURE OVERVIEW: Ezekiel sets the stage for the readings this week. In a vision, the prophet sees a seemingly hopeless situation, yet God restores flesh to the bones and brings them back to life by breathing into them. The psalmist calls out to God from the depths of devastation and waits confidently for God's redemption. Paul plays off the double meaning of the Greek word *pneuma*: "breath" and "spirit." Just as Ezekiel's dry bones are brought back through the breath of God, so are we raised through the Spirit of God. The Lazarus story provides a bookend resurrection story for the week. Here Jesus demonstrates in the physical realm the spiritual realities described in the other passages. These resurrection stories point us toward Jesus' resurrection and ultimately the promise of our own.

QUESTIONS AND SUGGESTIONS FOR REFLECTION

- Read Ezekiel 37:1-14. When have you heard from God directly or through others in times of devastation? How did you respond?
- Read Psalm 130. How can you listen for signs of hope and look for God's voice?
- Read Romans 8:6-11. What helps you remember that you cannot save yourself and to put your trust in God?
- Read John 11:1-45. When have you been disappointed in God's timing or response? What would be different now if God had met your expectations then?

Campus Chaplain and Assistant Professor of Religion at Greensboro College in Greensboro, NC.

Words have power. We say words cannot hurt us like sticks or stones, but the truth is words can wound us in ways that are hard to heal. If we have been told that we are not worthy or good enough, we begin to believe it. If we are continually called a disappointment or a failure, we begin to believe it. If we are told over and over that we are not beautiful or attractive, we begin to believe it. These words can come from our own family and echo in our lives for years. These words can come from commercials and advertisements that bombard us every day. These words can sound in our own voice. Words certainly have the power to harm. Words can wound us in ways that sticks and stones cannot.

However, words also have the power to build us up and restore our souls. In the passage today, God brings Ezekiel to a valley of loss, grief, and disappointment. The dry bones show there is no hope here. What can bring life back to this place? God's word. God commands Ezekiel to speak to the bones. The words spring to life, reconnecting sinews and flesh. The breath that carries those words brings new life from the dust. Ezekiel's words, which are God's words, are powerful, restorative, and transformative. The words of harm and hopelessness are no match and blow away like sand.

Hear the words of God's good news again. God overcomes sin and death. God forgives. God restores. God makes a way through the valley. Hear these words of life again and again. *You are loved. You are a beautiful child of God. You are enough.* Believe these words and then go speak them into a world in need of God's hope.

In a world full of words, God, help me to hear the ones that matter the most: your words of redeeming love and new life. Amen.

Wind is powerful. It can bend trees and topple buildings. It can refresh us on a hot day and make us shiver in the snow. We can have the wind knocked out of us, and it can fill our lungs with new life.

In the Bible, the word for *wind* is the same word associated with the *Spirit* of God. The Spirit or wind of God hovers over creation. Jesus tells Nicodemus that the wind (Spirit) goes where it pleases. Jesus breathes the Holy Spirit upon the disciples.

God tells Ezekiel to call forth this wind from the four corners of the earth to bring life to the bodies of the slain. The bodies that have rattled back together come alive when the wind fills their lungs. The wind is the breath of life. The wind is the Spirit of God giving new life to God's people so they can stand on solid ground.

One of the ways experts advise us to handle our fears and our anxieties is to focus on our breath. Breathe in and out and focus on being present and grounded. When we remember to breathe and focus on our own breath, we also remember the sustaining presence of God's Spirit.

When the world becomes overwhelming, remember to breathe. When frightened by the future and the uncertainty of tomorrow, remember to breathe. When stepping out in faith into a new job, a new ministry, or a new task, remember to breathe. Breathe in and breathe out, and in so doing remember the Spirit of God that sustains us, renews us, and leads us to new life.

Spirit of God, breathe new life into my being so that I can stand upon the solid ground of your hope and love. Amen.

The Hope for New Life

This is a prayer of lament, a prayer of complaint. The psalmist cries out from the depths of pain and sorrow. We do not know if this is a personal struggle or a situation outside the psalmist's control, but we do know the psalmist is in a season of disquiet, disturbed and uneasy. The psalmist prays for God to bring new life through forgiveness and redemption.

We can relate to the psalmist's cry. We find ourselves in situations when we have messed up. We have broken relationships. We have lost hope in others. We grieve losses of all kinds. We hold on to anger when nothing goes our way. We reside in the depths of misery and hopelessness.

The psalmist shows us how to be in an authentic relationship with God, bringing troubles, pain, and complaints to God. We do not have to come to God with a holy reverence or a happy heart. We do not have to have our lives all together before we talk to God. We can come to God angry and hurt. We can cry out to God in our brokenness and loss. We can come to God to demand that God hear us and listen to our cry.

The psalmist cries out even without the promise of God's response. The psalmist believes that crying out to God and vocalizing the trouble is enough. The psalmists place their trust in God even before God responds, putting their hope in God to redeem God's people and bring new life. God can handle our grievances. God can handle our anger. God can handle our complaints. God hears us, and being heard is sometimes enough.

Hear my prayer, O God. I lift up my worries and sorrows to you knowing that you hear me and want me to know your peace, forgiveness, and redeeming love. Amen.

Lent is a time of preparation and prayer. We spend these days before Easter engaging in disciplines that help us grow closer to God. We let go of bad habits. We pray. We fast. We study. We long for God to lead us into the new life that Easter brings. Growth in faith can take time. Good spiritual habits can take weeks or longer to become ingrained in us.

The psalmist cries out to God for forgiveness and redemption to come but does not expect a transformation to come right away. Instead, the psalmist waits on the Lord to act. Three times the psalmist repeats the word *wait*. Waiting, it seems, is a significant part of the life of faith. Waiting is a spiritual practice. We wait in hopeful anticipation of what God will do in our lives and our world. The psalmist waits with hope, knowing that the present days of grief and sorrow will not last. There will be a day when God's reign over sin and death will be complete.

Waiting on the Lord can be difficult in an impatient world. We expect our packages to be delivered by the next day. We expect our food to be ready in minutes. We want problems solved as quickly as possible. Waiting is difficult.

The season of Lent is coming to an end. Holy Week will be here soon, and the promise of Easter will shine brightly upon our souls. Until then, maybe we can lean into the waiting. Maybe we can learn to trust God in this waiting. We wait on the Lord knowing that one day sin and death will no longer wield their power. We hope for this promise of new life, even as we wait for its fruition.

God, help me wait on you and trust you more as I live into the confidence of your steadfast love and forgiveness. Amen.

The Hope for New Life

Have you ever ridden in a new car and then start to see cars just like it everywhere you go? Have you had a new song stuck in your head and begin to hear it everywhere? Have you made a mistake, and then every thought reminds you of your failure? Sometimes when we focus upon something, it becomes all we see in the world.

Paul tells the Romans that it is important where we focus our minds. Paul says that if we set our minds on our own flesh, it will lead to death. He is not arguing against our bodies or suggesting that our flesh is something from which we need to escape. Rather, he is warning against focusing on our human desires. This human focus often leads us to be self-centered, greedy, vengeful, and even fearful. If we focus on the flesh, it will shape how we see the world in a way that leads to our downfall.

Paul urges us to set our minds on the Spirit that resides in our mortal bodies. If we set our minds on the Spirit of God, we will set our sights on the new life offered in Christ Jesus. This life is an assurance of God's redeeming love that claims us as God's own. To focus on the Spirit is to focus on the goodness of God for us and the world.

In these days of anxiety, worry, and fear, we need to focus our minds on the Spirit of God. If we set our minds on the Spirit, we can focus our lives upon forgiveness; we can have hope for tomorrow; we can live without fear. Set your mind on the Spirit of God that fills us with the hope of new life and peace, so it becomes all you see in the world.

Spirit of God, help me to set my mind on your goodness, forgiveness, and love so that I see your righteousness in all I do. Amen.

We all know someone who is always late for a meeting or a dinner. It does not matter how important the gathering is, they are always late. We might become accustomed to a friend's tardiness, but what happens when that friend is Jesus? How do we respond when God is slow to act?

Jesus does show up in this passage, but Mary and Martha believe it is too late. They are furious. Jesus, disturbed by their grief and anger, begins to weep. He stands within the sorrow of his friends. Jesus' tears are a sign of a God who grieves with us.

That is the real heart of this story. Yes, in his sadness, Jesus calls Lazarus from the grave. It is a miracle, but it is only temporary. One day Lazarus will die again. One day, Mary and Martha will grieve again. Jesus is not a lucky charm that protects us from experiencing grief and sorrow. But the hope and promise of new life Jesus offers us in the midst of our heartache and pain are permanent.

This resurrection of Lazarus foreshadows Jesus' own journey through death. It is also a glimpse of God's desire for the world. Jesus enters our sorrow and dies our death in order to prove that sorrow and death will not have the final say.

We will encounter moments where it seems like God does not show up on time. We will be in places where it feels like all hope is lost. These moments of sorrow and grief feel lonely, but they are the very places where Jesus resides. Jesus weeps with us. Jesus cries out on a cross. Jesus banishes the power of sin and death. This is our hope right now, while we wait for new life to come.

God of compassion, help me see your presence in my grief, and give me hope for a better tomorrow. Amen.

The Hope for New Life   109

FIFTH SUNDAY IN LENT

Have you found yourself in a hopeful, new relationship, and yet the mistakes of your past relationships still haunt you? Have you taken a new job but do not feel qualified? Have you tried to forgive those who have hurt you, but a past heartache still holds you tight?

Jesus calls forth Lazarus to rise up to new life, but when Lazarus walks out of the tomb the cloths of death are still wrapped around his body. When the light of another day hits him, his face is still covered, and his hands and feet are bound. Sometimes when we hear the goodness of God's redeeming love for us, we still cannot fully claim it for ourselves. Our past failures, mistakes, and disappointments keep us from truly living a life of assured grace.

Jesus speaks again, but this time it is to the community around Lazarus. He tells them to unbind him from the cloth. Lazarus cannot unbind himself. He has to have help. Jesus asks the community to help set him free. It is through the community that Lazarus is able to live fully into the new life he is given by God.

This is why support groups are so helpful, especially for those who are grieving or are recovering from addictions. This is why small groups are necessary to help us discover God's love. This is why the church should be a place people can receive and offer forgiveness.

It often takes a community to help us find our way out of a gloomy past and into new life. Whom do you need to ask for help today? Maybe it's a counselor. Maybe it's a friend. Maybe it's a small group. Maybe you can take a step into becoming part of a community that helps others find freedom and new life in Christ.

God of hope, help me drop the burdens of my past that keep me from living freely and fully into the life you offer. Amen.

Preparing for the Journey

MARCH 27–APRIL 2, 2023 • KAREN OLIVETO

SCRIPTURE OVERVIEW: The Liturgy of the Palms readings prepare us for Palm Sunday, when Jesus enters the city of Jerusalem in triumph. The psalmist celebrates the one who comes in the name of the Lord, who is celebrated with palm branches. Matthew then tells the story of Jesus, who enters Jerusalem in this way and is greeted with joy, such that the crowds quote Psalm 118. The Liturgy of the Passion points to the end of that week and the coming suffering of Jesus. Isaiah and the psalmist describe being treated with contempt, beaten, and rejected. In reciting the earliest known Christian hymn, Paul in Philippians emphasizes how Christ surrenders his glory and is subjected to humiliation and death. Matthew recounts the passion of the Messiah, who is rejected as the prophets have foretold.

QUESTIONS AND SUGGESTIONS FOR REFLECTION

- Read Psalm 118:1-2, 19-29. How has God been steadfast in your life? How do you praise God for this continual presence?
- Read Matthew 21:1-11. How would you expect a ruler to enter a city? How is Jesus' entrance the same? How is it different?
- Read Isaiah 50:4-9a. What does being a servant of God look like? How does God help you live as a servant?
- Read Philippians 2:5-11. Consider the author's suggestion that Jesus manifests his divinity by being completely obedient to God. How does this change the way you think about the divine image within you?

Bishop of the Mountain Sky Conference of The United Methodist Church; author of numerous books, including *Together at the Table: Diversity without Division in The United Methodist Church* (Westminster John Knox Press, 2018).

Are you one of those people who wake up fully alert, energetic, and ready to leap out of bed to *carpe diem*? Or do you like to approach the day ever so slowly? Or perhaps you prefer to pull the covers over your head in hope that the day will pass you by.

Today's scripture provides a good foundation both to help us get out of bed each day and to prepare us for the quickly approaching Holy Week and the journey with Jesus we are invited to travel. The psalmist provides us an orientation to the journey, beginning and ending the passage with the same message of God's goodness and our joyful response. These bookends hold a story of rejection and redemption, of sacrifice and salvation. Through it all, the psalmist sings out, "This is the day that the LORD has made; let us rejoice and be glad in it."

How can we approach the new day, which will be filled with untold troubles and unexpected blessings, as an invitation to praise God? How can we start and end our day with the same kind of gratitude as the psalmist?

The psalmist invites us to "rejoice." The word *rejoice* means to give ourselves over to joy. Having joy is not the same thing as being happy. Happiness is often felt as a result of an experience. Joy, however, is a fruit of the Spirit and buoys us through anything life can bring us.

Tomorrow morning, pause before leaving your bed and ponder how you can live into joy in the new day, knowing that no matter what happens to you in the course of the day, nothing can separate you from God's love for you.

Recite this as a breath prayer: "This is the day that the LORD has made, let us rejoice and be glad in it."

As Jesus prepares for his triumphal entry into Jerusalem, he tells two disciples to enter the village to find a donkey and a colt tied together and bring them to him. He will ride both into Jerusalem, entering through the Golden Gate on the eastern side of the city. There is, on that same day, another parade entering the city: Pontius Pilate, complete with chariots and horses and soldiers, enters the main gate, located on the west side of Jerusalem.

There could not be a starker contrast: Jesus, riding humbly on a donkey and a young horse while common folks hail him as a king, versus Pilate, flanked by all the trappings of wealth and power, a Roman governor wielding authority over an occupied territory.

Where do the donkey and colt that Jesus rode come from? The disciples are not given an address or a name. They are just given instructions to tell anyone who might object, "The Lord needs them." Jesus assures the disciples that the owner will hand over the animals.

Jesus is confident that God will provide what he needs.

God has that same confidence in us. Can we be trusted with that confidence? When there is a need in the world, a thirst that seeks to be quenched, a hunger that longs to be filled, can God count on us to respond unhesitatingly as members of Christ's body?

God needs you. There is no one in the world who can respond to God's needs in the ways you can. Are you able to untie whatever constricts your soul and heart and say, "Here I am! Use me!"

Creator God, as I go about my day today, may I listen for your voice pointing out to me the ways I can honor you through my service. Amen.

In these nonstop days, smartphones not only allow us to work from anywhere but to work anytime/all the time. Many of us fall into bed exhausted, only to rise up weary as we reach for our phones to begin our day before we are even out of bed. Studies show that 80 percent of smartphone owners scroll through their phones within fifteen minutes of waking up! When half the people in the world own a smartphone, that means we are starting our day with the jolt that comes from having billions of people enter the space between our waking and rising.

That is not a good way to start the day.

It is not that those voices are unimportant. As followers of Jesus, we need to keep our ears open to the cries, needs, and concerns of others. We need to be aware of spaces and places in our world in need of healing, hope, and love. But starting our day by reaching for our phones means we are like a car with no gas—we won't get very far.

The book of Isaiah offers us an antidote with a daily ritual to begin our day: Set our eyes, ears, heart, and soul on God. Listen for what God has to teach as we rise each morning. Listen for what are we being called to do, so we can leave our beds saying, "Here I am, send me!"

Isaiah didn't shy away from all that was going on in the world. Oppression, brokenness, marginalization, exploitation, and political corruption were just as real in Isaiah's time as they are in ours. But the prophet set before his people—and all who will come after—a vision of the coming of Jesus. And this is the way to face the day!

Morning by morning, may I awake and set my attention to you, O God, so that I hear the ways I may serve you and your people throughout the day. Amen.

S ome days are better than others. Even when we are aware of the goodness of life, there are times when our well runs dry, we lack the reserves to deal with life's challenges and trials, and it feels as if the universe is conspiring against us.

We want to cry out: *Why does this always happen to me? Why can't anything go right? Is there no one I can count on and trust?*

Those are the times when we move into victimhood-thinking instead of belovedness-thinking.

The psalmist knows something about life's hardships. Psalm 31 is a lament from one who has experienced scorn, rejection, and alienation. Sighs too deep for words well up from the depths of despair the psalmist feels.

Yet the psalmist doesn't wallow in that place for long. Naming experiences with honesty and vulnerability, the psalmist moves to a place of peace by recognizing that God's goodness never fails. God will be the source of strength to get through the hardship and arrive in a place of wholeness.

When you are facing life's trials, how do you lean into God's grace? How do you trust in the One who created, redeemed, and sustains you? When the storms of life are so threatening, how can you remind yourself that you are a beloved child of God?

Remember the psalmist's words: "I trust in you." I trust that this hardship I am experiencing will not be forever. I trust that even when things feel so difficult, God is walking with me, guiding me through all that feels threatening. I trust that God will never leave me.

Some days my life feels really hard, O God. In the midst of the hardships, help me remember that I am your beloved child and trust that your love and grace will lead me through the hardships to a place of peace and wholeness. Amen.

Paul sought to unite the church at Philippi by reminding them of what Jesus modeled. Instead of wielding his power to force people to get along, Jesus pointed beyond himself to God's goodness and grace by emptying himself and becoming like a servant. Imagine what could happen in a world where Jesus' followers did the same.

I will never forget a time I spoke to the students in a seminary class about how much I love parish ministry. The professor said, "I couldn't stand to be a parish minister. I don't care what color the drapes are."

The professor's underlying assumption was that churches get caught up in arguing over the little things. Small disagreements snowball into grudge-filled camps that divide the congregation. We stop living humbly as followers of Jesus and instead puff ourselves up and push to get our way.

I don't care what color the drapes are either. But I care passionately about how we decide on the color of the drapes. It matters how we enter into disagreements—are we willing to acknowledge humbly that we might not have the right answer? Will we listen to all sides and let them inform our own thoughts? Can we talk not as opponents but as fellow Christians seeking the best for our community?

Something changes when we seek to have the mind that was in Christ. We recognize that other viewpoints are as worthy as our own. We listen more and talk less. We learn when to lead and when to be led. We seek to ground all our actions in an expression of grace and love.

When we share the mind of Christ, love and grace become contagious. Others see a community that is welcoming, creative, and open. We all then grow more fully into the likeness of Christ.

God of grace, help me live as one who has the mind of Christ.
May my words and actions reflect Jesus' humility. Amen.

Our bodies have within them a natural fight-or-flight response to stress and danger. For some, however, there is a third option: sleep. Researchers note that this response is due to early experiences of trauma and feeling a lack of control. It is called "learned helplessness" and can manifest itself by sleeping when we are confronted with stressful and difficult situations.

The disciples who walked with Jesus over the course of his public ministry had known a road filled with unpredictable crowds and suspicious leaders. But what could have prepared them for Jesus' final days? Jesus spoke to them about all that lay before him, but were they able to grasp the seriousness of his words? As Jesus grew "grieved and agitated" in the Garden of Gethsemane, they felt the full impact of Jesus' words. Instead of praying with him as he wrestled with his fate, the disciples did what many of us who don't fight or flee do—they fell asleep.

All Jesus wanted was for them to be by his side as he prayed and struggled. That is all anyone who is in distress asks of us: *Sit with me. Pray with me.* Seldom do we hear a request to fix it, change it, make it not happen. Just be present and share the journey together.

As we get ready for Holy Week, may we not leapfrog from Palm Sunday to Easter, seeking to avoid the painful, crucifying parts of Jesus' journey. May we not slumber as the Son of Man faces betrayal, a trial, lashings, and finally, death on a cross. May we stay awake and enter into the fullness of Jesus' last days.

Jesus, may I stay awake with you as you make this journey to Golgotha. I want to be a companion to you and all who suffer. Amen.

PALM/PASSION SUNDAY

The journey from Palm Sunday to Easter is filled with shocking twists. Jesus' triumphant ride into Jerusalem quickly sours, and the shouts of "Hosanna" turn into cries of "Crucify him!" So many of us want to skip those pages in the Gospel story and run to—and then from—an empty tomb. Keep the joy alive!

But Holy Week calls us not to turn away but to study what happened to Jesus. Between today's packed church and the even fuller Easter service, there will be other services with smaller crowds. Like the women who refused to leave Jesus as he hung on the cross, they will listen to the story and take their parts in the Passion play. They will mourn as they sing with trembling voices, "Were you there when they crucified my Lord?"

As a child, my Mum had us save our palm branches until next Palm Sunday. We would come home with those waxy palm fronds and turn them into crosses. We cut the palm frond, made two slits on one of the pieces, and threaded the other piece through the slits. The cross was placed above a little picture of Jesus that hung above my bedroom light switch.

I give thanks that at such an early age I was taught of the solemn connection between Palm Sunday and the cross of Good Friday.

Enter into the joy of Palm Sunday. But don't turn away from the events that followed. There are important lessons for us all to discover: that life can take unexpected turns; that betrayals happen; that the powers and principalities that be will forever be threatened by those who stand with those on the margins; that too often, death feels like it has the upper hand over love.

O God, give me the strength and perseverance to walk with Jesus this week. Amen.

Holy Week

APRIL 3–9, 2023 • JOE E. PENNEL JR.

SCRIPTURE OVERVIEW: Although we anticipate the celebration of Easter, this week's readings remind us to slow down and walk through Holy Week. Monday's passage in John has Jesus in Bethany in full knowledge that he would be betrayed. Tuesday's Gospel concludes Jesus' public ministry. The crowd does not understand now, but they will. On Wednesday Jesus tells the disciples that they do not know what he is doing, but later they will understand. On Thursday, the reading in John shows us that even when facing death, Jesus continues to model selfless love. Friday brings pain and rejection, but Sunday is the greatest day in human history. He is risen indeed!

QUESTIONS AND SUGGESTIONS FOR REFLECTION

- Read John 12:1-11, 20-36. How is this story like the voice from heaven the people heard? What does it mean for us to walk in the light?
- Read John 13:1-7, 21-32. Consider someone who has disappointed, hurt, or betrayed you whom God might be calling you to love. How could a posture of service help you act in a loving way even if you cannot feel affection for this person?
- Read John 18:1–19:42. What new detail did you notice in rereading this long passage? Why might John have included that detail in the account?
- Read Matthew 27:57-66. Sometimes all there is to do is sit with someone in their grief. Think of a time when someone's presence has made a difference in your life.
- Read John 20:1-18. The disciples saw and heard and believed. What has helped your belief?

Bishop of The United Methodist Church (retired); currently Professor for the Practice of Leadership at Vanderbilt Divinity School, Nashville, TN.

I do not enjoy the scripture readings about Judas. I think it is because I see myself as being somewhat like Judas. In today's reading, the Gospel of John does not mince words. John says that Judas, one of the disciples, was to betray Jesus. Do I betray him too?

I see myself as a disciple of Jesus. I live in this world as a baptized person who belongs to the church, which is the body of Christ. I try to keep the spiritual disciplines of prayer, meditation, searching the scriptures, and deeds of mercy and kindness. Yet there are still times when I betray Christ by not doing what love requires. There are times when I do not engage life as Jesus did. Jesus was present to the sick, forgave sinners, ate with outcasts, and spread the good news to all he encountered. By not following Jesus' example, I betray him.

Judas did not follow the model of Jesus when he objected to what Mary did. She took a costly ointment and anointed Jesus' feet. Judas said the expensive ointment should have been sold for money to give to the poor, but he did not really care for the poor. There is a difference between simply giving money to the poor and truly loving the poor.

As a pastor for more than sixty years, I have taken offerings for the poor without challenging my congregations to be present and lovingly engaged with the poor. Did I betray Jesus as did Judas? Perhaps. I should have known better than to betray Christ in this way because I have been taught that we meet Christ in the poor.

Help me, God, during this Holy Week to practice confession and repentance with the assurance that you will forgive my betrayals. Amen.

Several years ago, I was a student in a Master Gardener class. It was most helpful because there was so much that I needed to learn. In particular, the instructor stressed the importance of having the garden soil tested so that we would know how it needed to be treated.

We were also told that the planted seeds needed time to die so that they could be glorified by becoming beautiful plants. I had always used the term *germinate,* but he preferred the *death* of the seed as being a better term.

My wife and I live in a retirement community where we are assigned a small garden plot. Our section is just large enough to grow six tomato plants, a few sunflowers, and about a dozen other flowering plants. The plot is small but very productive.

In today's reading, Jesus was foretelling his soon-to-be death. He said, "The time has come for the Son of Man to be glorified." He was letting Andrew and Philip know that he would not be physically present with them much longer. He said, "The hour has come for the Son of Man to be glorified. Very truly, I tell you, unless a grain of wheat falls to the earth and dies, it remains just a single grain; but if it dies, it bears much fruit."

Jesus would die like a planted seed, but his life and teachings would continue to bear much fruit. The seed of his life has been planted in the soil of countless lives from then until now. His love will not be stamped out.

His seed will bear the fruit of love in the prepared soil of our lives. Holy Week is a good time to test that soil.

Creator God, help me worship, search the scriptures, pray, and practice deeds of mercy and kindness so that the soil of my life will bear the fruit of love. Amen.

The writer of Hebrews used some strong words to describe how we are to follow Christ. He wrote that we are to run with perseverance the race that is set before us. To run with determination is not like a walk through a shopping mall. It is to run with tenacity and persistence. Christ has set the goal of the race before us as individuals and for the church. We should run with our minds and hearts open to Christ and to the needs of the world around us.

As we run, we are to lay aside the weight of sin that clings so closely to us. Sin is any thought or deed that separates us from God, others, or ourselves. Sin can block us from running the race of love. As we move toward the Cross this week, we need to confess and repent so that the heaviness of sin can be lifted.

We also run this race by looking to Jesus who showed us how to run the race of love even if it meant hanging on a cross. When we want to understand how to run this race, we study and meditate on the way that Jesus ran his race.

Tradition refers to this day as Spy Wednesday, the day when Judas planned to betray Jesus by helping to orchestrate his ambush and arrest. Judas did not run with Jesus to the finish line. After he dipped the bread into the cup, he took the money with him and went out into the night.

We want to say that we are not like Judas. None of us wants to be known as a betrayer of the Lord. But like Judas, we are tempted to go our own way. We must not forget that Jesus also died for Judas—and for us.

Dear God, hear my confession and forgive me for being like Judas. Amen.

MAUNDY THURSDAY

What would we do if we knew that it was our time to depart this world? Have a party? Take a trip with our family? Do one last good deed? I once had a congregant who knew that she had only a few days to live. As she was able, she spent her remaining time writing notes of love and concern to people who were sick or troubled.

When Jesus knew that his time had come to physically depart from this world, he got up from the table and washed his disciples' feet. Some did not understand, and some got upset. When Jesus was washing the feet of his friends, it was an act of humility and love directed toward ordinary people. He was demonstrating an upside-down kind of leadership. He was practicing what he had taught the disciples. When the disciples had argued about who would be the greatest in the kingdom, Jesus told them that he had come to serve and not to be served. If the disciples wanted to follow in his way, they should do the same.

Let this Maundy Thursday remind us that we follow a Teacher whose life was humble service to others. Since Jesus has washed us with love, we are to wash one another's feet with the same love. We are to do as Jesus did.

After Jesus had served the meal and washed the disciples' feet, he gave a new commandment: "Just as I have loved you, you also should love one another." After we have partaken of the bread and wine today, let us truly believe that we are to be a living sacrament in today's world, no matter how much time we have left. May it be so.

Dear Jesus, I want to feel you washing me with your love so that I feel emboldened to do the same for others. Amen.

GOOD FRIDAY

As a pastor for more than sixty years, I have been present with a large number of congregants who have experienced the death of a loved one. It was not uncommon for those grieving people to share the last spoken words of the person who had recently moved to the birth of a new life. For some families and friends, these last words are never forgotten.

John did not forget to write about the last words of Jesus. As he was hanging on the cross, Jesus looked at his mother, his mother's sister, and Mary Magdalene. One of the disciples whom Jesus loved was standing by his mother. All who were present that day must have been experiencing great pain as they watched Jesus nearing death on the cross.

According to John, Jesus looked at his mother and the beloved disciple, and both looked at him. Here we see the pained yet loving gazes of a mother and a dear friend. Next, Jesus invited them to look at each other. Then he said, "Woman, here is your son." Then he said to the disciple, "Here is your mother." I feel that Jesus was inviting them to truly see each other, not just with their eyes but also with their hearts.

The love of Christ continues to call us to look at each other with love. With all of our painful problems in the church and culture, we need to gaze at one another with forgiveness and grace. When we do this, we are living out the image of the Suffering Servant, despised and rejected. Here we see the image of compassion in place of the image of power and judgment. This is what allows us to call this Friday "good."

Forgive me, O God, if I have not gazed at others with love in my mind and heart. Help me do what Jesus requested of those who stood beneath the cross. Amen.

HOLY SATURDAY

What Joseph of Arimathea did was a prelude to Jesus' resurrection. He acted contrary to the customs of his day that said that the bodies of crucified persons were to be thrown into a ditch and covered with dirt so that they would not be eaten by vultures.

Joseph decided to take care of Jesus' body in a different way. He went to Pilate and got permission to take Jesus' body from the cross before the Roman soldiers could throw it into a ditch.

Joseph was a rich man, so he could afford to wrap Jesus' body in clean linen and take it to his own new tomb. He then rolled a great stone in front of the door and went away. It is interesting that Jesus was not buried by any of the Twelve. They had abandoned him. Neither was he buried by members of his family or by a benevolent member of the opposition.

None of the men who had heard Jesus speak about the promise of the resurrection was present. Even Joseph, who had rendered this last touching and costly act for his teacher, went away, having honored Jesus' life but not expecting or even hoping for a resurrection. The resurrection would take place without any of them present.

Only the two Marys showed some expectancy by keeping the silent vigil in front of the tomb. Perhaps they believed what Jesus had promised. On this day before Resurrection Sunday will we be present to the risen Christ, or will we go away?

Dear God, I want to keep my mind and heart open to the risen Christ. Help me not go away. Amen.

EASTER

Mary Magdalene had a passion for Jesus' ministry. It all started when Jesus cast seven demons out of her (see Luke 8:2). But it did not stop there. The Gospels of Matthew, Mark, and Luke tell us that she was devoted to Jesus. She participated in his mission in Galilee and contributed financially to this effort. She went with Jesus and his followers to Jerusalem for his final appeal to the nation. She was present for his crucifixion, and she came to the tomb to anoint Jesus' body. There is no wonder that she wept.

It is possible that she continued to weep as she went to the Eleven to report the empty tomb and the message of the angels. She is rightly described as the apostle to the apostles. She was the first witness to the resurrection, and Jesus sent her to tell the good news to others. When we experience the resurrection, we, like Mary, are sent to tell others. We do not keep it to ourselves.

I believe that it was Mary's passion to be with Jesus that drew her to the garden tomb on Easter morning. I think it was this singular unifying passion that Jesus recognized and responded to when he gave her the commission, "Go to my brothers and tell them." Jesus saw a lot in Mary that others probably did not see.

In today's reading, Mary sees Jesus, but she does not "see" him until he discloses himself to her. She mistakes him for a gardener. Easter Sunday will not let us forget that the risen Christ has been unveiled to us and that we are being sent to witness that the Cross did not defeat love. They tried to put love to death, but it would not die. Christ sends us—as he sent Mary—to tell other people this great news.

Loving God, help me to look at all people through the eyes of undying love. Give me the passion of Mary. Amen.

This Jesus God Raised Up

APRIL 10–16, 2023 • KATHERINE WILLIS PERSHEY

SCRIPTURE OVERVIEW: Psalm 16 and Acts 2 fit together, since the latter quotes the former. Both celebrate God's presence in human life and the powerful expression of that presence. In his Pentecost sermon Peter sees a messianic application of the psalm to the resurrection of Jesus. First Peter affirms that resurrection creates community, stressing the faith and love of Christians that arise without the experience of physical contact with Jesus. For later generations, belief and commitment are born out of the witness of others.

QUESTIONS AND SUGGESTIONS FOR REFLECTION
- Read Acts 2:14a, 22-32. How should the reader (or preacher) acknowledge Peter's troubling language of blame toward the Israelites without losing the point of the passage?
- Read Psalm 16. In what way does God provide protection and refuge for you?
- Read John 20:19-31. What does it mean for Jesus to bless "those who have not seen and yet have come to believe?"
- Read 1 Peter 1:3-9. How do Peter's words speak to Christians who do not live with the threat of persecution?

Minister, author, yoga instructor; one of the pastors at First Congregational Church of Western Springs, IL, a Chicago-area congregation affiliated with the United Church of Christ.

Peter speaks these fiery words on Pentecost Day, but the theme of his address is pure Easter. The message Peter and his fellow apostles have for the Israelites (and, in good time, all the world) is extraordinary. Jesus died a horrible death, but God raised him up.

While Jesus' crucifixion took place in public, thereby becoming an all-but-indisputable fact, the resurrection of the Messiah is a different matter. On this topic we settle for the testimony of witnesses. To believe the Easter story we must first determine if we believe Peter. We know well Peter's less-than-stellar record as a follower of Jesus. We not only remember Peter's density and desertion; we cringe at the way he incriminates the Israelites. You crucified and killed him, Peter taunts; his accusation reverberates throughout history, leaving a shameful wake.

Why should we believe this imperfect apostle? Is his biblical interpretation pointing to the incorruptibility of Jesus' flesh persuasive? Is his confident delivery convincing? Can we perceive the power of the Holy Spirit at work in his words?

In all honesty, I can come up with no good reason to believe Peter—at least no reason that relates to Peter himself—or any of the other eleven witnesses with whom he stands that Pentecost Day. The person bearing witness of the good news may be a reformed scoundrel or a sinful saint, a relapsed drunkard or a child with a reputation for crying wolf. I believe Peter's testimony because what he says about Jesus is profoundly true in my own experience and that of others through the millennia.

Jesus, the holy man from Nazareth, the one through whom God did deeds of power, wonder, and signs, could not be held in death's grip—and because of this, neither can we.

God of Easter, we hear the good news with glad hearts; make us witnesses with Peter. Amen.

When reading the psalms, I tend to hurry through the harsh parts. I linger on the psalmist's intimate expressions of faith and doubt but avoid the vitriol spoken against the psalmist's enemies. Accordingly, I often skip past the line about the maligned others who choose other gods when I read Psalm 16— to my detriment. It casts a shadow, no doubt, but the contrast illuminates. Fixing our eyes on the darkness often makes the light more brilliant.

I know something about sorrow-multiplying idolatry. We all do, I think, even if we don't call it by its proper name. The false god I am most frequently tempted to serve is the god of absolute security. As a person who suffers from bouts of anxiety, I desperately desire assurance that nothing bad will befall me or my family.

I find it much harder to take refuge in the true God than to seek absolute security in a false god. The true God will not swoop in and catch my daughter when she tumbles from a concrete step or guarantee that the cells of my loved ones will never be besieged by cancer. (As it turns out, no matter how many metaphorical drink-offerings of blood I pour out, the false god can't do these things either.)

The protection our devotion to God affords us is not always the protection we think we want. But the boundary lines fall around us in a most pleasant place, indeed: They embrace us within God's eternal grasp. Nothing can remove us from that everlasting refuge. Even if our voices tremble, let us say to God, "You are my LORD; I have no good apart from you."

O God, we take refuge in you and trust that no matter what befalls us, we are yours forevermore. Amen.

The disciples cower behind locked doors, frightened and, I imagine, ashamed. They have failed their prophet, their teacher, their leader, their friend. If the tomb truly is empty and Jesus is walking the streets of Jerusalem again, are they ready to face him? Cowards in the hour of Jesus' death, they now allow their fear and shame to make cowards of them in the wake of his resurrection.

Suddenly Jesus stands among them. Isn't this the stuff of ghost stories? Don't only intangible haunts pass through doors? Aren't we to focus on the real and tangible body of Christ, present and fully alive? I used to roll my eyes at this kind of detail. But through the eyes of faith, Jesus' sudden appearance inside a locked room becomes more than a special effect thrown in for pizzazz. Yes, it signals God's impressive power, but God doesn't waste power on empty miracles.

In this passage, the Christ breaks and enters—and not just into a house. Jesus breaks the chains that bind God's children to fear and shame and enters their hearts.

"Peace be with you." This is what he says to the disciples gathered there. Not, "How could you deny me, Peter?" Not "Why did you not go looking for me when Mary told you she had seen me?" Simply: "Peace be with you." The disciples might have expected anger and disappointment. Instead Jesus greets them with the ultimate sign of reconciliation—his peace.

Jesus breathes on them. As they inhale the gift of the Holy Spirit, the disciples experience release from their cage of fear and the bond of shame and receive the authority to forgive—to break the shackles of sin that yet cling to their brothers and sisters.

Lord Jesus Christ, break into our hearts. Grant us the peace that delivers us from fear and the forgiveness that releases us from shame. Amen.

No wonder Thomas is ticked. No wonder he stubbornly announces that he won't believe a word unless he can see and touch Christ's wounds for himself. He has missed out on the encounter with Jesus Christ in the flesh, who grants peace and exhales the gift of the Holy Spirit. Wherever Thomas was that evening, he wasn't in the right place.

Thomas often gets a bum rap throughout Christian history; no one wants to be a "doubting Thomas." But how can we blame him? He becomes the first person pressured to affirm Christ's living presence without having seen for himself.

So Jesus does it again. He enters through the closed doors of the house. He issues the same greeting of peace and addresses Thomas personally, offering Thomas exactly what he needs to believe and offering it with no condemnation. Even as he concedes the special blessing in having faith without the benefit of proof, Jesus gives Thomas the chance to touch the hands and side of his Lord.

Sometimes we focus our attention on Thomas, whether we judge him or relate to him. Certainly, we find his struggle with belief and unbelief compelling. But we wisely turn our gaze to the One who was raised from the grave. Here we witness a resurrected Christ who willingly encourages a man to touch his tender wounds in hopes that he will believe in God's glory.

We may not have seen, but we believe. And if we do not believe, Jesus will find a way to make it so. The breath of his peace still rests upon us.

Jesus, give us what we need to see you for who you are and the courage to confess that you are our Lord and our God. Amen.

This Jesus God Raised Up   131

Enough is as good as a feast." Thus says Mary Poppins, ever the arbiter of wisdom. The children in her care want more, as children tend to do—as most of us tend to do, if we're honest. One slice of decadent chocolate cake is surely sufficient, but the temptation to go back for just one more forkful is fierce. More dessert, more money, more power, more time—we often struggle to make peace with enough, even though enough is not only enough, it is often preferable to profusion.

Here, the Gospel of John divulges that there is more to the story. It delights me to envision a host of undocumented miracles, conversations, and encounters with Christ. Sometimes that unrequited imagination even finds an object of fascination when an ancient manuscript or mysterious relic is discovered.

Yet even as John teases the reader about the many other signs Jesus did in the presence of his disciples, in the very same breath he confirms that the stories written in his Gospel are, quite simply, enough. In the text of our sacred scriptures, we encounter Jesus, who challenges and invites us to believe that he is the Messiah, the Son of God.

We can choose to accept his invitation and live it out every day. We need nothing else to have life in his name: no hidden knowledge, no higher pathway, no magic prayer.

This story is enough. Our humble response is enough. Jesus is enough—and, sure enough, Jesus is as good as a feast.

Jesus, you are the Messiah, the Son of God. We entrust ourselves to you and give thanks for the life we are granted in your name. Amen.

Thomas sees and believes. The author addresses this letter to Christians who have not seen and yet believe. These believers find themselves in crisis; their acceptance of Christ makes them exiles. They have received the gift of salvation only to be faced with unthinkable persecution.

How can this reminder of the troubled history of the early church follow so quickly on the heels of Easter's glory? Surely, the good news that rang out last Sunday means that suffering is no more. And yet this epistle tells us that the faith of these early Christians—some who surely joined the unnamed class of martyrs—will be tested and refined by fire. Didn't Christ's death and resurrection put out for good the fire of evil and oppression?

Easter does not promise that we will be whisked away from suffering. Indeed, many believers throughout the centuries have experienced increased suffering because of their faith. Today, in some places in the world, openly professing belief in the name of Jesus Christ can be dangerous.

Jesus' resurrection brings new life, fostering the growth of a new community of persons who nurture and support one another. Christians rejoice in the face of persecution and pain, for as the author reminds us: We have an inheritance coming, one that is imperishable, undefiled, and unfading.

The promise of salvation doesn't render our life on earth meaningless, but an eternal perspective has an impact on how we approach each day. It gives us a new birth into a living hope. Life will overcome death.

The world around us may feel like Good Friday, and sorrow may touch our lives. But we are transformed by Christ in the here and now. The glory of the hereafter resides in our bones.

O God of living hope, no matter our circumstances, we rejoice with indescribable and glorious joy. Amen.

This Jesus God Raised Up

When I lived near the ocean, I always enjoyed driving the road that ran along the shore. On a clear morning, I would ponder the blue ocean and the spray of the breakers. I marveled at the curve of the land, how the mountains and the peninsula stretched to embrace across the bay.

But what I enjoyed most was the chance to observe the people on the sidewalk who were taking in the grand seascape. I caught fleeting glimpses of people who stood transfixed. Being in the presence of something so deep, so mysterious, so big, grasps people. I've heard it said that gazing at the ocean causes a soul to expand; the soul grows in response to what it sees.

I find it interesting that Peter in his sermon quotes rather extensively from this psalm to support his belief in Jesus' resurrection. (Read Acts 2:22-25.) This week's passages propel us to consider our response to what the Resurrection might mean for our lives. The Gospel emphasizes belief. The letter of First Peter weds belief to celebration: "You believe in him and rejoice with an indescribable and glorious joy."

Today's psalm sets the tone for such rejoicing. It serves to remind Christians—when read in the context of the other lectionary texts during the Easter season—that the Resurrection is not merely a doctrinal point to which we grant our intellectual assent. The Resurrection is something to behold and experience.

Our hearts are gladdened, our souls freed to rejoice. The Lord holds our cup and portion; our living is not restricted. And our bodies, often a source of pain, can rest, trusting that nothing can wrench us from the Lord's grasp. The believer will not descend to Sheol. The faithful will not tumble into the Pit. Easter reveals the breadth and depth of God's glory and leads to the path of life. May our souls grow in response to what we behold.

Lord, we believe; receive now the rejoicing of our souls as we delight in your wondrous presence. Amen.

Listen In, Call Out

APRIL 17–23, 2023 • EMMA JOY BUSHONG

SCRIPTURE OVERVIEW: As we consider further the power of Jesus' resurrection, how should we respond? This is the question posed to Peter in the reading in Acts. Peter's first instruction is to repent, to change course in our thinking and our living to align more with God's way. The psalmist proclaims his gratitude to God because God has heard his cry, but the process began with the psalmist's turning to the Lord. The letter of First Peter states that because we have turned and have faith and hope in God, we ought to love one another deeply from the heart. Luke tells the story of two men who meet Jesus on the road to Emmaus. They recognize him only as he breaks the bread, symbolizing that Christian fellowship is also part of a changed life.

QUESTIONS AND SUGGESTIONS FOR REFLECTION

- Read Acts 2:14a, 36-41. How might you allow Jesus' crucifixion and resurrection to disrupt your life or your faith? How would such a disruption change you?
- Read Psalm 116:1-4, 12-19. When have you learned of God's great joy for you? How do the Psalms remind you that you are beloved?
- Read 1 Peter 1:17-23. How can you take the author's advice to "act like someone who knows [you are] loved"?
- Read Luke 24:13-35. Recall times throughout your life when Jesus has been revealed to you. Which of these encounters have been logical? Which have been supernatural?

Recent graduate of Belmont University currently serving the young people of Belmont United Methodist Church in Nashville, TN; plans to pursue further theological education to follow her passion of helping the youth and families of The United Methodist Church navigate mental health and faith.

The best conversations happen on walks. They create a special space that seems to transcend societal laws of vulnerability. Somehow the mix of fresh air, light exercise-induced endorphins, lack of eye contact, and movement toward a shared destination allows us to share what's on our minds and take conversations to more intimate places.

We see this happen between Jesus' followers when he joins them on their walk to Emmaus. Jesus approaches them while they're deep in conversation about everything that has just happened regarding Jesus' death. I like to imagine that they're using their walk to process the emotions and traumatic events they've just endured, and that maybe in between the heavy somber moments they crack jokes and rehash the family drama going on back home. Jesus' followers were simply people, after all. Then a man, a stranger, engages them. Their walk has lowered their barriers, so without screening questions, a name, or any kind of second thought, they loop him into the story. All of it. Jesus lets them tell him the story he already knows, the story he lived, because the followers needed to share it.

Despite God's omniscience, we are invited to tell our stories. To bring our experiences to God. To approach God with lowered walls, deep conversations, and the desire to move forward. God engages us, knowing who we are and what we're going through because God wants to walk alongside us as we work through it. Christ may first appear like a stranger, but as we share and listen and travel, he will be revealed to us in the stories we tell, the memories we have, and the moments we experience.

God who meets us wherever we may be on our journeys, thank you for inviting us to share our stories with you. Forgive our imperfect retellings, and bring clarity to the truths we've experienced. Reveal yourself to us, and guide us as we walk toward hope and healing. Amen.

There is something sacred about breaking bread with people. A professor of mine once said that her favorite way to get to know someone was over a meal because a barrier comes down when we eat. You can't eat in front of someone without recognizing that you're both human and that you both need this food to live. It's humbling and brings vulnerability to both.

Jesus loves breaking bread with people. Early theologians suggested that it's one of the ways we know he was fully human and not just a divine apparition. Eating equals humanity. In Jesus' last moments before his crucifixion and then after his resurrection, he chooses to break bread with those he loves—to humble himself before them once again, and to share in their most human activity.

It's in that moment, the moment he blesses the bread at the table in Emmaus, that they realize who he really is. In this mundane action, Christ reveals his presence. He could've chosen any moment to do this—perhaps earlier on the walk, or when he was invited into the house, or when he was hearing them retell the events of the week—but he chooses this moment. It's the moment where their need is acknowledged and blessed.

As soon as they realize who they are about to dine with, Christ disappears. Poof. I can imagine how his two followers must've felt. They longed to hear his voice again. They wished they had said something different and listened to him more closely. And they realized they were still hungry.

God, thank you for revealing yourself to us in our most human moments. Help us to see you in the humanity of others. Amen.

Can you imagine having the confidence that Peter has? Maybe I'm just more timid than some, but the idea of standing in front of a large crowd and commanding them to listen to what I have to say is foreign to me.

I like to compare Peter's actions in this verse with what we saw of him just weeks before. During the hours leading up to Jesus' crucifixion, Peter lost all confidence and sense of self. He denied his relationship with Jesus not once but three times. Despite his love for and commitment to Christ, the fear of the situation overtook his voice. Yet here he is so soon after, boldly sharing the truth. His single voice, willing to stand and face a crowd full of skeptics and naysayers, added fuel to the movement that Jesus started, and it ignited believers to create something new. They united, organized, struggled, failed, succeeded, and ultimately built the church that we're still working to make better today.

The power of a single voice cannot be overstated, but it can be hard to believe that on a personal level. We've seen countless times that God chooses to speak the truth through those who don't want to speak, who have been broken or interrupted, and whose confidence has taken a hit. God chooses those like Moses, Esther, Mary, and Peter. When it comes to speaking on behalf of God, it doesn't matter who you are, what you look like, where you fit in to society, or how loud your voice is if God has chosen you.

God, help us know when to listen, when to speak, and when to stand up and shout for your glory. Amen.

The best sermons are the ones we preach to ourselves. Whenever we listen to preachers or read devotionals, we filter the words through our own experiences. We take hold of the narrative and shape the external message to fit our internal monologues. It's our way of engaging with the words around us, and it's natural for us to re-preach the sermons to ourselves, rehashing things in our own voices and adding our own context.

In this passage, Peter preached to thousands of people. His words were so compelling that three thousand people were baptized and joined the church that very same day. I've heard a lot of great preachers, but I've never seen anyone do that. How could one message reach all those people? They all had their own experiences, their own struggles, and their own pain. How, then, could they all walk away with the same decision?

In this story, Peter tells the crowd to "change their hearts and lives" (CEB), and I'm certain that as they heard those words, they saw a different part of their life flash before their eyes: a different sin that held on to them, a different person they had wronged, a different wound they needed healed. Though they all heard the same words, each journey was unique.

While I'm sure that Peter's words were compelling, God was doing most of the work in the people that day. Their inner narratives—the voice of the Holy Spirit that dwells in all of us— preached the real sermons in their hearts. God is doing the same work in our hearts today. We need only listen and ask the voice of the Holy Spirit to do the rest.

God, help us hear your voice within us, and give us the boldness to rely on your word, presence, and wisdom. Amen.

Listen In, Call Out

The word of God has set us free. I always find it interesting when someone talks about the gospel like that. When we read this phrase, we know that it really means that the truth about Jesus' sacrifice has broken our chains of sin and given us eternal life. Somehow that whole, big idea has been boiled down to simply "the word of God." As someone who loves writing and literature, I cherish the idea that words can set us free.

Words are more than just letters in a row or lines and shapes that we've learned to associate with sounds and meanings. There is a unique power in them. They can carry our stories into the world, bring truth, and connect us to others. They allow us to share our hearts.

The two wordsmiths I feel nearest to despite never knowing them are Rachel Held Evans and Taylor Swift. Though one wrote Christian nonfiction and one is a songwriting pop star, both string their words together in a way that feels like they were meant just for me. The specificity of their experiences creates a sense of universality that makes each reader or listener feel known.

Encountering the gospel can feel this way too. Though it can be difficult to devote time to reading scripture and sitting with it long enough for the meaning to sink in, the words are meant for us. The truth in the story of Jesus was written for us to hear. It is real, compelling, specific, and life-changing. Within the stories of the Bible lie the universal truths of our own struggles and pains. Peter invites us to accept this truth and live in the story that God is writing for each of us.

God, help us choose to be part of your story—to see your divine creation in our lives and to live in the truth of your word. Amen.

If no one has told you so recently, I hope you hear me when I say that your voice matters. It is worthy of being heard. This truth is harder for some to grasp than others, but it is true all the same. As one who often has trouble accepting this truth, I find Psalm 116 a helpful reminder that even if no one here on earth cares to hear me, God does.

When we start to turn down the volume on our own voices, it's far too easy to let the many voices of negativity speak over us. What we hear matters. We know that we start listening to the world around us when we are still in the womb, and those early sounds inform our experiences once we're born. As we grow, the noises, songs, and sounds we hear shape the development of our own voice. Did you know that our musical ears naturally bend toward the scales that are most common in our culture? Children will naturally sing tunes in the scales that their society finds acceptable. Of all the notes and intervals in existence, Western children will nearly always choose the same few to make their melodies. From day one, the voices around us affect how we shape, use, and value our own voice. That is a powerful concept.

Our voices can get overpowered when we hear only the voices of death and sorrow. But our voices aren't lost; they're stirring within us, working up the courage to burst out and cry "Please, LORD, save me!" just as the psalmist does. And our God is there to hear it. Every. Single. Time.

Lord, bend your ear to hear our voices, every word, every prayer, every breath, no matter how quiet. Amen.

Today I will call on the name of the Lord. I will use the voice I've been given to speak up, sing praises, shout, and make my voice known. With the psalmist I confess that my God has pulled me from dark depths and saved me countless times. I will never be able to thank God properly for pulling me from the pit of an eating disorder, surrounding me with a faithful community of people who love me, and slowly but surely revealing the call God has placed on my heart. But I can try. I can do everything in my power to follow God's call. I can love those around me boldly and fiercely. I can share my story with those who might be fighting the same fight I was.

In these closing verses of Psalm 116, the psalmist expresses the feelings a lot of us have when we're trying to express the greatness of God's mercy. It feels scattered, jubilant, and almost aggressively thankful. It drives the psalmist to call on God.

Wherever you are today, whatever you're feeling, call on God. Whether it's a quiet whispered cry for help, a silent request for the Holy Spirit to speak, a loudly sung doxology, or something in between, call out! God is ready, waiting to listen, wanting to hear your voice, and ready to respond with wisdom and mercy.

Holy Trinity, thank you for your presence. God, thank you for your willingness to bend your ear to listen to your children when we cry out to you. Thank you, Jesus, for humbling yourself, walking alongside us, and sharing in our humanity so that we may feel closer to you. Thank you, Holy Spirit, for being the guiding voice within us that gives us boldness, wisdom, and courage. Help us value our voices, knowing you have given us each a story to tell. Remind us to call on your name, knowing you will be there for us every time. Amen.

Listen In, Call Out

God Is Near

APRIL 24–30, 2023 • JEFFERSON FURTADO

SCRIPTURE OVERVIEW: The reading from Acts picks up the themes of mutual love and fellowship from last week and records that the display of these qualities captured the attention of the people in Jerusalem. When the church displays these qualities today, they still attract people to the Lord. The psalm and First Peter are linked by the theme of suffering. In Psalm 23, David is confident that God will stay with him even through the darkest valley. Peter encourages his audience to walk through that same valley, strengthened by the knowledge that God will never abandon them and that they are following the example of Christ. In John, Jesus declares that he is the way to safety for God's sheep, so we should listen to his voice alone.

QUESTIONS AND SUGGESTIONS FOR REFLECTION

- Read Acts 2:42-47. How have you seen the joy and goodwill of the people of the church attract new members?
- Read Psalm 23. How do this psalm's joys and comforts change when you consider the suffering of the psalmist in Psalm 22?
- Read 1 Peter 2:19-25. When you have been caught in a struggle, how have your actions helped or worsened your situation?
- Read John 10:1-10. How have you or someone you know attempted to enter God's abundance by stealth? What would it mean to rectify this and enter through the gate?

Native of Rio de Janeiro, Brazil; member of the Connectional Ministries staff of the Tennessee-Western Kentucky Conference of The United Methodist Church.

Though shepherds and sheep are the prevailing images for most of the readings this week, when we stand far enough away we can notice another connecting point: the constant presence of our triune God. The theme of God's presence permeates our texts. We see this clearly in Psalm 23 with God as shepherd, John 10 with Jesus as the Good Shepherd, today's reading with the presence of the Holy Spirit, and in Second Peter through Christ's example of life.

The presence of the Holy Spirit in the life of the community is an essential part of our story. The visible reality presented in our text is empowered by this invisible and constant presence. The power of the Holy Spirit enabled the early church to live in a way that showed the world an alternative to selfishness and brokenness.

Though we often focus on the external actions performed by Christians and the Christian community, we must also attend to the work God performed through them. Some people simply heard the good news, and God worked within them to add them to the church. Others experienced the material generosity and joy of the church and were attracted that way. These daily works of the Holy Spirit—works of faith and generosity—instruct, connect, and feed us all.

In *Jesus and the Disinherited*, the great theologian Howard Thurman pondered what the religion of Jesus has to say to those who find themselves in the margins of society. In a world where political, racial, social, and theological divisions are the norm, it can be difficult to imagine harmonious life in a diverse community. But the example of the early church shows that the dream can become a communal reality through the power of the Holy Spirit.

Dear Lord, your presence overwhelms our senses, and your love enriches our lives. Fill us with your love so that we may share your light with the world around us. Amen.

Psalm 23 is one of the most popular psalms in the Bible. The King James Version has immortalized the words of this psalm with poetic language that has endured through many centuries. It has offered comfort to those who face grief, courage to those in danger, hope for the lost, and encouragement for all who seek direction.

Something special happens to me when I hear "The LORD is my shepherd; I shall not want." Even though I live in a city and do not know any shepherds, the words take me on a mental trip to a place where I see God's love and care. The poetry is universal. Everyone knows what it means to fear, doubt, and feel alone. Everyone needs comfort and protection.

There is also a beautiful perspective presented here where God journeys with us even through the mundane parts of life—rising, eating, drinking, moving, and resting. When our needs are met, it is because God is our shepherd. This understanding moves us out of the center of the universe and places God in control, tenderly leading us into a life of abundance—even in the face of danger.

Whether we find ourselves in routine moments or times of trial, this psalm reminds us that no earthly presence or power can fulfill the needs of life; but God can. When we cannot see the path ahead, God shows us the way. When we feel exhausted and need rest, God refreshes our life. Even when darkness surrounds us and fear threatens to overtake us, we can rest easy when we trust our Shepherd.

Great Shepherd, your love for us is beyond our imagining. Open our eyes to see your presence and feel your guidance through all moments of our lives. Amen.

Our text speaks of a reality that often sounds foreign to the ears of most Christians in North America: unjust suffering. Though we live in an era of protest and digital indignation, most of us are far removed from the suffering described in our text. Yet unjust suffering continues to be a real crisis in our world, and those who experience it need a word of hope.

The apostle Peter begins his address in verse 18, which was omitted from the lectionary, speaking to Christians who are enslaved and are living in spaces that are not their own. Their social location places limits on their personhood and freedoms. Still Peter counsels them to live according to the example of Christ, who "entrusted himself to the one who judges justly."

Those who continue to suffer unjustly today need Peter's reminder that they, like all those who follow Christ, are "immigrants and strangers in the world" (1 Pet. 2:11, CEB). The reality of Christ in our lives leads us to yearn for and seek the blessings of liberation and peace for ourselves and others. But that is not an easy journey. The good news we hear in this text is that Christ is present with us.

The Good Shepherd, who became human and made his home among us, suffered unjustly. He stands by our side and journeys with us in our times of suffering. He also calls us to journey with others—to stand by their side in times of challenge and to work for God's vision of justice and righteousness so that it becomes a reality for all creation.

So be encouraged, even in your time of suffering. Christ is with us.

God of compassion and love, we live as immigrants and strangers in a world of strife and pain. Remind us that even here we are not alone. Help us to journey with faith, following the example of Christ. Amen.

I was an adult the first time I ever saw a sheep in person. I have to confess that all those paintings of Jesus and sheep radically undersold what real sheep look like. I did not find them to be cute or to have a particularly pleasant smell, but neither of those things seemed to bother those charged with their care. They simply stood guard, carefully watching and caring for the sheep. What a beautiful image. But still, sheep cannot permanently live in enclosures. They must go beyond the safety of those boundaries, moving through the gate, to find green pastures and freshwater. Jesus tells his listeners not to be mistaken; he is the gate and only through him can they find fullness of life.

The healing of the man born blind is an important context for our readings (see John 9:1-38). The words of Jesus in our passage are a response to and explanation of those events. Deep compassion and care are central themes in both texts. In the healing story, we see the disciples' inability to recognize an individual in need of help. But Jesus sees the need and offers grace. The Pharisees also failed to discern God's power at work and chose to exclude a sibling they did not understand. But when Jesus encounters that same person, he offers welcome and understanding.

This image of tender love and care is carried forward as Jesus proclaims that the shepherd calls his sheep by name and the sheep know the voice of their shepherd. There is a reality of intimacy in these words. The shepherd is not a stranger. The shepherd knows how to enter the sheep pen and guide the sheep so they can "live life to the fullest."

How might we follow Jesus' example and have compassion for those whom the world ignores, neglects, and judges?

Gracious Shepherd, give us eyes to look at the world with compassion and love. Help us to be your hands and feet to those in need of a gracious friend. Amen.

Early in my ministry life I was asked, "What would happen if one hundred new families suddenly showed up at your church?" This seemed so far-fetched that I hadn't given it any thought. I would be unprepared. But for the early church community this was a daily reality. We may idealize the life of the early church, but I imagine that any community that grows thirtyfold overnight faces challenges.

Luke tells us that those gathered before Pentecost numbered one hundred twenty persons (see Acts 1:15); after the outpouring of the Holy Spirit, the church grew extensively, adding three thousand new believers (2:41). But unlike the challenges I imagine we would face today, this growing Spirit-led community lived in harmony—a harmony grounded in their shared connection to Christ and the power of the Holy Spirit.

Today we can find communities of faith that share life together through teaching, fellowship, shared meals, and prayer. As in the early church, such connections are through Christ and the power of the Holy Spirit. But something stands out in the text that sets us believers apart: the radical generosity believers had for one another—a generosity in sharing possessions and life.

The reality of the early church may seem beyond our modern reach. But how can we practice daily a Spirit-empowered life that attracts those who feel abandoned by the world, those who can find a home with us?

The witness of the early church offers us a glimpse of a kingdom reality that is possible when we open ourselves to the movement of the Holy Spirit and live as a community of faith.

Draw us to your love, Lord, so we may grow in our love for others. Draw us to grace so we may live in grace with others. Help us to dream of a world where all people practice generosity and love. Amen.

My first memory of Psalm 23 does not come from a funeral or church service but a prayer meeting in my grandmother's backyard. Grandma's Saturday morning prayer meetings were a permanent appointment in our family calendar. We lived next door to her house, and each week she would rise much too early, calling each grandchild by name so we could attend her prayer service. Psalm 23 was a regular part of the readings and was one of the psalms we were expected to memorize. As I got older this psalm became a nightly prayer, a plea in times of trouble, and a mantra in moments of anxiousness.

Though we often hear this psalm at funerals, it speaks clearly and confidently about life. More specifically, these words speak about a way of life guided by God's faithful love that pursues us all the days of our lives. We are invited to draw near to the shepherd and place our full lives under his loving care. It is good for us to note the shift in language that happens in verse 4, where the psalmist switches from speaking about God in the third person to speaking to God in the second person.

The nearness of God in language and action is an important feature in the psalm. God does not stand at a distance as life events take place, God is near. God is ready to protect as life becomes dangerous. God is ready to provide when we face adversity. God welcomes us to the table of grace.

When we face difficult moments in life, we must remember that the Lord is indeed our shepherd. God is near—ready to protect, welcome, and provide.

Dear Lord, when challenges grow all around us, may we feel the nearness of your goodness and faithful love and rest in your peace. Amen.

There is one thing about being a sheep that we don't often hear in sermons: Sheep don't live by themselves; they are part of a flock. People who actually know things about sheep say that sheep naturally gravitate toward one another—they flock together. Whether they find themselves in times of feeding or fear, sheep will group together. Even though we can find a great assortment of "Jesus and I" theology in the world, the good news of Jesus calls us to life in community. The good news of Jesus invites us to be a part of the sheep pen.

We often forget that we are called to listen to the voice of the One who knows our name and walk through the gate into abundant pastures. There are times when we become so distracted with the concerns of life that we end up following voices that seek to steal our peace, kill our joy, and destroy our communion with others. When we move away from the voice of the Shepherd, we become vulnerable to a world of pain that divides, distorts, dehumanizes, and harms us. But even when we find ourselves far away, the voice of the Shepherd calls and leads us back through the gate, into the safety of the fold. When we turn our hearts and ears to him, we find safekeeping, care, and provision.

Now we may find ourselves as sheep that have already walked through the gate, heard the voice of the Shepherd, and are living happily in community. But we cannot forget that there are others who still need to hear the comforting and healing voice of the One who offers fullness of life. Perhaps through our living and witness we can help them find their way home.

Good Shepherd, we hear your voice of love call our name. Help us to follow wherever you lead. Amen.

Focusing on Christ

MAY 1–7, 2023 • TANYA MARLOW

SCRIPTURE OVERVIEW: All of the readings this week include people facing hostility or suffering. In Acts, Stephen is stoned to death for his belief in Christ. In John's Gospel, the disciples in the upper room are anticipating Jesus' death. Peter tells the scattered believers not to fear despite the hatred in society, and the psalmist cries to the Lord for rescue from his persecutors. Another aspect the readings have in common is the solution to their suffering. For the psalmist, this means recalling God's character. In the New Testament passages, it's remembering Christ. God is a rock and fortress in Psalm 31, and Christ is the cornerstone, our firm foundation, in 1 Peter. Focusing on Christ shapes our response to suffering.

QUESTIONS AND SUGGESTIONS FOR REFLECTION

- Read Acts 7:55-60. Recall a time when you have seen God's power in action. How was God's power different than you might have expected?
- Read Psalm 31:1-5, 15-16. Contemplate your answers to the author's questions. How do the psalmist's hope and experiences reflect your own?
- Read 1 Peter 2:2-10. When have you experienced God as a loving Mother? When has Christ been your cornerstone?
- Read John 14:1-14. How do you experience God's presence through the life or actions of others?

Writer, theologian, and speaker whose work focuses on the spirituality of suffering and sacred storytelling (*narratio divina*); lives in Britain with her husband, who is a Church of England minister, and their one bouncy son; author of *Those Who Wait*. Download her book on Ruth at TanyaMarlow.com.

We are so accustomed to Stephen's serene posture in death that it's easy to forget the fiery speech that got him martyred. Stephen shocked the Sanhedrin by identifying his hearers as enemies of God, stiff-necked and uncircumcised of heart. Why? They had rejected Jesus. The speech was a blistering attack upon arrogant leaders oblivious to their sin.

By using the title *Son of Man*, Stephen referenced not only the humanity of Jesus but Daniel's prophecy that "one like a son of man" would be worshiped by the world (see 7:13-14, NIV).

At this so-called blasphemy, the members of the Sanhedrin ground their teeth (see Acts 7:54) and rushed him. (The Greek word for "rushed" is the same one used for the demon-filled pigs in the Gerasene in Matthew 8:32; Mark 5:13; Luke 8:33.) Luke's imagery connects the religious leaders with hell.

Stephen, in contrast, has a face like an angel (see Acts 6:15) and receives a vision of heaven. By focusing on the resurrected Christ, Stephen is emboldened to keep proclaiming the unpopular truth against an angry mob.

History shows us that we have always killed the prophets, and "we" includes committed Christians. All prophets tell confrontational truth that offends those in power. Like the council, we sometimes rush as a mob to silence uncomfortable truth. We may identify with Stephen, but we often act like the Sanhedrin.

What prophets today critique the hypocritically religious or powerful? May we differ from the Sanhedrin by listening to those in church or society who make us uncomfortable with their truth-telling. When we weep in frustration at the silencing of today's prophets, may we, like Stephen, lift our focus to the interceding, resurrected Christ.

Almighty God, when we see the persecution of Christians and the silencing of prophets, give us ears to hear truth, boldness to speak, and eyes lifted up to our resurrected Lord. Amen.

When the early church witnessed Stephen's death, they must have been struck not only by the injustice but the lost opportunity. Stephen was a persuasive and holy man who could have been a spokesperson for the early church. He was a rebel for Jesus, bold and erudite, who would have spread the gospel if he had lived.

Stephen, however, was already looking to the possibility of hope and redemption in his martyrdom. Rather than respond with hate, he died like Jesus, deliberately echoing the words from the cross for God to receive his spirit and forgive his killers. When we look closer, we realize that his holy rebellious streak came through even in his darkest moment: He committed his spirit not to the Father but to Jesus, thus once again equating Jesus with God. Jesus was killed as the prophets had been. Stephen found honor in his humiliating death by connecting it with Christ's.

When Jesus died, the disciples despaired. However, God redeemed their suffering. Because of Stephen's death, the church scattered in fear, fulfilling Jesus' command to go outward from Jerusalem to the ends of the earth. Where there is unjust suffering, God can bring vindication, redemption, and hope.

How should we respond when we witness grave injustice in the world? Like Stephen, many today are killed for speaking the truth or simply being a Christian. In yesterday's meditation, we noted that when we despair at the silencing of the prophets, we look to the resurrected Christ—truth personified. Here, as we reflect on Stephen's death, we look to the crucified, forgiving Christ. The focus on Jesus' death sustains us amid unjust suffering.

Lord Jesus, when see suffering, give us hope through your redemptive passion and death. Amen.

The disciples certainly have reasons to be troubled. What starts as a celebratory meal is ruined by Jesus' predictions of betrayal by Judas and denial by Peter. Similarly, Jesus is troubled because of his impending death. He informs them that he will be going somewhere they cannot follow, yet the very purpose of being a disciple is to follow. His announcement shatters their vocation, crushing their hope of victory.

But Jesus tells them not to be troubled: Although they can't follow him, he is going ahead to prepare dwellings for them. They do not need to take further action to reach their destination, for Jesus himself will come back for them. His death is not the end of hope.

At this point, Thomas sounds confused and asks what Jesus' destination is and the way there. Perhaps he misunderstands the dwellings as something geographical. However, he is the devout disciple who committed to die alongside Jesus (see John 11:16), so it is likely he understands Jesus' spiritual meaning and wants to know how to reach heaven. He probably expects an answer about fulfilling commandments or some heroic deed. Jesus' surprising answer is that he himself is the way: his suffering, his death, not Thomas' goodness or effort. Heaven's suites are opened to us through Jesus. It's not about us.

Today there is much that can distress us. Sometimes we also feel lost, like our purpose has shattered. It helps to return our attention to Christ who has promised not to abandon us and who, though troubled himself, comforted the troubled disciples. Jesus is our way to God and all that is good, the living embodiment of truth, and the giver of the fullness of life eternal.

Bring to God today what troubles you. Meditate on Jesus as the way, truth, and life.

If the first verses of John 14 are about going, the next part is about knowing. We may miss how shocking it is that Jesus asserts that the disciples have seen God because they have seen him. This was God the unseeable, whose face no one could see and live. Now, if we want to know the character and habits of God, we need only look at Jesus.

Jesus phrases it carefully: He is in the Father, and the Father dwells in him and works through him. Jesus doesn't say that he is the Father. Rather, they are two separate but interconnected persons of one essence; to know one is to know the other. In verse 12, Jesus hints at the full Trinity by pointing to the greater works the disciples will do when he returns to the Father, which is when the Holy Spirit comes.

I have been almost completely bedbound with chronic illness for more than a decade. I know better than most that when we experience sickness, or our world implodes, or we are betrayed or heartbroken, we need to know that God is with us in the darkness. This, I must confess, is not my initial prayer or immediate longing. My first cry is for God to fix whatever is wrong and make it better in just the way I want it made better. But that is not always what happens. Times of suffering can cause us to doubt not merely the existence but the goodness of God, and this is a terrifying thought.

To know Jesus is to know God. Jesus' appeal to his actions helps. If we focus on Jesus in our suffering, we can know the goodness of the God who heals the sick, forgives the guilty, pastors the weak, leads the lost, and suffers with us and for us. It doesn't fix it, but it helps.

Lord of the lost, be with my downcast heart today; let me know the certainty of your goodness. Amen.

The early church was a collection of rejects. It first appears that Peter was addressing diaspora Jews scattered across modern-day Turkey (see 1 Peter 1:1). However, many interpreters argue that his audience was most likely Gentile converts because of their former licentious behavior (see 1 Peter 4:3-4). Peter identifies these Gentiles as chosen people, aligning them with their Jewish brothers in Christ. Whether Jews or Gentiles, the recipients of this letter were misfits who were experiencing attacks and hostility from society.

Peter speaks compassionately into that feeling of lostness and loneliness by pointing out that Jesus was in that exact position: rejected by humans, chosen by God. Using the image of a stone that had initially been rejected by builders but which eventually became the cornerstone supporting the whole house, he links several passages from the Hebrew Bible, applying the stone images to Jesus.

When I was eight, I took a boring tour of a jewelry factory and was rewarded at the end by a visit to the "scratch patch," where rejected gemstones were expelled out into a yard. I rummaged and found the most perfect stone: a thumb-sized amethyst, jagged on one side, showing its layers, smooth and luminous on the other. I've kept it ever since.

First Peter is a message for people who don't quite fit in to a particular tribe—perhaps too religious for society but not religious enough for traditionalists, perhaps culturally different. It is for those who feel purposeless and insignificant in the kingdom of God. Whenever we feel out on our own, we have the reassurance that Jesus was similarly unpopular. In God's sight, we are deliberately chosen and treasured.

Lord Jesus, may I see myself and other Christians as precious and treasured. Build my life upon Christ, the cornerstone. Amen.

Peter's letter reveals that the early church was small and characterized by deep, communal, organic spiritual growth. The first metaphor he uses shows the members as infants craving spiritual milk. We all need spiritual food—scripture, prayer, and Communion—to grow. Yet the second metaphor shows that those same infants form the living temple and its priests who serve. Peter affirms the small gatherings as a continuation of Israel's gathered worship, still offering holy sacrifices. Note that these sacrifices are not an atonement for sin, which Christ Jesus alone achieved. Rather, Jesus is the means by which they can offer the other kinds of temple sacrifices, such as thanksgiving and fellowship offerings.

Addressing people who had not been born Jews, Peter tells them that they are a chosen race and people who belong to God by virtue of their faith in Christ. Speaking to a group consisting mainly of women and slaves, lower in class and respect, scorned and regarded as insignificant, Peter declares them to be royalty. Those seen merely as sinners, he names *priests*, light in the darkness. Among the plethora of affirmations of their identity, he gives only two instructions: Long for spiritual feeding and proclaim God's mighty acts.

We cannot grow as individual Christians unless we grow communally and in Christ. Consider what steps you could take today to help your church do good in your community or encourage a lonely church member. Ask for and offer prayer with your Christian family.

Lord, we have tasted that you are good. Keep us looking to you, knowing our true identity, longing for deep spiritual growth. Build us together as a church. Amen.

When someone misrepresents me, I feel hot rage. I suspect you do too, but often we're powerless to defend ourselves publicly. When David was slandered, which is the context for Psalm 31, he took his frustration to God in lament. He prayed he would not be put to shame, that God would save him from his enemies' traps, and that he would be saved from persecution.

Note that David only discovers trust in God after he has prayed for it. He begs, "Be a rock of refuge for me" and then declares, "You are indeed my rock and my fortress." Likewise, David fears being given into the "hand" of his persecutors, so he commits his spirit into God's hand. By verse 6, he can affirm that his destiny and life events are indeed already in the trustworthy hand of God. Desperate prayer results in reassurance.

The psalm is well-known for a phrase Jesus quoted as he died: "Into your hand I commit my spirit." Jesus, too, knew the pain of being falsely accused, with a raging mob refusing to hear the truth about him. As we have seen, Stephen also experienced this and prayed the same prayer.

Whenever we face slander, we can focus on Jesus and once more surrender our life and reputation into his hands. When we are under siege, asking God to be our refuge shows us that God already is.

This week we have seen the power of focusing on Jesus: the resurrected Jesus for truth-telling boldness; the dying Jesus for redeeming suffering; the eternity-guaranteeing Jesus for uncertain times; the wholly good Jesus for when we're troubled; the misfit Jesus chosen by God; the misunderstood Jesus who empathizes with us.

Lord Jesus, may we always look to you. Into your hands we commit our circumstances anew. Amen.

Knowing God

MAY 8–14, 2023 • RICK QUINN

SCRIPTURE OVERVIEW: In Acts, Paul visits Athens and finds the people worshiping various deities. He attempts to show them the one true God not by open confrontation but by understanding where they are in their own thinking and then engaging in conversation. This model is confirmed in First Peter: We should always be prepared to give reasons for our faith, but this should be done with gentleness and respect, not confrontation. The psalmist promises to make offerings in the Temple to the Lord because God has brought the people through a period of testing. The psalm thus also ties into First Peter where the believers are being tested. Jesus tells his disciples in John that God will send the Spirit to empower them to demonstrate their faith by keeping his commands.

QUESTIONS AND SUGGESTIONS FOR REFLECTION

- Read Acts 17:22-31. When have you searched for God? How did God's nearness surprise you?
- Read Psalm 66:8-20. What tests have you endured? How have you known God's presence through times of difficulty?
- Read 1 Peter 3:13-22. How does your faith help you determine what is right? How does it give you courage when doing what is right brings you suffering?
- Read John 14:15-21. When have you felt encompassed by the Trinity? When has your identity as part of this family felt fragile?

A writer who lives in Goodlettsville, TN; member of McKendree United Methodist Church, a multicultural community in downtown Nashville, TN.

To an unknown god. The inscription on the altar might seem to be an example of people hedging their bet just in case they have missed something. If that is the case, then Paul is correcting the naivete of the religiously curious Athenians.

But notice the language. Paul is not making plain what had been hidden. Instead he acknowledges and affirms their recognition of mystery. And—get this—he deepens it.

Have you ever thought your task was to explain away all doubt to someone struggling to believe? Or have you felt inadequate because you were grasping for God, unsure of which direction to take?

We do this story a disservice if we view Paul as a lecturer to the ignorant, pulling back a secret curtain to reveal all the answers. Instead, he invited those gathered to consider the mystery of radical relationship and the way the God who acts in Christ is close to each of us yet cannot be pinned down, defined, or confined in our structures or comprehended in our thoughts.

At a time of profound loss in my life, too many well-meaning friends attempted to provide an explanation, a key to understanding tragedy in a system of meaning. It felt cold and distant, a barrier that held them off from my pain. Those who were more comfortable with the mystery didn't try to explain my loss but rather reminded me of whose I was. As Paul reminded the Athenians of what they already knew from their own poets, my friends reminded me of what I already knew at a level that words or gold or silver or stone image cannot contain.

God, in this moment free me from grasping to control, and teach me to dwell in you. Amen.

When was the last time you experienced awe or wide-eyed wonder? When have words escaped your ability to give expression to beauty? Or grief? In these moments we get a glimpse that the words we have for the deepest things can fall short. Could this lead us into new vistas of relationship to God?

Paul honors the vertigo that inspired the Athenians' marker to the ungraspable by inviting them deeper into the contradictions rather than resolving them. The God of creation, of the vast expanse of reality, cannot be housed in shrines formed by human hands or in ideas formed by our minds. Yet God has made us in such a way that we grope and search for God.

To go deeper into contradictions is not the invitation we want most days. We want to make sense of the world, and we want to understand the plan. Inevitably, life upends all our efforts to make it all make sense.

Paul reminds us that we are part of a story more profound than a set of instructions. Invoking Creation, he hearkens back to the mystery of God's Spirit hovering over the chaos and bringing forth life, and this is our connective grounding to the mystery of creation and life.

In God we live and move and have our being. Indeed, we are God's offspring. Sit with that for a moment. Don't try to resolve the logical contradictions of being within and without a logical puzzle but instead invite an awareness of profound relationality, an awareness that all that is and happens is not separate from the love that raised Jesus from the dead.

God beyond understanding, give me patience to sit with the unknown and broaden my imagination beyond a need to contain you in my ideas. I live and move and have my being in you. Amen.

Knowing God 161

Communities have stories. If you think about it, there really is no hard and fast distinction between the story of me and the story of us. Every individual's story contains numerous acts of grace and assistance from a wider community. We don't get many places by ourselves.

It's difficult to see clearly in times of suffering. Pain is acute and focus narrows. Sometimes we need to be reminded that our story is part of a larger narrative. A community can remind us of who we are and from where we came when our vision of the path ahead is obstructed by the present.

The language used by the psalmist in the first five verses of today's passage is plural, the language of the community, before it switches to singular for the rest of the psalm. Verse 9 proclaims, "God has preserved us among the living; [God] didn't let our feet slip a bit" (CEB). The hearer is drawn into a collective story of resilience and deliverance only attributable to the presence of the Divine in their midst. It is the story of the Exodus, a deliverance of a whole people from death to life. The suffering of individuals in the wilderness can often cause us to forget the larger story. We need the corporate world and word.

Several years back, our family was rocked by a sudden and profound loss. It was during the Easter season, and I was scheduled to lead the liturgy on Easter Sunday. Reeling and wounded, I did not feel the "alleluias" of the season. I could only continue forward by recognizing that this was the language of the community of faith and not just my own individual story. Without denying the specificity of my pain, the corporate liturgy—like this psalm—declares, "We got you." This is our story, and it has a trajectory set by the One who steadies our feet.

God of deliverance, steady my steps today by reminding me of my place in your grand story. Open my eyes to your guiding presence today. Amen.

I recently visited Maine's Acadia National Park, an expansive natural treasure of 49,000 acres. The breathtaking landscape was carved out by glaciers in a past so distant that it stretches the imagination.

While there, I attempted to hike the Bubble Rock trail, a "family-friendly" trail according to our guide. For a difficult hour I couldn't focus on anything but taking the next step in front of me and attempting to catch my breath. At one point I had to stop and sit for a while. When I did, my attention shifted from the trail immediately in front of me to a vast expanse of lakes and peaks and foliage. I was lifted out of struggle and enveloped in a breathtaking landscape. I was a sojourner in a community with co-travelers past and present and with the natural world that sustains us all.

In today's passage, the psalmist exhorts the community to join in hymns of praise to the God of creation and the God whose deliverance was manifest in the Exodus. After struggling to give an account of the corporate struggle and suffering of the community, the psalmist shifts attention back to God's deliverance in the midst of struggle.

The NRSV translates this act of deliverance by declaring that God has "brought us out to a spacious place." The transformative work of God gives rise to many striking metaphors. Suffering narrows our field of vision. This psalm witnesses to the work of a God who lifts our eyes to the wider hills from whence our deliverance comes.

Maker of heaven and earth, bring me out into a more spacious place this day. Reveal to me where my vision is limited, and give me a glimpse of the breadth and depth of your love. Amen.

Knowing God

Now who will harm you if you are eager to do what is good?" It turns out that this does not promise followers of Christ that they will be free from discomfort. In fact, inasmuch as the Resurrection disrupts the categories of the cycle of life and death, so too does living in the community of the resurrected One. It puts one out of step with a world dominated by the cycle of death.

Early communities of faith formed in the wake of Easter found themselves at odds with the status quo. The transformative encounter with the resurrected Christ formed communities who, like their Savior, transgressed the boundaries of the world. Christians don't seek discomfort nor should they wear it as a badge of superiority, but the discomfort will come. The writer here frankly cautions us to expect it.

Our experience of suffering is mapped within the context of Christ's own action, which, as verse 18 says, was his suffering in order to bring us into the presence of God. This is the boundary-shattering impact of the gospel. There is no experience outside of the intimacy of the divine reach. In even the most seemingly godforsaken scenarios, God is suffering for and with us to bring us into God's presence.

The suffering of Christ reveals God's presence in the broken places of life, on the margins and the outskirts of the hierarchy of values set down by existing powers. Disrupting the status quo means our allegiance lies with the God of resurrection who brings down the mighty and lifts up the lowly. The waters of destruction give way to the waters of baptism. The disruption of the Resurrection leads to new life that ultimately is the opposite of harm.

O Resurrected One, lead me deeper this day into your presence in the most unlikely of places. Amen.

Language about God is a tricky business. A mentor stressed to me that speaking about God means trading in metaphors. They flutter between yes and no, opening vistas of understanding and encounter while giving way to inexhaustible mystery. We grasp on to insights, but any attempt to control them is like trying to hold water in your hand. They inevitably seep from our grasp.

Today's reading comes after Thomas and Philip struggle with Jesus' claims about how one comes to God. Much of what Jesus says in this chapter is about how intimacy with God is inseparable from a relationship with Jesus. I am often surprised that Jesus' closest followers were confused about this (as if I have a perfect understanding of my relationships!).

Take a look at the three verses set aside for today. Jesus is in the midst of a difficult conversation with his disciples around loss, limits, and a projected absence of his presence. Grief, disruption, and feelings of abandonment creep in, and often our reflex is to anchor ourselves in certainty, to find something that doesn't change. In such a scenario, the offer of an "Advocate," the "Spirit of truth," might seem grounding. But as quick as we start to hold on, we are reminded that this Spirit is not received in the world. It is neither seen nor known. Too often, we are told that knowing God is the control of correct beliefs. Jesus pulls us back to a deeper truth—to know God is relational. It is in abiding that we are transformed day to day.

Spend some time in silent prayer today. Find a place where you are comfortable and open yourself to God's presence. When you find yourself distracted or grasping, don't fight it. Just say "Abide" as a prayer of returning to openness to God's indwelling Spirit.

Knowing God

I remember specifically the terror I felt as a child in the basement of a Sears department store when I discovered that my curiosity had separated me from my mother—who was only an aisle over. So much of what we take for security in relationships is tied to physical presence and certainty.

"I will not leave you orphaned," Jesus asserts, foreshadowing the grief to come for his companions. We read these texts in the season of Easter in light of the Resurrection because, honestly, sometimes we need assurance. Even still.

The passage in John that ends our week points back to Paul's address in Athens at the beginning of the week. In God, we live, and move, and have our being. Here in the "farewell discourse," Jesus evokes presence and absence (of sight or proximity) in ways where the hard lines between them blur while never disappearing. It is tempting to read Jesus' words here as a series of transactions or obligations: If we do this, then we are loved by God. But this is just another example of the temptation to nail it down, to swap a transformative relationship for certainty. Jesus is assuring those with him that the loss and disruption they will soon feel in relation to him is bound up in a larger context. This context is not a formula that we master to anchor ourselves in storms but a glimpse into the mystery that no place is "God-forsaken."

To live in the Easter season is to experience without being able to define in words the enveloping fullness of God's love.

Creator, Redeemer, Sustainer, I give you thanks for the mystery of your abiding presence that absence cannot negate. Lead me into the mutuality of love where your word and presence find me. Amen.

Witnessing (to) the Journey

MAY 15–21, 2023 • MAUREEN KNUDSEN LANGDOC

SCRIPTURE OVERVIEW: Though Jesus has taught his disciples that God's kingdom is not an earthly one, following the Resurrection some are still expecting him to set up a kingdom on earth. Instead, Jesus ascends into heaven in front of them, being taken up in the clouds. The scene recalls Psalm 68, where the Lord is described as one who rides on the clouds across the expanse of the heavens. In the Gospel reading, Jesus anticipates his coming departure and prays for his followers. Peter talks about a trial—literally a "fiery ordeal"—that is testing Christians. The reference to fire may be specific, for the Roman historian Tacitus records that Nero killed Christians in Rome by burning them alive. The author may therefore be speaking about suffering that is not just metaphorical.

QUESTIONS AND SUGGESTIONS FOR REFLECTION
- Read Acts 1:6-14. When have you experienced the power of community?
- Read Psalm 68:1-10, 32-35. Recall a time when you recognized God's power with fear and joy. How might that have been a foretaste of God's kingdom?
- Read 1 Peter 4:12-14; 5:6-11. How have you walked with faith through suffering?
- Read John 17:1-11. What does it mean for you or your congregation that Jesus prayed for unity among his followers?

———————

University Chaplain and Associate Dean at DePauw University in Greencastle, IN; elder in the Indiana Conference of The United Methodist Church.

Are we there yet?" This question captures a weariness from travel and an eagerness to arrive. Whether on a family road trip or working toward a professional goal, exhaustion and excitement often merge on a journey.

In today's passage, the disciples had already been on quite a journey with Jesus. They were with him when he healed the sick and preached good news to the poor. They wilted as he was beaten and crucified. They were astounded to discover he had been raised from the dead. They could not recognize him on the road to Emmaus. Now they have gathered together for a meal with their resurrected Lord. After this sort of journey, how could their question not come from deep exhaustion and eager anticipation: "Lord, is this the time when you will restore the kingdom to Israel?" *Are we there yet?*

Jesus' answer is twofold: Such things are not for them to know, and they will receive power. Power, Jesus seems to say, doesn't mean having all the answers. Although the disciples' journey to be Christ's witnesses to the ends of the earth will require tremendous power, Jesus does not supply answers. Rather, he gives purpose and the promise of God's Spirit. Jesus equips his disciples with what they need (power) when they need it (purpose), and then he ascends into heaven before their very eyes.

Surely this must have prompted more questions! And this reading says it did—not from the disciples but from two angelic figures: "Why do you stand here looking up toward heaven?"

We are part of God's purpose. You are empowered with God's Spirit. This is our journey, questions and all.

God, when unanswered questions seem to block the path, open our eyes to the purpose we have been given and our hearts to the power of your Spirit. Amen.

"Hurry up and wait." Anyone who's ever taken a family trip knows the feeling. The destination is in mind and the itinerary all planned out, but so much of the journey is occupied with waiting, wondering, or worrying. Preoccupied by the frustration of just trying to get out the door, we overlook the people around us and the purpose of the journey.

That's why it's important to observe what the disciples do after Jesus' ascension. They have a big task ahead of them: being Christ's witnesses to the ends of the earth. But they don't immediately go. Following Jesus' instruction, they gather in Jerusalem to wait for the promised Spirit.

Bearing witness to Christ is not so much striving toward somewhere but resting in someone. To spread the good news throughout the world, we must grow in awareness of God's presence and receptivity to God's indwelling Spirit. This waiting supplies both the power and the purpose necessary for the journey itself.

It is absolutely true that the disciples are not "there yet." They have miles ahead to travel. Yet as they congregate in the upper room and devote themselves to prayer, they are precisely where they need to be—in fellowship with God and one another.

Being Christ's disciples means we bear witness to Christ not only in our going and doing but also in our being and waiting. In fact, here in Acts 1, the former depends upon the latter. Waiting ("where two or three are gathered") is part of the journey itself—a journey more focused on going deeper than on going forward.

So the disciples trust Jesus' instructions and pause in Jerusalem. Here they will discover the promised power of the Spirit at Pentecost, not in frenzied frustration but in patient anticipation.

God, are you asking us to wait? (Pause)

Witnessing (to) the Journey

Journeys can feel risky, especially when you feel like no one is in charge. Today's passage takes us back to an earlier stretch of the disciples' journey, when Jesus had just told the disciples they would see him no more. Jesus would soon be betrayed, arrested, and crucified. After three years doing life together, the time had come for Jesus to leave.

Why? Because, as Jesus explained, he had finished the work the Father had given him to do. But how could his work have been finished when there clearly was (and is!) so much left to do? As we know, the disciples would soon be tasked with being Christ's witnesses to the ends of the earth. *Jesus,* they thought, *are you really sure this is the best time for you to leave?*

But the hour had come. Jesus had finished his work on earth, making the Father known to the world and sharing the gift of eternal life with his friends. *Eternal life,* Jesus says, *is to know and to love God.* The very promise and purpose of the journey is relational.

We see this in the prayer Jesus offered for his disciples. He acknowledged that they would face trouble in this world, but he did not pray for invincibility or riskless journeys. Instead, Jesus prayed that his disciples would know and experience the intimate unity he has with the Father—that they may be one. Oneness, closeness, and togetherness are at the heart of the journey—that we may be one, even amid the troubles of this world.

Yes Jesus left his disciples, but he did not abandon them. The disciples were not alone. They would be given a Helper—the Holy Spirit—and the fellowship of beloved community. These same gifts are offered to you this very day. How might you receive them?

Leading God, grant us the close companionship of fellow travelers. Strengthen these life-giving relationships, and help us make room for others through your Spirit. Amen.

ASCENSION DAY

Have you ever flown with young children? "Mom, look at those mountains!" "Dad, what's that out the window?" Caught between the beauty and the novelty, they want us to join their experience of wonder. Not unrelatedly, they also want us to stop looking down at our screens and start looking up at all we are missing!

Even when our phones are off and we attend to the scenic views before us, we often still need help understanding what we are seeing. What kind of bird is perched in the tree? Why is this historical monument significant? Sometimes we simply cannot see what is right before our eyes.

In today's passage, Jesus' followers are gathered in Jerusalem, talking about the recent encounter two of them had with the resurrected Jesus on the road to Emmaus. Suddenly, Jesus stands among them. They think he is a ghost, but he offers them peace and guidance to the scriptures about him. He explains that everything must be fulfilled that was written about him: The Messiah will suffer death but rise again three days later. This message of repentance and the forgiveness of sins will spread throughout the world, and the disciples shall be witnesses of these things. *This is what you saw,* Jesus points out; *this is what you need to see.*

Today, you will encounter many things. Some experiences will appear straightforward and simple. Others may be painful or perplexing. While being attentive to both the present moment and our community surely widens, deepens, and focuses our perspective, we still may struggle to understand what we see. Thank God we worship the risen Christ, who not only calls us to be witnesses of many things but also opens our minds to understand what is before us.

Teacher, open our minds to understand. What are we witnessing? What do you want us to see? Amen.

Witnessing (to) the Journey

While driving through a storm can be scary, making a journey when you feel sick or are in pain can be absolutely excruciating. The early church knew that following Jesus would mean they would suffer. *Do not be surprised,* the writer of First Peter exhorts, *when you are reviled for the name of Christ.* Suffering on account of the One leading this journey is not something strange.

But does the fact that it is not strange, not unique, not a surprise make it hurt any less? We are called to be steadfast in our faith, knowing others around the world are suffering similarly. Should we take comfort in the knowledge that others are also in pain? No matter how we respond, we are bound to be left uncomfortable and with further questions.

This is why it bears noting that nowhere in this passage are we told that suffering is necessary or even necessarily purposeful. We are not given a clear purpose for the pain. But we are given a promise: *The end is glory.* God will restore, support, strengthen, and establish God's beloved. Be surprised neither that your journey resembles the One you follow nor that glory follows suffering.

Though the journey may be terribly painful, suffering is not the end of the road. You are called to eternal glory in Christ. First Peter beckons us to live as though we know this is true. When glory feels so far away, we are to humble ourselves, be alert, resist the enemy, remain steadfast, and cast our cares on Christ. In so doing, we do more than endure; we bear witness to the hope we have in Christ. His journey does not end with suffering, and suffering will not end this journey. To God be the glory forever and ever.

Dear God, this hurts. Here it is. Here I am. Carry this, and carry me. Amen.

A good road trip needs a good playlist. Sure, luggage and itinerary are important, but what music will you listen to along the way? What song will you sing at the top of your lungs, forever to be associated with the summer you traveled out west?

In today's passage, the psalmist sings praise to God and invites others to join along. For those journeying with Jesus, it should sound familiar: *Sing to God!* God who cares for orphans and protects widows, gives a home to the desolate, leads prisoners to prosperity, provides for the needy, and restores a heritage to the languishing. *Sing praises to God!*

Over and over again, the song recalls who God is and what God has done. Praise springs from remembering, and remembering is crucial for bearing witness to Christ. In order to testify, we need to know the story. How shall we remember?

This is precisely what God's people do when they gather in worship: We proclaim God's mighty acts of salvation throughout history in song and sermon, sacrament and scripture, service and study. This is our liturgy—the "work of the people." This is the soundtrack that scores our journey as Christ's disciples. And it is no accident that so much of this liturgical work has been set to music.

Researchers have long noted a powerful connection between music and memory; they have even observed singing's restorative effects on those who have suffered brain trauma. Witnessing this is nothing short of miraculous because remembering is sacred work. But as we journey in discipleship, we can often forget where we are going and get discouraged by our distractions. To be faithful travelers, we must remember God's faithfulness—who God is and what God has done. *What do you remember?*

O God, what refrain have I been singing lately? Is there a song I have forgotten? Open my lips, that my mouth may declare your praise. Amen.

Traveling with others can be . . . complicated. You have to negotiate restaurant choices, broker musical selections, keep your cool in confined spaces, adjust to another's rhythms, share way too much. No wonder many prefer to travel solo!

But in today's passage, we are reminded of who calls us to this journey. As the psalmist declares: The One who rides across the highest heavens, who thunders with a mighty voice, whose majesty is over Israel, whose power is in the heavens—this is the One who invites us to walk this path. In so journeying, exhorts the psalmist, we are to "proclaim the power of God!"

The disciples witnessed this power during Jesus' earthly ministry, as well as when their resurrected Lord ascended to heaven. When they were called to be Christ's witnesses to the ends of the earth, they were able to do so only because they had received the power of the Holy Spirit.

As the psalmist concludes, we are also reminded with whom we are to journey. God gives power and strength to God's people. God does not hoard power. On this journey, being together is better than being in control. "Being together" is the purpose of Christ's journey. It is the desire of God's heart to be with us now and for all eternity.

And so, let us proclaim the mighty power of God: a power that provides for the poor and defends widows, a power that raised Jesus from the dead and exalted him to the right hand of God, the Father. This is the power we have been given for our journey. No matter what distractions, roadblocks, or detours we may encounter, God is present with us. Ultimately, power and purpose point to personal presence. This is why God strengthens and empowers God's people. God desires being-together. May this be the desire of our hearts as well.

Praise be to God who gives us power and strength! Amen.

Power and Authority

MAY 22–28, 2023 • EMANUEL CLEAVER III

SCRIPTURE OVERVIEW: Many contemporary Christians wrestle with the theology of the Holy Spirit. Some are perceived as emphasizing the Spirit too much, while others talk about the Spirit only vaguely or even not at all. Both extremes can mislead us. The Spirit is powerful and active, and we understand the role of the Spirit within larger truths about God and God's activities in the world. God empowers the disciples on Pentecost by the Spirit, and the psalmist emphasizes the role of the Spirit in creation. Paul tells the Corinthians that the Spirit enables us to recognize Jesus as Lord and serve one another. Jesus gives the power of the Spirit to his disciples. May we also seek God's help in receiving the power of the Spirit to serve and reach those far from God.

QUESTIONS AND SUGGESTIONS FOR REFLECTION

- Read Acts 2:1-21. What moments from your life might you consider Pentecost moments? How have you seen the Spirit empowering God's people in these moments or movements?
- Read Psalm 104:24-34, 35b. When have you experienced God's rhythm of withholding and releasing? How can your breath remind you of your place in this rhythm of creation?
- Read 1 Corinthians 12:3b-13. How does your faith guide you to a tension between sameness and difference that might help you create a diverse unity among your family or faith community?
- Read John 20:19-23. How does your relationship with Christ help you break through fear?

Senior Pastor of St. James United Methodist Church, Kansas City, MO.

On the Day of Pentecost, people from all over had gathered in Jerusalem for the Feast of Weeks. Once the apostles were filled with the Holy Spirit, they were able to address every member of this diverse crowd in a language they could understand. The amazing thing about the story of Pentecost is that it is a picture of what the church should be. It shows God's vision for what those of us who are followers of Jesus should work for.

It is God's intent that the body of Christ reflect the multiplicity of cultures and peoples created in God's image. The role that we as believers play is similar to what the apostles did over two thousand years ago. We are to speak love and truth to all, including those who are different from us. When the crowd heard the apostles speaking all these different languages, someone asked, "What does this mean?" Peter addressed this question in the next few verses.

I believe there are a few questions that the church must answer: Why do the majority of congregations lack diversity? How did we get here? And finally, what can we do to build multi-ethnic and multi-generational churches?

I truly believe that what happened on that Pentecost Day was meant to show us how God is moving us to be more inclusive and united: "They were all together in one place." Every believer should use the season of Pentecost to consider how they can help make a reality here and now of God's vision of a diverse people united in Christ.

Holy God of love and life, I am grateful that you love every person. Help me to return that love to you and share it with everyone I encounter. Amen.

The blessing of the Holy Spirit that was promised through the prophet Joel and was received on the Day of Pentecost is still available today. Jesus' apostles taught, performed miracles, and stood on their convictions through the power of the Holy Spirit. Believers today have access to that same power. How could God expect us to carry on the movement that Jesus began and the apostles continued if we are not given those same gifts of the Spirit?

It is important to remember that the Holy Spirit that was promised and given is for young and old alike. God does not want only an ethnically diverse church but also a multi-generational church. It is commonplace that young people give energy and life to a church, but we must not forget the wisdom and stability of older people. You can't have an Acts 2 kind of church unless you have both young and old.

It has been stated by many leaders throughout history that the church is always one generation away from extinction. Perhaps that's why when we read scripture we see how important it was for one generation to share the stories of what God had done for them in years past. It was a way of keeping the message alive as well as connecting each generation with the movement of God. The same is true today; every generation must learn to pass on the good news of Jesus in a manner that resonates with those coming behind them.

The true lesson for us is to make sure the faith community we belong to provides ministries for people of all ages. All generations are important and a blessing, and we ought to treat them as such.

God of the young and old alike, fill me with your Spirit. Grant me the ability to appreciate the gifts of every generation. Amen.

It is simply breathtaking to consider that God created everything. God didn't use the same pattern when designing the animals of the land and the creatures of the sea. Everything relies on God for life.

Just imagine that God knows every intimate detail about everything we see and all that we cannot see with the naked eye. God is not simply a creator but also a provider who sustains all life. We have the privilege of experiencing God's beauty and wonder simply by noticing the sights, sounds, and smells of everything around us. We can touch God's creation and feel God's handiwork.

We can see God not only in creation; we can experience God in every moment of life. The words for *breath* and *spirit* are the same in both Hebrew and Greek. Every time we take a breath we are filled with God's Spirit. Each breath we take is a reminder that God's love is filling us; exhaling reminds us of how we can share our experience of God with the world.

God's glory is all around us, and we should make a habit of recognizing it, acknowledging it, and appreciating it. Nature is God's autograph, reminding us of God's love and care for all creation.

Loving God, I thank you for creating and sustaining me. You are my provider, and I give you praise. Move me toward a greater awareness of your presence in all of creation. Amen.

Devotional exercise: Take a moment to notice one particular part of God's creation—something you can hear, see, or feel. Reflect on its intricate makeup and thank God for it.

Some have suggested that it is strange to say, "Bless the LORD." Strange, because how can a mere human bless the omnipotent Creator of the universe? Many would argue God does the blessing and we do the receiving. But one thing that scripture teaches is that it is right to give God our praise.

Early in the story of the people of God, Exodus 7 teaches that God wanted the Hebrews released from bondage so that they could go into the wilderness to worship. At the other end of the story, Revelation 4 shows twenty-four elders and four living creatures continually praising God in heaven. Praising God is what God's people do.

Pentecost is an opportunity to bless the Lord in recognition of the gift of the Holy Spirit. Praise is what we should do continually when we are commemorating what God has done and is doing. I consider Pentecost to be the second holiest day of the year, behind only Easter, because it is the birth of the church. In honor of the church's birth by way of the Holy Spirit, we should do all we can to "bless the LORD."

Another way of understanding the phrase "bless the LORD" is simply recognizing that it is a call to express gratitude for God's love and care. It can be a formal Sunday worship service, or it can be as simple as singing a song or saying, "I love you." So let us bless the Lord with all our heart, soul, mind, and strength.

All-loving Creator, may my praise of you be constant and authentic. Remind me that praising you should not be limited to one place or day of the week. Help me, O God, to live in a way that truly gives you praise. Amen.

After the Day of Pentecost, the apostles of Jesus walked in power and authority as a result of being filled with the Holy Spirit. That same Spirit still empowers believers today. I've heard that the spiritual gifts that the apostles had were only for the first-century church. But God didn't put a limit on the gifts of the Spirit.

Until the earth completely reflects the kingdom of heaven, work needs to be done. Spiritual gifts are the divine attributes of God given to believers for the sake of continuing the work of Jesus. The gifts of the Spirit are the very characteristics of God manifested in the person of Jesus of Nazareth, given to the apostles, and now present in believers for the work of kingdom building. While there are a variety of gifts, we are united by them because they all come from one source—God's Holy Spirit, which is what Paul is trying to help the Corinthian Church understand. When spiritual gifts are used for the church, they draw us closer to becoming like Jesus.

Operating in the gifts of the Spirit helps to produce the fruit of the Spirit. As a body of believers, our purpose is to grow into the fullness of Christ's power, knowledge, and love through the gifts of the Spirit. The body of Christ is glorified through the ministries of the church, the unity among believers, and the maturity in Jesus by way of God's gifts of grace. So, whether you possess some of the nine gifts listed in 1 Corinthians 12 (this is not meant to be an exhaustive list) or some of the many other gifts of the Spirit, use what God has given you.

Merciful Lord, we thank you for blessing us with the gifts of the Spirit that unite us with other believers. Your gifts empower us to continue the work of Jesus. Help us recognize, develop, and exercise these gifts. Amen.

There is something special that happens when believers come together in one accord. In Matthew 18:20, Jesus explains that when two or more people gather in his name, he is right there with them.

On the first Easter Sunday, the followers of Jesus assembled together in fear that they too could be executed like Jesus had been. They were in the same place, trying to make sense of the arrest, trial, death, and rumors of Jesus' resurrection. They had gathered in the name of the Lord, and, lo and behold, Jesus appeared among them!

The first thing to note from these two short verses is that Jesus' presence calms our fears and eases our doubts, and his presence is often experienced profoundly when we gather with others. The second is that the disciples were filled with joy once Jesus showed them the scars on his hands from the nails of crucifixion.

We too can gather with other believers and be bursting with joy because of what Jesus has done for us by way of the cross. When Jesus extends his hands to show the disciples his scars, it is a way of suggesting to everyone that he is ready to receive us all with open arms. Regardless of where you are in life, Jesus has extended his hands to you to offer unlimited joy and peace that passes all understanding.

Mighty and eternal God, thank you for your presence among us. Help us accept and embrace you as you continue to extend your hands to us, offering your redemptive love. Amen.

PENTECOST

After his resurrection, Jesus appeared to his disciples as they gathered together in a locked room. The scripture says that Jesus breathed on them and they received the Holy Spirit, empowering them for ministry. There is no greater honor or responsibility than being a part of the Jesus movement, and like the first-century disciples, we have been blessed with the Holy Spirit and endowed with gifts to carry on the work that began two thousand years ago.

The first disciples of Jesus received two gifts on that day, and those two gifts have also been given to us today. First was a mark of authority. Jesus passed on to his followers the right to recognize sin and also to forgive those sins. Second was the ability to do the work of ministry. The gift of the Holy Spirit means that we have the power and authority to serve as the eyes, ears, feet, and hands of Jesus in the world today. We are more than his followers; we are representatives who have been authorized to release the prisoners and free the captives.

If believers actually lived into the power and authority we have been given, the world would look more and more like the kingdom of heaven. Let us walk in that authority and power to continue the mission of sharing the good news that there is freedom through Christ Jesus.

Lord God, you are amazing and generous. Out of your loving-kindness you have blessed us with many gifts of your Spirit. Continue to empower us to stand firm on your truth and continue the work that Jesus began. Amen.

Interdependent from Beginning to End

MAY 29–JUNE 4, 2023 • GINGER E. GAINES-CIRELLI

SCRIPTURE OVERVIEW: Our first reading is arguably one of the most controversial passages in the Bible. Even among those who believe that God created the world, there is controversy. For example, should the days be understood as literal or symbolic? Much time and trouble have been spent in arguing about these things. A different approach is found in Psalm 8, where the author simply praises God for the majestic work of Creation without needing to work out all the details. Perhaps this approach would lead to more love and peace among the people of God, as Paul hopes for in Second Corinthians. Matthew describes the Ascension, where Jesus tells his followers to baptize in the name of the Father and the Son and the Holy Spirit, an appropriate passage in preparation for Trinity Sunday.

QUESTIONS AND SUGGESTIONS FOR REFLECTION

- Read Genesis 1:1–2:4a. When has reading the Bible in a new way or with new knowledge changed your experience of the text?
- Read Psalm 8. How do you feel called to care for the earth God has given us?
- Read 2 Corinthians 13:11-13. How does your faith community heed Paul's advice to the Corinthians? How does it fall short?
- Read Matthew 28:16-20. Recall a time of doubt. How has that experience made your faith stronger?

Senior Pastor of Foundry United Methodist Church in Washington, D.C.

In our biblical tradition and ancient Near Eastern traditions that influenced the biblical texts, any large body of water was symbolic of chaos. "In the beginning . . . the earth was a formless void and darkness covered the face of the deep, while a wind from God swept over the face of the waters." The "formless void" of the "deep waters" in the original Hebrew is *tohu wabohu*, in effect, "formlessness and normlessness." *Chaos.*

There is always some level of chaos in human life—unpredictable and dangerous forces all around us, natural disasters, political or relational strife, disease, and the overload of expectations, activity, and unknowns in an over-programmed, increasingly complex culture. Chaos in any form stirs fear, anxiety, and defensiveness. Chaos can make us feel unmoored, alone, swamped, and without strength to withstand the flood.

God's first recorded act is to address the "formlessness and normlessness" that can evoke such reactions. God's *ruach* (breath, wind, spirit) dances across the deep, and God's word speaks beautiful diversities into being: day and night, earth and water, rooted things and flying things, the singing and the silent, the swift and the sluggish, all finding their place and connection in a created order.

In the beginning, a diverse God—Creator, Word, and Spirit—created a diverse world, all interdependent, all profoundly good. God reveals what can emerge out of chaos: order in which all things have a valued place, harmony in which difference makes the song richer and more interesting, a world in which all belong and have a role to play, a world in which God continues to recreate, speak, and breathe life into our lives, raising us up again and again.

Loving Creator, recreate us to delight in your beautifully complex world and to trust you will be our anchor when sea billows roll. Amen.

The first Creation story in the Bible can be interpreted as God creating order out of chaos by separating things into either/or categories. But what is clear from the text—and from the created world all around us—is that there is a multiplicity of "kinds" of everything in creation. God speaks trees and seeds and living creatures "of every kind" into being. And the order and harmony described in the first Creation is accomplished not by separation but by naming as "good" every part of the diverse creation and acknowledging its relationship to the whole.

This is true for humans as well. Notice the plurals in the dialogue on the sixth day: "Let us make humankind in our image, according to our likeness." Some interpreters suggest the "us" points to an ancient understanding of God among heavenly beings. Others recognize the "us" as the persons of a Triune God.

In any case, the Creator God makes humans in many "kinds." No two persons are the same, even if they share things in common. It is tempting to think that if someone looks like us or shares a cultural heritage with us, then that person also shares our perspectives or experiences. But how many of us can point to siblings within our own family who are very different people from us?

Among the factors that make humans unique is gender. We're told God creates humankind male AND female in God's image. Isn't it interesting it's not male OR female?

Modern psychology and medicine understand that every human has male and female elements of both body chemistry and spirit, and these manifest in a beautiful diversity of ways.

What if we allowed ourselves to consider that either/or ways of thinking about God, humans, or anything else in creation likely limits our perception and experience of the fullness of relationship with God, others, and ourselves?

Wondrous God, thank you for creating all human kinds. Amen.

Reflection upon scripture often brings to mind hymns, poetry, or images. As you ponder Psalm 8, is there anything that comes into your consciousness?

Two familiar hymns bubble into my spirit: "How Great Thou Art" and "All Creatures of Our God and King." These songs marvel at the wonders of Creation and, like the psalmist, burst into refrains of praise: "Then sings my soul . . . how great Thou art!" "O praise ye, Alleluia!" "O Lord, our Sovereign, how majestic is your name in all the earth!"

It's common for people to identify nature as a place where they feel particularly close to God or experience moments of transcendence in nature. Imagine the psalm-writers in a beautiful part of God's creation, walking or sitting or even working. They become aware of just how amazing it is to live in such a world. From the heavens to the depths of the sea, God's wonders abound. Then all at once, an awareness of being one creature amid the vastness of God's world emerges, bringing with it a question: "What are human beings that you are mindful of them, mortals that you care for them?"

What a question that is. Why should the eternal God, the Creator and Sustainer of all that is, care about the likes of us? Why are we "crowned with glory and honor" and given responsibility to care for what God has made?

Libraries are filled with books trying to answer the question. But this psalm invites you simply to pay attention to the world all around, humbly acknowledge your place in it, marvel at God's trust in you, God's grace for you, God's love for you. And then, together with others, burst into praise.

Gracious God, thank you for the wonders of your creation, the wonders of your love, the wonders of your faith in us. Help us honor these gifts through our lives. Amen.

Greet one another with a holy kiss." This is an early reference to a practice in worship that some love and others loathe: the "passing of the peace." Regardless of where you fall on the love or loathe continuum, the practice has an interesting history.

The "kiss of peace" dates to the earliest days of Christian worship and the celebration of Holy Communion. In the ancient rites of the church, after the confession and the affirmation of God's pardon, the deacon would say something like, "Embrace one another; this kiss is the sign that our souls are united and that we banish all remembrance of injury."

Years ago, when I was a young church staffer, a sermon I preached inspired an email "bomb" filled with attack and accusation. The hurtful message included no invitation for conversation. So I simply avoided the sender—until one Sunday when, at the passing of the peace, I came face to face with the person who had hurt me. In that moment, the church invited me to reflect the love of God, the love that is offered whether it's accepted or not. I extended my hand and the words of peace. And the woman responded. We didn't become best friends, but it was a beginning.

This practice is one way the church trains us to put into flesh the sacrificial love of God that reaches across difference and even injury to reconcile us with our siblings in Christ. It is a way we seek to reflect the grace, love, and communion of God in our lived experience and to be people of peace.

Sometimes it may seem that things we do in church don't matter. But congregational life is where we learn and become skilled in the ways of God so we can put these practices into every area of our lives.

Merciful God, teach us the ways of peace, whether through ritual or relationships. Give us courage to seek reconciliation in the broken places. Amen.

Interdependent from Beginning to End   187

The so-called "Great Commission" includes words that drag around a lot of baggage, words like *authority, obey, commandment,* and even *make disciples.* In the context of Christian history, these words can conjure images of exclusion, authoritarianism, cultural theft, colonialism, forced conversion, and violence inflicted to make people conform to "our way." The teachings of the Bible have undeniably been twisted and used to do harm over the centuries.

But such abuses are directly counter to the heart of the gospel. Jesus didn't usurp authority from anyone but was given authority by God. Jesus never used divine authority to manipulate or do violence. To "make disciples" is not to frighten or bludgeon people into some thin profession of belief but to help them know God's liberating love.

We're asked to teach others to obey the commandments of Jesus, including the challenging teachings in the Sermon on the Mount—like loving your enemies and praying for those who persecute you. The parables and teachings of Jesus require careful, prayerful thinking and interpretation, not mindless box-checking.

The greatest commandment in the law according to Jesus is to love the Lord your God with all your being and your neighbor as yourself (see Matthew 22:35-40). That, Jesus said, is the heart of it all. Love is not enacted through violence, control, or manipulation. The law of love is upheld through doing justice, loving mercy, and walking humbly with God (see Micah 6:8).

The commission Jesus gives us truly is "great": to share with others a way of life filled with purpose, love, and grace.

Lord Jesus, open our hearts and minds to receive with humility and with joy the commission you give us. Help us share with others the life-giving wisdom and way you have so lovingly revealed. Amen.

Here's some Christian math: One, one, and one equals . . . ONE. Our God is both three distinct persons *and* one God.

This may seem an outdated or useless head-trip. But understanding God as Trinity undergirds core Christian values and affects concrete practices in life and community. Things like unity in diversity, the sacred worth of every person, mutuality, self-giving love, justice, and interdependence all find their theological grounding in the Trinity.

Even so, Jesus' Great Commission isn't about getting people to declare their belief in the Trinity or any doctrine. Rather, the invitation is to enter a new way of life. To be baptized in the name of our triune God is to become part of a messy, diverse, grace-fueled community that tries to follow the Way of love and justice revealed by Jesus. And this communal life is interconnected and interdependent. We who are many are ONE.

But these days (you might point out) one, one, and one make . . . three opposing factions. And unity is often equated with sameness or likeness of mind. But in Matthew 28:17 we see that those closest to Jesus aren't all on the same page. Some are openly doubtful right in Jesus' presence after the Resurrection! Following this revelation of doubt, Jesus extends the Great Commission to all present. Those who doubted weren't rebuked; they didn't get their disciple membership revoked or their place in the commissioning service canceled. Clearly, the goal is not unity through intellectual agreement.

Doubt is possible—even expected—because the main point is not to believe a certain set of teachings but to enter a relationship. Doubt or difference of opinion do not exclude you from being called into the life for which you are created, the life that reflects God's own life of love, justice, and joy, the life that makes we who are many . . . one.

Triune God, help our lives reflect yours. Amen.

Interdependent from Beginning to End   189

TRINITY SUNDAY

In the beginning . . . to the end of the age. These are the first and last phrases in the first and last texts for Trinity Sunday. They hold the promise of God's steadfast, tender presence with the whole of creation and with all of us in the depths of our suffering and at the heights of our triumphs. In the beginning, God brought life and flourishing out of formless void and chaos. At the end, Jesus says, "I will be with you."

Between the beginning and end, we are commissioned by Jesus to follow his Way—to proclaim the good news of God's reign, to heal, liberate, and usher in new life (see Matthew 10:7-8), to baptize, to teach others "to obey everything he commanded," and to do it all in the name of the God whom Jesus reveals most fully. Just as Jesus was the presence of God in flesh, so now we are given power to be Christ's presence in the world.

As it was in the beginning, is now, and ever shall be: God creates, breathes Spirit into matter, and calls it good, creating one beautifully diverse human family. God strengthens weak knees and binds up the wounds of the brokenhearted, is compassionate and merciful, scooping us up from the pit to save us. God continues to lift up and anoint every kind of human to participate in the work of making the world more gentle and just, more in the flow of God's amazing grace.

May we be baptized daily into that flow, immersed in that grace, anointed by the Spirit, to receive and invite others to share in God's liberating life and love. May we pour out our lives in humble, loving service after the Way of Jesus Christ. And may we do that as steadfastly as our God is with us—from beginning to end.

Steadfast God, guard and guide us as we seek to live worthy of your call. Amen.

Faithfulness > Obedience
JUNE 5–11, 2023 • ANDREA ROTH MURDOCK

SCRIPTURE OVERVIEW: The readings for this week share the theme of our faith and God's faithfulness. In Genesis, God calls Abram to leave his country and promises to make of him a great nation. Abram has faith in God's faithfulness and goes. In the Gospel, Matthew follows Jesus immediately, and there are two stories of healings that show great faithfulness. In Romans, Paul explains that God calls Abram and Matthew and us—even though we are all sinners—and reckons our faith as righteousness. The psalmist reminds us that all God's "work is done in faithfulness."

QUESTIONS AND SUGGESTIONS FOR REFLECTION

- Read Genesis 12:1-9. Think of a time you chose to follow God's leading. How were you blessed by the decision?
- Read Psalm 33:1-12. Where have you seen God's faithful actions in your life? Among the nations?
- Read Romans 4:13-25. How is the promise that our faith will be reckoned to us as righteousness good news for you?
- Read Matthew 9:9-13, 18-26. How is Jesus calling you to get up and follow? What would that kind of faith look like?

Chaplain at the University of Kansas Hospital and a probationary elder in the Great Plains Conference of The United Methodist Church; married to Russ and together they have three sons and two Boxer dogs.

Do you ever read scripture and say to yourself, "I could never be that obedient, even to God"? We read stories from the Old and New Testaments where the main characters just drop everything and do what is asked of them. They are immediately obedient. It leaves us as readers today feeling like we are destined to fail as disciples.

But let's look at it from a different perspective. This week's readings all tie in to the idea of following and pleasing God. At times, they read like a list of examples of obedience. Yet we have free will. We are offered the choice to obey God, to follow Jesus, to listen to the guidance of the Holy Spirit. What if what God wants is for us to *choose* to answer our call rather than blindly obeying laws and rules? We often read this passage in Genesis 12 as if Abram's reward for obeying God was to have his name and descendants blessed. Using our change of perspective, we see it is Abram's faithfulness that brings about his choice to do what God calls him to do, after God has offered blessing.

Another important piece of information about Abram's amenability is that his choice affected a large group of people, as referenced in verse 5, and required livestock for labor and food, not to mention all the household supplies that were needed. Then there were stops along the way. Yes, Abram built altars along the way, always taking a moment to thank and praise God, but the commitment to the journey was what truly exemplified his faithfulness. Likewise, for us the effort to make choices and follow through on them comes from our faithfulness to God's will.

When I am anxious, O God, about knowing how to be faithful, renew in me a spirit of desire to choose the next right step toward you. Amen.

We all know rule-followers, those people who need to read the instruction booklet before playing a new board game, the ones who know you are required to buy or auction off each property in Monopoly the first time you land on it. Maybe you are one of them.

There is nothing inherently wrong with being that way. The challenge to daily life comes when following rules to the letter subverts the purpose of the rule or interferes with a more important goal. Maybe your family does not like the dynamic of auctions in Monopoly and has more fun ignoring that rule. Of course, in circumstances of safety, it is critical to attend to the details. But in this passage, Paul is clear that adhering to the law is not in and of itself a path to righteousness.

To exemplify his point, Paul harkens back to the story of Abraham (Abram as he was then called) to remind his readers that the earliest stories of the founders of the Hebrew people show that faith was the determining factor in a life that honors God. Paul is also setting up his argument that one need not be Jewish to become Christian, a central theme in the book of Romans. Therefore, being a descendant of Abraham by living a life of faith offers us the promise of God's grace, even over those who follow the same rabbinical law of the Hebrew scriptures.

So go ahead and read those instructions. Paul isn't saying knowing the laws and understanding how they can help build and maintain a faithful community is bad. He is instead saying that following the rules just because they are there isn't enough to please God. Your heart has to be in it too.

Are you a rule-breaker or rule-follower? Do you see rules as a way to create order or impede freedom? What does your relationship to rules say about how you offer or expect to receive respect?

Faithfulness > Obedience

Ever read a really good novel where everything seems to go wrong for the protagonist? Most epic novels and comic books start that way. A great person is down on their luck or faces seemingly insurmountable odds. From Frodo of the Shire to Bruce Wayne to Emma Woodhouse, well-written characters often have resources like family, friends, food, and shelter, but their stories show them discovering their strength by hoping against hope for the redemption that seems beyond possibility. This is where we find Abraham in today's passage.

Paul is reminding us that Abraham had every reason to scoff at the promises of God. His body was old, and his wife, Sarah, was barren. Yet he continued to have faith. But Paul goes a step further, telling us that it is not just about Abraham anymore; it is about us too. Abraham was not called *righteous* just so we can honor a righteous man who lived thousands of years ago, but so that we have a way to understand what faithfulness looks like in relationship with God. For Paul, that relationship is made complete through Christ. We are offered freedom from the urgency of the law by believing in the redemptive power of the resurrection of Jesus Christ. It is faith in him that offers us the position alongside Abraham as a part of the household of God.

What makes you feel weak today? Does your body or your spirit feel as good as dead? What or who is planting a seed of distrust in your gut?

Where might you be able to give glory to God anyway?

God of Abraham, infinitely faithful to your word, take away my sense of weakness or distrust. Bring me into a life of promise in you. I offer my praise to your glory today in hopes that I will remember that I, too, am justified in Christ. Amen.

We've been working this week to step away from the mindset that God expects blind, almost mindless obedience, and then we have this verse where Matthew, in fact, jumps up and follows Jesus without question or hesitation. But check out what happens in the very next verse. In verse 10, it says tax collectors and sinners were sitting with Jesus and his disciples, as if those were entirely separate groups. But look at where Matthew was just one verse earlier—sitting at the tax booth! We have a tendency, or at least I do, to think of the disciples as better-than-the-rest followers of Jesus, but they were really part of the reason the Pharisees were critical of Jesus. It wasn't just that there were some tax collectors and sinners hanging around his faithful followers. They were within the tight-knit group too.

We know everyone falls into that category of "and sinners." We all fall short of the glory of God, but the amazing thing is we have a God that reaches across the divide to us. Jesus sat with them and broke bread with them. The Holy Spirit invites us to the same table. All we have to do is show up.

But showing up is sometimes harder than it sounds. Maybe it requires getting past our negative inner dialogue to offer compassion to someone who needs a kind word. Maybe we need to forgive someone who hurt us so we can release that pain and rediscover joy. Maybe showing up will come from sitting down with the word of God on a regular basis so it can really sink into our heart. I can't say what showing up looks like for your life. But whatever it is, give it a shot. Then try again tomorrow.

Christ, I commit today to see you in those around me and accept the challenge to show up in my life today and going forward, not in blind obedience but in renewed faithfulness. Amen.

Upon reading this passage, I was struck by the phrase "and they laughed at him" in verse 24. The "they" is a group of people in active, demonstrative mourning for the death of a young girl. This is not a moment of giggles breaking out to break the tension of an uncomfortable moment. This is sardonic laughter meant to mock and ridicule Jesus. Even people who loved and cared for this family—or at least respected them because the father was a leader of the synagogue—were unwilling or unable to hope that there was truth in what Jesus said. They were obedient to the laws of nature and to the power of group think rather than faithful to the message of Jesus in the power of God.

We all fall victim to this kind of lack in faithfulness from time to time. Whether losing confidence in our favorite professional sports team, lamenting the longevity of a season of unemployment, or lacking trust that God is with us during difficult times, we all can find it easier to join in with the groups that encourage disillusionment and disappointment. That tendency is why we all know the idiom "misery loves company." But guess what? Joy loves company too. We all have a natural proclivity to become more like the people around us. So what happens if we decide to join the people living in faithfulness? What happens if we become determined to believe in the possibilities that come from faith in God? Daring to remain faithful in the face of sardonic laughter takes courage. And often our courage is rewarded by an experience of God's miracle-working power.

God of unexpected outcomes, today I pray for daring and the boldness of thought to believe the best is possible even when those around me laugh at my optimism. Amen.

Faithfulness > Obedience

When you have found a trustworthy mechanic, a gentle dentist, or a new favorite workout, you want to share the news. That's where today's psalm comes in. When we live faithfully and see the results of mindfulness and commitment to practicing our faith, we feel the blessing of the Lord and want to share it with others.

Maybe like Abram you are in the middle of a long journey where the odds are stacked against you. Perhaps you are like the early Christians debating about how to follow your faith even when the rules seem prohibitive. Or you might be stuck in the muck of a mob mentality, laughing at God's promises.

Then again, you may have worked through those struggles or had your own version of them and come out on the other side. Are you someone who can be found building altars to God at every opportunity? Are you someone who looks to see how God's word speaks to you each day? Are you someone who can step away from the crowd and forge your own path toward Christ?

Each of us is on our own, yet we are not alone. No matter where we are in our faith, we can find people to journey and praise God with us. We cannot play all the instruments and sing all the songs called for in our psalm today if we are alone. It takes a choir. And our psalmist reminds us in verses 4 and 5 that all God's work is done in faithfulness with steadfast love. That sounds like something to share with the world.

O Lord, I sing your praises even if I can't carry a tune. You are steadfast, faithful, and worthy of my praise. Amen.

Faithfulness > Obedience

Our psalm ends today saying "happy [are] the people whom [the LORD] has chosen as [God's] heritage." We have come full circle. We began with God's promise to bless all the generations of Abram's descendants should he faithfully respond to God's instructions. Now, we are told the results. God has blessed and continues to bless those who accept the thoughts of God's heart.

Take a moment to remember part of the passage in Matthew from earlier this week. Jesus, like a physician, came not for the well but for the sick. We all need God's grace, and the best way to experience God's grace in our life is to seek it faithfully. Being blindly obedient to the rules of the church or small portions of scripture does not convey the mutuality of a relationship with the God of creation. It does not inspire us to stand in awe of God.

Most Christians consider Sunday their day of rest, their sabbath. Today is the perfect time to think about ways we can transform the small things in our life a little at a time to create a major shift in our path toward faithfulness. Choose your scenery—a mountain hike with pines on either side, a beach with the ocean and dunes flanking your journey, wide-open plains with a worn-out dirt path among the tall grass and prairie wildflowers, or wherever you feel closest to God's creation and the nudging and nurturing of the Holy Spirit. Picture yourself there. Now breathe in and out a few times and pray the following prayer.

God, I choose faithfulness. It may look like blind obedience to others only because I trust in you. I strive to live in awe of you. May it be so. Amen.

Responding to God's Grace

JUNE 12–18, 2023 • MAX O. VINCENT

SCRIPTURE OVERVIEW: The readings this week lack a common theme. Genesis recounts the promise of Isaac's miraculous birth and the fulfillment of that promise—a key story in the history of God's people. The psalmist cries out with thanksgiving to the Lord, for we are God's people and the grateful recipients of unending faithfulness. Paul rejoices because we have peace with God through our faith in Jesus Christ. This is not because of anything we have done or could do; rather, God's love sent Christ to die for us when we were distant from God. In Matthew, Jesus calls his disciples and declares that God's harvest is vast, but there are not enough workers willing to go into the fields. It is a call for us to go as the disciples did.

QUESTIONS AND SUGGESTIONS FOR REFLECTION

- Read Genesis 18:1-15; 21:1-7. How does your faith invite you to laughter?
- Read Psalm 116:1-2, 12-19. How do you make a thanksgiving sacrifice to God? Consider trying a new practice of thanksgiving.
- Read Romans 5:1-8. How has God's love for you prompted you to "the second movement of the symphony," to share God's love with others and all creation?
- Read Matthew 9:35–10:23. How are you called to participate in Christ's ministry of healing?

Senior Pastor of St. James United Methodist Church in Atlanta, GA.

Reading this passage makes me wish I were an artist. I would love to paint this last exchange between God and Sarah, the moment when God calls Sarah's laughter out into the open. Many images of this passage focus on Abraham's hospitality, welcoming God by preparing a feast for the three visitors. Occasionally, I see a picture with Sarah in the background snickering. But I cannot recall a painting of God exposing Sarah's laughter.

If I painted this exchange, I would show God smiling as God looks at Sarah and says, "Oh yes, you did laugh." This passage reminds us that laughter is as appropriate a response to God's grace as hospitality. Too often, we highlight Abraham's hospitality at the expense of Sarah's laughter, as if we are embarrassed by the laughter, afraid it is the wrong response at the wrong time.

When God visits us, promising new life where we thought there was no chance of life, maybe laughter is the best way to acknowledge just how unexpected God's grace is. Perhaps God calls Sarah out of the tent and names her laughter publicly because God is glad we get the joke that grace surprises and astounds us, changing our lives and our future.

Years later, amazed to return to a rebuilt Jerusalem and a new Temple, the descendants of Abraham and Sarah sang, "Then our mouth was filled with laughter, and our tongue with shouts of joy" (Ps. 126:2a.) Sometimes laughter is the perfect way to respond to God's grace turning our expectations upside down, reminding us that our destiny is not determined by the laws of nature but the gracious presence of God.

God of grace, give us the courage to rejoice in your presence in our lives. Amen.

I don't remember my parents saying that boasting is a sin, but boasting was not welcome in our home. If I talked too long about one of my accomplishments, my mother would caution me, "Don't blow your own trumpet." Once while my brother was struggling with some math homework, I remarked about how easy it was for me to learn math. My father quickly responded, "Don't pat yourself on the back for a gift God gave you."

In these verses from Romans, Paul is encouraging us to boast—in our hope and in our suffering. That's a lot of boasting for someone taught to shun the practice. Do I follow the exhortations of Paul or stay true to the warnings of my parents?

On closer examination, I think Paul and my parents might not be so far apart. The boasting my parents warned me against is boasting that puts me at the center of attention. Paul is calling us to focus on what God has made possible in our life through Jesus Christ.

The hope we boast in is not our desired outcomes but the hope of sharing in God's glory because Christ has reconciled us to God. It's a hope that comes to us in Jesus Christ. The sufferings we boast of are the sufferings that shape us into faithful followers of Jesus Christ. Even the ability to endure these sufferings is a gracious gift of God's Spirit working within us.

The boasting Paul encourages among us is another way of responding to God's grace. It is an acknowledgment that the peace we have with God results from God's gift offered to us and is not based on anything we have done or earned. It is not boasting about ourselves but about the new selves we are becoming through God's work in us.

God, keep me focused on your presence today so I may walk in your peace and grow in your love. Amen.

Is this a cause worth dying for? I hear that question when those around me know that I am on the verge of making a decision that will upset others. The question may come from another staff member or a member of our congregation. Sometimes I hear it from my District Superintendent. None of us thinks the decision I am about to make will lead to my death. The question is a warning to consider the cost of the conflict my decision could provoke.

So what is a cause worth dying for? We tend to think that those who sacrifice their lives for the sake of others die for a worthy cause. It could be death in service to one's country or rescuing others from danger, but we often assume those saved are somehow worthy of the sacrifice, worth dying for. Paul says God's love for us is proved through Jesus' sacrifice for us when most people would have thought we weren't worth dying for. That Christ offers himself as a sacrifice for us is amazing. Even more astounding is that this sacrifice is proof of God's love.

We often expect the unfaithful partners to be the ones who must prove their love to restore relationships. In our relationship with God, we are the ones who turned away, whose loved failed while God's love remained constant. But God does not wait for us to prove our love. God acts first to demonstrate that our unfaithfulness has not separated us from God's love.

One of the refrains throughout the Old Testament is that God's love is steadfast, and God's mercy endures forever. God's love is not bound by our perceptions of who is worthy. In fact, God's love makes us worthy, justifies us, and makes us righteous.

God, thank you for reaching out in your love to restore me to your presence. Amen.

In response to an experience of God's grace, we find ourselves asking with the psalmist, "What shall I return to the LORD for all his bounty to me?" We long to express our gratitude in some way. We want God to know we are aware of God's gifts and do not take them for granted. What sacrifice can we offer in response to Christ's sacrifice for us? The psalmist points us to the sacrifice of thanksgiving.

An expression of thanks might seem inadequate in light of what God extends to us. Saying thanks can seem like such an insignificant thing that we may struggle with the expression "sacrifice of thanksgiving." Is offering thanks worthy of being called a *sacrifice*?

Leviticus 7:11-18 describes a sacrifice of thanksgiving for the children of Israel. It was not a sacrifice that was prescribed for a certain time or as an atonement for sins. This sacrifice could be presented whenever one wanted to give thanks in recognition of God's gifts. The sacrifice involved flesh and bread. Gifts were offered back to God as a sign of thanksgiving. However, part of the ritual was a feast following the offering. Part of the offering went to the priest and some was consumed in fire, but the rest became a meal to be shared with others.

Christians have a similar practice in Communion. We offer up bread and wine in thanksgiving to God. God then blesses those gifts and offers them back so that they can be used to extend God's blessing to others. God blesses the gifts we offer and invites us to share them with others so that they too may know the joy of God's blessings.

Thank you, God, for the gift of life and the gifts that sustain our lives. Guide us to faithful stewardship of your gifts that others may share in your blessings. Amen.

Once we experience God's grace, we want others to experience it as well. We see the whole world in need of God's grace, like fields ready to be harvested. So Jesus tells us to pray that God will send workers into the fields.

This call to prayer is followed by the commissioning of the Twelve. They are sent out to extend the ministry they have witnessed Jesus performing—healing and casting out demons. This ministry is what the world is ready to receive. They are being sent to help supply God's answer to the prayer Jesus told them to pray.

Is our commitment to God's grace so strong that we are willing to be used by God to invite others into this experience? Are we content simply to receive from God, perhaps going so far as to stop and give thanks to God for God's gifts at work in our lives? We might even go a step further and say that we want others to have this experience, but are we willing to be a part of God's mission to extend this grace to others. Or do we think this is someone else's responsibility?

Jesus encourages us in joining this mission through his instructions to the disciples. Jesus sets an urgent tone, instructing the disciples to travel lightly, not waiting until they feel like they have enough money or an extra set of clothes. I think Jesus is saying more than "let the mission drive your activity." I believe Jesus is teaching us to go forward trusting in grace. Trust that the same grace that first brought you to Jesus will be with you as you join God's mission. God's grace is not a one-time experience but a lifelong journey. Jesus asks us to make that journey in service to others, so they too may know the joy of God's gifts in their lives.

God, use me for your work today. Amen.

Sometimes we think that everything will work out well if God's grace is with us. Then any opposition we experience is evidence that we are not doing the right thing, as if God were creating obstacles to our efforts. However, Jesus tells us quite the opposite: Our work for God will produce opposition, but God will be with us through it all.

Jesus sends us out, warning us that being a part of God's mission brings persecutions and dangers. He talks of religious and civic opposition. He warns of the most personal betrayals, family members turning on each other. Jesus is not giving a rosy recruitment speech. It is an honest caution of the peril involved in following God's direction. Not everyone is going to thank us or agree with what we are doing. Some may even hate us and our association with Jesus.

Jesus reminds us that sometimes people and powers oppose us because we are doing God's work. So he calls us to stay true and let the urgency of the mission, not the circumstances we encounter, set our course to new locations where we may get a better response. Jesus wants us to trust God's grace, even in adverse times.

God's grace does not mean that things will always be easy or go well for us. Grace means God will not leave us but will travel with us in difficult times. Jesus emphasizes this by telling us not to worry about what to say in our defense because God's Spirit will speak through us. His life and ministry caution us that even the most devoted adherence to God's work does not protect us from danger and persecution. But his resurrection shows us that nothing can separate us from God's love.

God, may I trust your continued presence in my life and not let circumstances become a sign of your nearness. Amen.

When I hear a good joke, I can't wait to share it with others. When I witness other people laughing, I find it hard not to join them. Sometimes the laughter is so contagious that I find myself laughing before anyone can tell me what started the laughter. I wonder if we have neglected laughter as a means of sharing our faith.

Sarah's child is named Isaac, "laughter," as a reminder of her response to God's promise to give her a child, her experience of God's grace in her life. Sarah offers the name as an invitation for others to join in her laughter. Sarah's witness gives us another way to view evangelism. I know many Christians struggle with the idea of evangelism because they think it means a particular presentation of the faith and requires new believers to respond in a certain way. What if we began to think about sharing our faith the way we long to share a good joke?

In some parts of the early church, the Sunday after Easter was referred to as "Holy Humor Sunday" or "Bright Sunday," an ongoing tradition in many Orthodox churches. In some places, the week of Easter was a time of sharing jokes and feasts as a way to celebrate Jesus' resurrection. Early preachers like Augustine and Chrysostom compared the resurrection to God's practical joke played on the devil.

Too often, we depict a life of faith as somber, a dour commitment to take every moment seriously. Our faith does deal with matters of life and death, but at its heart it is a story of life from death. That is a surprising, joyous turn of our expectations. What if we took time to laugh at the unexpected ways God opens up new possibilities in our lives? What if we invited others to come and laugh with us?

God, use me to invite others to join the laughter your surprising work in our lives brings. Amen.

Provisions in the Wilderness

JUNE 19–25, 2023 • LINDSEY KRINKS

SCRIPTURE OVERVIEW: The story of Hagar and Ishmael being cast out from Abraham's house reminds us that even when we are in our darkest hour, God doesn't abandon us. God is faithful and meets us in the wilderness. The psalmist calls out to God from a place of desperation, yet even in desperation there is confident hope in God. Paul reminds us that as Christians, we participate in the death and resurrection of Christ. The powers of sin and death no longer have the final say over our lives. Jesus teaches us that discipleship will not be easy, but that God's care for us is great. It is only when we're willing to lose our lives that we will find them.

QUESTIONS AND SUGGESTIONS FOR REFLECTION

- Read Genesis 21:8-21. Consider a time you've excluded someone. What do you wish you would have done differently? How might a daily Examen practice help you right the wrongs you caused or learn from your mistakes?
- Read Psalm 86:1-10, 16-17. In what ways do you need God's help in your life today? Consider writing a prayer to more deeply connect with God about your needs.
- Read Romans 6:1b-11. Consider the author's question "What does freedom from sin look like?"
- Read Matthew 10:24-39. In what ways have you become too comfortable in your discipleship? Where is God calling you to be more faithful?

Street chaplain, co-founder and Director of Education at Open Table Nashville; author of *Praying with Our Feet.*

We all experience seasons of life that wring us out. These are times of wilderness where we tread through tangles of uncertainty, pain, frustration, and loss. Seeds of desolation take root in our spirits. We wonder where our help will come from.

David, the author of Psalm 86, was no stranger to dark times. He was intimately acquainted with anxiety, betrayal, regret, and loss. He also knew that the most powerful tools he had for perseverance were his prayers and his relentless trust in God's faithfulness.

Perhaps the most universal prayer ever uttered is the prayer for help. Asking for help is difficult for many of us, partly because of the vulnerability that accompanies being in a position of need. But David knew that the God he served listened to the cries of the downtrodden and bereft.

God heard the cries of the Israelites in their bondage. God heard the cries of David as he fled for his life. Again and again, God hears the cries of God's people. And today, God hears our cries too.

One of the most compelling features about the book of Psalms is that each prayer offers us words when our own words fail. Each prayer reminds us that God invites our vulnerability and welcomes every emotion we feel. So let us lean into the psalmist's words today.

Bend your ear to us, O God, and hear our prayers for help. Uproot the feelings of despair that crowd out your light. Be our compass when we've lost our sense of direction. Help us find comfort in the shelter of your steadfast love. Amen.

At the center of today's passage is Hagar, an enslaved Egyptian who bore Abraham a son named Ishmael. Because of her status, Hagar occupied a marginal place in society and experienced great vulnerability. When Sarah, Abraham's wife, saw Ishmael as a threat to her son Isaac, she told Abraham to cast Hagar and her son out of his household. Abraham followed Sarah's orders and sent Hagar and Ishmael into the desert with no more than a little bread and a skin of water.

The newly homeless mother and child wandered in the wilderness, and when their provisions were gone, Hagar and the boy both cried out. God heard them and sent an angel. "Do not be afraid," the angel told Hagar. The angel promised her that even though she had been utterly disinherited by Abraham, God was faithful and would make a great nation from her son.

While few of us will be able to comprehend Hagar's absolute marginalization in this story, we know what it's like to feel like we're wandering in the wilderness. We know what it feels like to be empty, rudderless, and to lose relationships that matter to us. We know what it's like to despair because the present seems perilous and restoration and redemption feel unreachable.

What can we learn from Hagar's story? What can we learn from her resolve and grit? What can we learn from her willingness to trust that God would provide and carve out a new life for her and her family?

God meets us in the wilderness. We may wander, but we are not abandoned. "Do not be afraid," said the angel. No matter what we are facing, God hears our cries and draws near.

Meet us in the wilderness, God of Hagar. Drive out our fear with your presence. Remember all who have been disinherited, and make a way to flourish for all who struggle. Amen.

Discipleship has never been easy. The tenth chapter of Matthew chronicles Jesus' words of advice to the twelve disciples as he sends them out for the first time. At this point, the Twelve are ordinary men—former tax collectors and fishermen—following someone extraordinary who defies the laws of nature and makes those in power squirm. They are given authority to heal the sick and cast out unclean spirits, and they're sent to proclaim the good news to the poor.

They soon discover, however, that this mission means putting themselves at odds with those who enjoyed religious and political power and benefited from maintaining the status quo. Jesus tells the twelve to expect conflict and even persecution. This road will be difficult, but have no fear; God's ultimate justice will prevail over everything done in the darkness.

When we are going up against overwhelming odds, not to mention the "powers of this present darkness" as Paul puts it in Ephesians 6:12, we can feel tiny and powerless. No doubt the twelve disciples sometimes felt this way. One of the smallest birds commonly known in Jesus' day was the sparrow. Sparrows were sold for pennies and were among the least expensive offerings that the poor could buy for their Temple sacrifices. Jesus reminds the Twelve of their significance by reminding them that God pays attention to even the tiniest creatures and knows each of us intimately.

What advice to the Twelve stands out to you from this passage? What wisdom for the journey do you need today?

Whatever you need, whatever anxieties you are facing, Jesus says again and again, "Do not be afraid." God will provide. God's care for you is great.

Loving God, may we, like the disciples, have the courage to follow in the footsteps of Christ and embody the gospel. Amen.

As Jesus is concluding his instructions to the twelve disciples before sending them out, he warns them about just how costly their discipleship will be. Their new commitments will stir up tensions. Not only will their allegiance to Christ put them at odds with those in power, but it will also challenge their relationships with their closest family members, partners, and friends.

Jesus isn't interested in a fan club. He's interested in disciples who take his teachings to heart and walk the walk. "Take up the cross and follow me," Jesus says, foreshadowing the ultimate cost that he and many of his disciples would pay. Jesus' contemporaries knew that carrying one's cross was reserved for outlaws, rebels, enslaved people, and political dissidents who challenged the laws of the Roman Empire or the lordship of Caesar.

The path of discipleship is not one of comfort, success, wealth, or worldly accolades. "Lose your life for my sake," Jesus says, "and you will find it."

Just as the Twelve were invited to undergo a shift in their core identity and allegiances, we too are invited to examine who we are. Where do we find our ultimate identity? Is our discipleship a hobby, or is it our defining trait? Where do we place our ultimate allegiance? Is it to our family, profession, denomination, political party, or nation? Or is it to a homeless carpenter and the borderless kin-dom of God?

If we find that our discipleship has become too comfortable and easy, it is time to ask what Christ we are following.

Draw us deeper, O God, into a faith that walks the walk. Give us the strength we need to reexamine our commitments. Teach us that we will find our life in you only when we're willing to lose it. Amen.

What does it mean to be baptized not only into Christ's death but also his resurrection?

Oscar Romero, archbishop of El Salvador, lived deeply into this mystery. At a time of sweeping injustice and shocking violence against those who worked for change, Romero listened to the cries of the poor and oppressed and stood in solidarity with them. His belief that the image of God was embedded in every person led him to fight for the dignity and rights of the poor. This put Romero in direct conflict with the powers of his day. He ended up following Christ all the way to his death.

"But if we have died with Christ," writes Paul, "we believe that we will also live with him. We know that Christ, being raised from the dead, will never die again; death no longer has dominion over him."

On March 24, 1980, Romero was assassinated while presiding over Mass. Just before he was murdered, Romero preached about how a grain of wheat will only bring about the harvest if it dies to itself. He encouraged all who listened to get involved in "the risks of life which history demands of us." Indeed, he had found his purpose and even a sense of liberation in using his life to create a better society. He lived as if the powers of death and injustice had no dominion over him. "If they kill me," Romero told a journalist just two weeks before his death, "I will rise again in the people of El Salvador."

Every day, we choose to live either for ourselves or for some greater narrative, mystery, and cause. What risks are history and our faith demanding of us today? What does it mean for us to be baptized not only into Christ's death but also his resurrection?

O God, teach us to stand in solidarity with the poor. Amen.

Journeying through our own times of wilderness can be all-consuming. The anxieties, worries, and fears swirl around us and within us and cloud our vision like a dust storm. This passage reminds us that just as God did not forsake Hagar and Ishmael, God will not forsake us.

Whatever we are going through—however dark the woods, however dry the desert, however deep the valley—we can take heart. God doesn't abandon us in the wilderness; God meets us there.

What is fascinating, and perhaps a little frightening, about this passage is that God does not rescue Hagar and Ishmael from the hardships of the wilderness. How many times have we wished and prayed that our struggles would vanish? That we would escape intact? Sometimes, we may experience a kind of immediate rescue, but often help comes in different and unexpected ways.

Indeed, Hagar and Ishmael were not pulled out of the wilderness. They were given the provisions they needed to survive in it. A well for water. A bow for food.

"Do not fear," the angel told Hagar as God opened her eyes to the nurturing, sustaining resources that already existed around her.

What fears do you need to lay aside? Where is God directing your vision? What wells are waiting for you?

God of the wilderness, the desert, and the valley, meet us in our despair. When our vision is clouded, open our eyes to your presence and provisions. Amen.

There is none like you among the gods, O LORD," the psalmist sings in today's passage. The God we serve is radically different from all other gods and Caesars and idols. Instead of favoring the strong and mighty, our God chooses the outcasts and underdogs. Instead of demanding perfection, our God uses fissures and gaps to let in the light. In God's kin-dom, the last are first, the poor are blessed, and the hungry are filled. This is indeed good news.

As you reflect on today's passage of praise, turn your attention inward. Where have you felt God's presence? Where have you found provisions? What do you feel most grateful for today?

God of the marginalized and homeless like Hagar,

God of the disinherited like Ishmael,

God of the underdogs like David,

God of ordinary workers like the disciples,

God of all with sullied backgrounds like Paul,

God of the desert and valley and wilderness,

God of inclusion and emancipation,

God of second, third, and fourth chances,

God of liberation,

Your steadfast love endures throughout the ages. You show up for us again and again and remind us that we are never beyond your care. Teach us to channel the gratitude we feel into love for others and a suffering world. Help us plant seeds of your upside-down kin-dom in the here and now, trusting in the day the harvest will come. Amen.

God Provides

JUNE 26-JULY 2, 2023 • SHIRLEY BROSIUS

SCRIPTURE OVERVIEW: The passages this week highlight several different themes. Abraham is put to the ultimate test. There is no denying how terrifying God's request must have been, yet Abraham ultimately is commended for his faith. We will not face this same challenge, but are there things dear to our hearts that God is asking us to give up? The psalmist is in deep despair and weary from awaiting God's deliverance, yet even now there is confidence. Paul continues to instruct the Romans about the necessity of living a new life, no longer being slaves to the desires of the flesh. Jesus teaches that when we receive those doing his work, we receive him. When we interact with pastors, missionaries, or nursery workers, do we treat these servants as Jesus himself?

QUESTIONS AND SUGGESTIONS FOR REFLECTION

- Read Genesis 22:1-14. What has this familiar story meant to you in your faith? How do you embody or struggle against this type of obedience and trust?
- Read Psalm 13. When has your lament allowed you to move from anger with God to praise? How long did that process take?
- Read Romans 6:12-23. How does the definition of death as a life cut off from God rather than a biological reality change your understanding of this passage? How might incorporating this definition of death change your life?
- Read Matthew 10:40-42. Who is in your wider community of witnesses? How does their example prompt you to turn to others in service?

Author of *Sisterhood of Faith* and coauthor of *Turning Guilt Trips into Joy Rides* with her speaking ministry team, Friends of the Heart; holds a master's degree in Christian Education and attends First United Methodist Church, Millersburg, PA.

A picture of Abraham holding a dagger above Isaac alarmed my granddaughter. "Nana, what is that man doing?" Rachel asked. I explained as best I could to a six-year-old that God was testing Abraham's obedience. Actually, as I've studied, I've learned God was "proving" Abraham was a man of faith.

In Hebrew, the same word is used to mean "tempt," "try," or "prove." Many translations of scripture translate that word as "test." As a former teacher, I gave tests so students could prove to me they had mastered the subject matter. I certainly wasn't tempting them to do anything wrong or to tax their minds, although a test might do that. I wanted them to show me what they had learned.

Abraham had already left his father and his homeland to obey God (see Genesis 12:1). Now God was asking Abraham to prove his love even further by sacrificing his beloved son. Abraham proved that love when he reached for his knife.

Abraham's actions revealed his heart. He loved God so much that he offered his son, even though God had told him that it was through Isaac that "your offspring will be reckoned" (Gen. 21:12, NIV). Since God had promised to bless Abraham through Isaac's descendants, Abraham believed God could bring Isaac back from the dead if he killed him (see Hebrews 11:19). But an angel of the Lord stopped Abraham and provided a ram.

Tests and temptations regularly come our way. Are we faithful to our word and our vows? Are we honest when we file income tax? Do we stand for what's right and good—even when friends do not agree?

Dear Lord, strengthen my faith, my confidence in your promises, so that I stand firm no matter the temptations or tests that come my way. Amen.

God has provided for my family in countless ways through the years. When we once needed a car, an elderly relative who could no longer drive gave us his. When I was grieving the death of an infant daughter, God gave me a psalm to memorize that has become a source of great comfort.

In proving his faith, Abraham willingly offered his son Isaac as a burnt offering. But an angel stopped him from this terrible act. Then God provided a ram that was caught in the bushes.

In gratitude to God for sparing Isaac, Abraham named the place "Jehovah Jireh," meaning "the LORD will provide." This happened on Mt. Moriah, which later became the Temple site close to Calvary where Jesus was crucified.

Christians often see both Isaac and the ram provided to Abraham as Old Testament pictures that foretold Christ. Isaac is seen this way in the beginning of the story because he did not question his father's actions when Abraham obeyed God by offering Isaac as a sacrifice. And the ram works as a type of Christ because it dies so that Isaac—who is no longer functioning as the Christ figure in the story at this point—could live.

These biblical stories of sacrifice and obedience and faith can be inspiring, confusing, and horrifying at the same time. We are lucky that we can jump to the end of the story and know that John called Jesus the Lamb (see Revelation 5:8) because John knew Christ came to take away the sins of the world and end the system of sacrificing animals to God.

What God prescribes, God provides.

Dear God, thank you for the times you've met my needs. May I always trust rather than despair and hope rather than feel helpless. In Jesus' name. Amen.

While praying a psalm such as this, we can identify with the psalmist. Who has not felt as though God is distant in their suffering? According to rabbinical writers, this psalm might have applied to the Hebrew people as a whole. The verses may have expressed their sorrow when enemies threatened them and they cried for God's help.

It may also express the feelings of people seeking God while suffering. First they protest. If God is good, why is this bad thing happening? Surely God could have prevented this injury, financial collapse, this death of a loved one.

Then someone points them to scripture. They read the book of John and learn about Jesus, who called himself the Light of the world (see John 8:12). Their eyes are opened, and they see the Light. They understand that Jesus was the light of all people, and that the darkness did not overcome it. Yet they also learn that Jesus suffered and died before conquering death in his resurrection. They learn of God's Spirit who comforts those who weep. And scripture softens their hearts.

After they understand the gospel, they pray: "Consider and answer me, O Lord my God! Give light to my eyes." And they become believers and accept that they are children of God and are loved by God.

Finally, they praise, and it's like sunshine after the rain. This psalm by David brings light to our eyes and hope to our hearts. And we join the psalmist in song.

Dear God, forgive us when we doubt your care and concern. Fill us with the light of your presence, and give us hope. In Jesus' name. Amen.

In 1967, a diving accident left Joni Eareckson Tada paralyzed from the shoulders down. She was an artist, but at first she spit out the mouthsticks her therapist suggested she hold between her teeth to paint. Joni must have felt forgotten by God. But she went on to paint and to inspire millions through writing and speaking ministries. Her suffering developed her compassion, and she touches people challenged by disabilities through her ministry, Joni and Friends.

This psalm of David expresses anguish at feeling forgotten by God. It may have been written while he was on the run from King Saul. Feeling threatened by David's success in battle, Saul tried to kill David, and David fled.

We don't know exactly how long David was forced to hide from Saul, but we know he spent more than a year at Ziklag (see 1 Samuel 27:7). Since David had already been anointed to be king by the prophet Samuel, not only not being king but running for his life must have made it seem like God had abandoned him, or at least that God had made a mistake.

In Psalm 13, David prays an honest prayer, expressing his frustration and begging God for answers. But then he leaves things in God's hands and praises God for his salvation: "I will sing to the LORD, for he has been good to me" (NIV).

We too sometimes feel forgotten by God. Physical challenges, relationship problems, or unfair treatment may make us miserable. When we are angry, we don't feel like praising God. But just as Joni and David grew and praised God in their suffering, we too can sing to the Lord even when our circumstances do not meet our expectations.

Dear God, help me to see my circumstances as opportunities to know you better and, like David, praise you for your goodness and salvation. In Jesus' name. Amen.

We face many choices every day. Shall we serve chicken or fish for dinner? Shall we exercise or watch television? Most choices do not much matter. But some choices have major consequences for our health or the development of our Christian character.

According to Paul, our choices should honor God. Christ freed us from the law, but that does not mean that our actions are without consequences. We want to honor Christ with the parts of our bodies that do things. Paul calls them our "instruments" or our "weapons," and he means such things as eyes, mouth, ears, hands, and feet.

Just as a knife can be used for good or evil, so can the parts of our bodies. Our feet can carry us to commit adultery, which could lead to the death of a marriage. Our mouth can spread words of shame and condemnation, which could lead to the death of a reputation. Or our mouth could ingest poisonous drugs, which could lead to death itself. Sin always leads to death of one kind or another.

"Sin is a dethroned monarch; so you must no longer give it an opportunity to rule over your life" (TPT).

Since Paul could not visit Rome, he wrote a letter reminding Roman Christians who they were in Christ. Converted Jews may have felt self-righteous as they followed the law, and Gentile converts may have felt self-righteous as they believed that no law applied to them.

Jew or Gentile, we live holy lives not to gain salvation but to express appreciation for our salvation and to become more like Christ in our character.

Dear Lord, give me strength to resist temptation. I want to be like Jesus, so use the parts of my body to do his work and represent him well. In his name I pray. Amen.

John Newton, writer of the hymn "Amazing Grace," was converted as a slave trader. While at sea in the middle of a violent storm, he prayed for God's mercy. The storm calmed, and he reached port. Newton then began reading the Bible and avoided drinking, gambling, and profanity. In time he realized the slave trade was evil and gave up his participation in it. He was eventually ordained a priest in the Church of England.

While explaining the concept of "grace" to the Romans, Paul posed the question: "What then? Shall we sin because we are not under law but under grace? By no means!"

In Greek, the word for grace is *charis*, which means a gracious favor or benefit. The law came through Moses, and grace and truth came through Christ (see John 1:17). and this grace and truth shows us that the sum and substance of the law is love.

When an expert in the law asked Jesus which commandment was the greatest, "Jesus replied: 'Love the Lord your God with all your heart and with all your soul and with all your mind . . . . And . . . 'Love your neighbor as yourself'" (Matt. 22:37-39, NIV).

Through reading scriptures such as this, Newton must have realized he could not continue to trade slaves. While the law of the land did not prohibit slavery, the law of love, which Jesus taught, did not allow it. How can you enslave someone whom you love? In time, Newton disavowed his association with the demonic slave trade and became an abolitionist. In appreciation for God's grace and firmly holding to the promise that no sin is too great to be forgiven, Newton changed his life. So can we.

Dear God, point out to me anything that makes you sad, so I may honor you with my life. In Christ's name. Amen.

Like the Shunammite woman who kept a room on her roof ready for the prophet Elisha (see 2 Kings 4:10), I keep a spare bedroom ready for a former pastor whenever he and his wife visit the area. Jesus commends hospitality for his servants, and this is my privilege. I enjoy interacting with people, especially church leaders.

In Matthew 10, Jesus commissioned twelve disciples to go into the world to announce that the kingdom of heaven had come near. Then after informing the disciples they would face persecution, he encouraged them by saying, "Anyone who welcomes you welcomes me."

Just as ambassadors represent a nation, Christ's disciples were ambassadors for him. The Jewish people had a common saying: "A man's messenger is as himself." Entertaining a disciple, a prophet, or a priest was like entertaining Christ himself. That's because Christ identifies with his followers, whether they are persecuted or blessed. Whether it's a cold shoulder or a warm bed, Christ experiences what they experience.

We will be rewarded if we offer hospitality to God's prophets and righteous persons. Jesus may have been referring to the latter when he said a person will be blessed for so much as giving "little ones" a cup of water. These "little ones" may have been the less famous, perhaps teachers instead of preachers or prophets. Or just plain ordinary Christians. Or poor people.

As a Christian speaker, I have stayed in homes countless times. Sometimes I'm quite comfortable, and other times pets harass me. But I've always written my hosts thank you notes, and I've often left them books for their kindness. I know they've also stored up blessings in heaven. So can we.

Dear Lord, bless those who host Christ's ambassadors going out to share their faith. Reward them with a sense of your presence in this life and eternal rewards in heaven. Amen.

Continuing the Miracle

JULY 3–9, 2023 • KAYLA CRAIG

SCRIPTURE OVERVIEW: The reading in Genesis shifts our attention from Abraham to his son Isaac. When Isaac comes of age, Abraham sends a servant to find a wife for him. When the servant meets Rebekah, her kind hospitality convinces him that she is the one. Isaac marries her, and the reading in the psalm celebrates nuptial love as a symbol of God's love. Paul in Romans reflects on the human condition. We desire to do what is right, but we fall short over and over again. What is the solution? God delivers us through Jesus Christ. In Matthew, Jesus emphasizes his intimate relationship with God and invites all who are weary to enter into Christ's rest.

QUESTIONS AND SUGGESTIONS FOR REFLECTION

- Read Genesis 24:34-38, 42-49, 58-67. Which of these or other biblical stories model for you the relationship between God and humanity?
- Read Psalm 45:10-17. How have you seen God at work in the way loving relationships have transformed you?
- Read Romans 7:15-25a. How might participating in Communion in times of strife or sin help you be reconciled to God and others?
- Read Matthew 11:16-19, 25-30. The life of faith holds many ironies. How do you hold together the seeming opposites of Jesus' and John's focus in their ministries? of seeking to be yoked to God when your burden is too heavy?

Author of *To Light Their Way: A Collection of Prayers and Liturgies for Parents* (Tyndale, 2021); writes nuanced, nurturing prayers at *Liturgies for Parents* on Instagram; lives with her family in a former convent in her Iowa hometown; connect at kaylacraig.com.

In our humanity, we doubt. We wonder and wrestle. We try to reason our way into the mystery of God's story within us and around us. Try as we might, it's difficult to fathom the divine miracle of the God of all things choosing to co-create with us. How could it be that God is continuing the covenant with Abraham here and now?

Throughout scripture, we're reminded that the God of all things is not squeamish about our flesh and bone. Our humanity doesn't hinder the promises of God. God chooses—and keeps choosing—to continue the covenant with humanity, to further a kind of love that brings new life to the womb of a woman who is crowned in gray. It is the kind of love that keeps every promise even when it seems far too good to be true.

In today's reading, we're reminded of promises made and kept between God and Abraham. God did not need Abraham but chose to be a co-creator with him anyway—a promise steeped in a deep and abiding love.

Wedding ceremonies remind us that the partners are entering into a covenant, a sacred binding together, a commitment that their love, human though it is, will bear all things and endure all things.

That kind of love never fails even when we do. It flowed into Isaac's life and across centuries and bloodlines and nations, choosing us and drenching us even now.

Covenantal love persists in working together to make a new reality, to piece together a new whole. When we don't feel equipped or adequate, God reminds us of the promise, begins a new thing, and invites us to behold it (see Isaiah 43:19).

O Creator God, maker of heaven and earth, thank you for your covenantal love. Help me see the ways you are co-creating with me so that I may cultivate a life rooted in your love. Help me remember that you keep every promise. Amen.

In today's reading, we see an answer to prayer unfold as God once again uses regular women and men to continue the miracle of covenantal love. Abraham's servant petitions God, asking for help in the high-pressure task of finding a wife for Abraham's son Isaac.

The clear answer to this bold prayer was given in the form of Rebekah's generosity of spirit and kindness toward the servant who was a stranger to her. Through Rebekah's hospitality at the spring, we see a picture of God's mercy for us. When Abraham's servant asks for water, Rebekah gives with no hidden agenda.

Rebekah does not have to offer her water but gives it freely. She does not operate with a scarcity mentality but gives out of abundance as God does. And at this moment, Abraham's servant knows that God has answered his prayer. Rebekah is the person he's been looking for. She could have never imagined what her yes would lead to. But her yes has reverberated across generation upon generation into eternity.

When we are generous, when we extend kindness to a stranger and share what we have, we enter into God's cosmic plan of redemption. We will never know how many times our acts of mercy and hospitality are the very clear answer to someone else's prayer. When the comings and goings of our daily lives overflow with God's abundant love, we become answers to prayers. As we're reminded in Romans 8:28, "We know that all things work together for good for those who love God, who are called according to his purpose."

Just as God works through Abraham's servant and Rebekah in this passage, God is still working in us and through us today.

O God of Living Water, help me live into rhythms of mercy and generosity in my daily comings and goings. Amen.

Road trips are full of choices. You can veer right or turn left or turn off the car altogether. Even when you run out of gas and find yourself a bit stranded, you can choose to call a tow truck, trek to a gas station, or take a moment to have a good cry.

Life is made up of choices, from the seemingly ordinary, like navigating the finer points of a road trip, to the most confoundingly extraordinary, such as deciding to get married or choosing to embark on a big move. God is a God of abundance, allowing us to choose the paths we'll take and how we'll get there. God is also a God of love. We are given agency to enter into the mystery of God's love. In the seemingly mundane moments and in the biggest transition points of our lives, we decide. We refuse. We accept. There's always a choice.

In today's scripture, Rebekah has a choice. A big one. Will she accept this invitation to leave her home to marry a man she's never met? Will she leave with a stranger—Abraham's servant— and wave goodbye to all she knows to enter into a bigger story?

"I will go," she says. And she does. But she doesn't make this decision in a vacuum. Her decision to offer kindness and hospitality to a stranger begets this choice to enter into God's story. And her yes is an answer to Isaac's prayer.

We never know when our yes to the Holy Spirit will be an answer to a stranger's prayer. When your conscience is pricked, when the Spirit whispers into your heart, you have a choice. Will you welcome the stranger? Will you enter into God's covenantal love?

O God, be near in my decision-making. Help me choose what is right and just, and help me trust you in the unknowing. Amen.

The Wedding Industrial Complex is a multi-billion-dollar worldwide industry. It's not uncommon for couples to go deep into debt paying for all the trappings of a wedding. The clamor is cultural, but the root of it is not; as humans, we have an innate desire for perfection. The debt, the stress, the work—it's all for the "perfect day."

But no matter how many spreadsheets there are and how dutifully an event planner works, a wedding will never be perfect. Not the venue or the people in it. The flowers will be slightly wilted, a dress will get stained, a caterer won't show up. Our human desire for perfection will never be filled this side of heaven, no matter how we try.

Marriage relationships aren't perfect either. Marriage is a mystery. A coming together of two completely different hearts and minds, bodies and souls. A covenant made by two imperfect people, entering into a promise that reflects a glimmer of God's perfect love.

In today's reading, we're invited into a picture that Christians have traditionally seen messianically, where the universal church is wed to Christ. The psalmist evokes wedding imagery to help us understand God's never-ending, always committed, perfect covenantal love for us.

The Creator of all things invites us here to imagine ourselves as his bride. Our imperfections are known and accepted. In this picture of covenantal love we are treasured, gowned in gold, and called beautiful.

Throughout scripture, God continually chooses flawed people to covenant with to continue the story of a love that delights, commits, and never gives up.

O God, help me see myself as you see me. Release me from shame, and help me receive the joy that comes from the way you love me. Amen.

Continuing the Miracle

There's freedom in saying, "I don't know." We can almost see Paul fall to his knees and throw up his hands in today's reading. We can almost hear the desperation in his voice: *I don't know, God. I don't understand. I. Don't. Know.*

How often do you feel the pressure to get things right? Certainty reigns supreme in our world of black-and-white thinking. Religious legalism pushes us to strive for an elusive perfection that only brings us shame—but the covenantal promise of our Creator frees us from this pressure.

In this passage, Paul is frustrated with himself. He keeps repeating the same scripts and falling into the same traps, and he's exhausted. He doesn't know why he falls into unhealthy habits, but he does. He doesn't want to keep repeating these cycles and doesn't understand why they keep happening. Throughout this passage, Paul shows he's aware of his very real shortcomings and is wrestling with himself—or as he says, "waging war against the law of my mind."

Paul knows that God is his deliverer through Jesus Christ, and yet that covenantal promise of a redeeming love does not take away the realities of being human. The good news for Paul and for us is that in every failing and frustration, we are invited to share our every anxiety and worry with a God who hears, sees, and knows. As 1 Peter 5:7 says, "Cast all your anxiety on him, because he cares for you."

Just as we cannot be perfect, we don't have the perfect words to pray. God's promises do not rely on our perfect confessions. Our prayers can be honest and raw. God wants the in-process us. The real us. We can release the shame and the guilt and turn to the One who knows us intimately and loves us with an everlasting love (see Jeremiah 31:3).

O forgiving and merciful God, I don't always understand. In the unknowing, make your perfect presence and promise known. Amen.

The liberating love of a God who enters into covenants with us and makes a way for miracles in the mundane—who brings heaven to earth and has been weaving a sacred love story since before time began—frees us to live in a new way. We are no longer bound by old laws; the promise has been fulfilled in Jesus.

This changes everything. We are not weighed down by the constraints of what the world says is important. We are children of the promise (see Galatians 4:28). But to our world that prefers pomp and performance, power and prestige to the radical reordering of Jesus Christ, it doesn't make sense. Following the way of Jesus doesn't seem logical or rational.

In today's reading, it's clear that the way of Christ is confounding. John fasts and prays, and the religious elite think he is demon-possessed. Jesus eats and drinks with folks on the margins of society, and church leaders call him a drunk. The upside-down kingdom of God doesn't make sense. It challenges cultural norms. It looks like eating locusts and honey, like having friends in low places. It feels dangerous to someone who hasn't tasted and seen that the Lord is good.

Be encouraged that God's extravagant plan for a new way (through love-made-flesh in Jesus) includes you. And while you may be misunderstood at times as you continue in this rhythm of faith where the last are first and the first are last (see Matthew 20:16), you'll be in good company, walking the same sacred paths as John and Jesus.

As the reading for today concludes, "Wisdom is proved right by her deeds."

O Jesus, friend of sinners, I belong in you. Thank you for making a way when there was no way. Help me find worth in you alone when the world does not understand your liberating love. Give me wisdom as I live in your upside-down kingdom. Amen.

Continuing the Miracle

We worship a God who took on flesh—who intimately understands the heaviness of being human. Jesus knows our burdens. He feels our weariness. And he doesn't leave us to hold all of it alone.

As a loving father has compassion for his children, so does God offer us extravagant compassion (see Psalm 103:13). In our passage today, after Jesus thanks the Father for the accessible, inclusive love that perplexes the wise but makes perfect sense to the youngest child, Jesus offers a word of comfort to his followers. He knows their every pain, their every fear and struggle, and their unspoken prayers.

"Come to me, all you that are weary and are carrying heavy burdens, and I will give you rest. Take my yoke upon you, and learn from me; for I am gentle and humble in heart, and you will find rest for your souls. For my yoke is easy, and my burden is light."

Jesus' comforting words have much to teach us today. They remind us to lay down our armor and our white-knuckling ways of getting through the world. We no longer have to carry it all. We can stop trying to carry what was never ours to hold in the first place. Jesus gently reminds us that he embodies a true strength that is tender, reflecting the Father's compassionate love to us even now.

O compassionate Christ, in you I find rest. I give all that I carry to you. When I am weary, hold me in your gentle arms. Help me to be more like you, gentle and humble in heart. Amen.

God's Surprising Salvation

JULY 10–16, 2023 • FRED EDIE

SCRIPTURE OVERVIEW: Even great people in the faith have moments of imperfection. Not all biblical stories are biblical examples. Jacob should feed his brother out of concern, but he takes advantage of the situation and robs Esau of his birthright. The psalmist asks the Lord to show him how to live. God's word is a lamp to his feet and a light to his path. Paul in Romans contrasts the life of the flesh and the life in the Spirit. Without the power of God, we are doomed to repeat our mistakes in the flesh; but the Spirit sets us free. Jesus reminds us in Matthew that the effectiveness of the gospel is not based on our efforts. We sow the seed, but we cannot control whether it takes root.

QUESTIONS AND SUGGESTIONS FOR REFLECTION

- Read Genesis 25:19-34. How do you experience God's "nevertheless"—God's grace—as you work through the baggage of your birthright?
- Read Psalm 119:105-112. What offering of praise do you feel led to bring? What can you learn today from God's precepts?
- Read Romans 8:1-11. In learning what spiritual practices strengthen you, what practices did you try that did not work? Now that you know what works, how might working on practices you once found unhelpful grow your faith?
- Read Matthew 13:1-9, 18-23. In what unexpected place might you sow seeds of God's love?

———————

Veteran youth worker, United Methodist pastor, and Professor of the Practice of Christian Education at Duke Divinity School; most recent book is *Nurturing Faith: A Practical Theology for Educating Christians* co-written with Mark Lamport.

Stories of the matriarchs and patriarchs of the Old Testament read like plots from juicy reality television. The second half of Genesis 25 finds an aging couple, Rebekah and Isaac, unexpectedly expecting. What's more, the tumult in her womb signals to Rebekah that she is carrying twins who are already clashing in-utero. The Lord (an off-camera voice?) indicates that these are just the opening skirmishes of what will become an intense sibling rivalry, one not only pitting brother against brother (and parent against parent) but also changing the course of history. More incredibly, the Lord claims to be working out the divine purpose in the midst of this hot mess. (More about this below.)

When her time is at hand, Rebekah gives birth to hairy, red Esau first, and Jacob comes second, clinging to his brother's heel. Does this gesture portend a lifetime of the younger "tripping up" the elder? Esau grows up to be a "skillful hunter," a "man of the field" favored by Isaac, while Jacob matures into a "quiet man, living in tents" loved best by Rebekah.

This drama compels as much human interest today as it did in the past. Sibling rivalry, parental favoritism—these tropes never get old. What else ought we notice? First, the story is of the "Just So" variety, explaining the origins of the geopolitical rivalry between *Israel*—the name Jacob receives in chapter 32— and *Edom*, the dominion of Esau's descendants. Perhaps it also reassured Israel of God's protection from their better-established and more powerful neighbor to the east. In addition, we may read this story as evidence of God's surprising love, choosing a people to love despite human antagonists who are at best beset by mixed motivations. God's relational love for Israel is an abiding love; it is an early sign of God's profligate grace.

We thank you, O Lord, for choosing Israel and for grafting us into Israel's vine through your son, Jesus Christ. Amen.

One day, returning famished from a hunting trip, Esau sniffs out his brother's famous lentil stew and demands a bowlful. Jacob agrees to his request . . . in exchange for the elder's birthright. Swearing an oath, Esau accepts these terms—really, who does their best thinking on an empty stomach?—and the die is cast for Jacob to become the father of the nation of Israel.

Once again we see the story reassuring God's people that, with respect to Esau's Edom, Israel is indeed God's beloved. We also witness the freedom of God to surprise, to love whom God will love, to turn the tradition of the birthright on its head by favoring the younger Jacob over the elder Esau.

The birthright seemed as immutable as day following night. By transferring most of a family's wealth to the oldest male child, it provided a practical means to ensure a family's legacy through the generations. In this story God is not so much canceling the birthright as refining the rules to suit God's purposes, an early instance of God's unexpected support for the weaker, the lesser, and the undeserving.

But what about Jacob's trickery and deceit? Does God condone or even orchestrate it? Let us allow that not everyone, especially oppressed peoples who find themselves under the thumb of an empire, has the luxury of standing on details like this. Surely Israel, who had been bounced like a ping-pong ball between Egypt and Babylon, squeezed by regional powers including Edom, and sacked and exiled, didn't waste time over Jacob's manipulation of his brother. Instead, the story evoked joyful praise for God's grace and surprising subversion of the status quo. Like Jesus' parable of the unjust steward, this story applauds Jacob's scrappy improvisational imagination, God's approved kind of scheming in the face of imperial power.

O God who saw in Jacob the hope of Israel, teach us to imagine as you do. Amen.

God's Surprising Salvation

For God's people, Israel, the Mosaic law became the heartbeat of life. It was the ubiquitous communal curriculum (to be written on doorposts, strapped to foreheads, recited upon going out and coming in) and was therefore critical to shaping Israel's identity as God's chosen people. It also provided a pathway to the good life; obedience to the law begat God's blessing. No wonder the law has become for the psalmist "a lamp to my feet and a light to my path," and God's decrees are "the joy of my heart."

Yet all is not entirely delightful in Doxology Land. The psalmist also complains of affliction and a risk of entrapment by "the wicked." In this passage and throughout the entire psalm an undertone of lament is juxtaposed with the strikingly beautiful language of praise and thanksgiving. Why the minor key dissonance in the midst of all this glory?

Perhaps the psalmist is gingerly probing the law's promise that obedience leads to blessing. The poet wants to affirm this conviction but can't help notice that being good sometimes places a target on one's back. As I write this, more than a dozen Christian missionaries in Haiti, seeking only to provide relief to Haitians from a hurricane, an earthquake, and the collapse of government services, have been kidnapped and held for ransom.

Biting insects and other phantoms of the night are drawn to lamps lighting paths through darkness. To put this in terms of a different kind of surprise, the law appears less than capable of sponsoring the good life. What is intended for freedom begets bondage instead.

Or perhaps as Paul the apostle will spell out tomorrow, the problem is not the law but the power of Sin to corrupt it.

Teach us, O God, to walk the lighted path of righteousness as its own reward, trusting always in your Word, whom darkness cannot overcome. Amen.

Paul contrasts life in the flesh with life in the Spirit, but not in the way we typically assume. Our distorted interpretive legacy of equating *flesh* with the *body* has led to a destructive dualism in which the human spirit is thought to host the things of God while our flesh stews in the juices of sin. Salvation, therefore, seems to require escape from the body. This dualism was employed historically by free, able-bodied men to judge and marginalize those who were deemed to be confined to their bodies or whose bodies gave the appearance of otherness—women, children, the aged, the disabled, enslaved peoples (the usual list of suspects).

But Paul uses a different term for "flesh" (*sarx*) than for "body" (*soma*). Flesh, for Paul, is coincident not with the body but with the fallen human condition. Flesh signals idolatry, the devotion of the person to lesser gods or to the self as god. Thus, embodiment isn't the problem; sin is.

Which forces a deeper contemplation of "sin." For many, sin equals the list of regrettable things confessed before we get to go to Sunday brunch. Paul, however, also envisions Sin (capital "S") as a cosmic power contending against God. This Sin is an agent; it corrupts the relations between and among God, humans, and the non-human creation. Sin enslaves those in the flesh into a cycle of sinning, making us at once Sin's victims and its deputies. Even the good gift of the law, for which the psalmist praised God just yesterday (and also expressed a certain prescient foreboding), has been twisted into an instrument of judgment by the power of Sin.

Life in the flesh is death. In response, Paul envisions life in the Spirit of Christ.

Cause us to flee the flesh, O God, even as we cling to the body of your Son, Jesus Christ, by the power of the Spirit. Amen.

God's Surprising Salvation   235

Thanks be to God for the gift of life in the Spirit! Made members of Christ's body through baptismal washing into Christ's life, death, and resurrection, we are "set free from the power of sin and death." Sin can no longer bind us to the flesh. Indeed, in Christ the law's requirement of us is "fulfilled."

This gospel represents an astonishing inversion of conventional thinking. Paul testifies to God's turning the world upside down then rebuilding it on a new foundation—the Son of God, likened to sinful flesh, condemns sin in the flesh by dying to it.

Yet even as Christ defeats Sin and frees from its power those joined to him through baptism, Sin is not yet vanquished. Yes, the new creation is underway, and yes, the future belongs to Christ. But Sin continues its rear-guard action. Though freed from enslavement to life in the flesh, Christians may yet forget or misuse their freedom.

The solution? To set our minds upon the Spirit to "receive life and peace." First, we embrace the baptismal life as a communion of Spirit-filled reconciliation and inclusion, one that will reestablish human interdependence with God, each other, and with the non-human creation. Second, we continue to battle against Sin, confident in Christ's ultimate victory over that dark power. This battle is personal but also social and even cosmic.

Paul sees that Sin can cause communities to misapprehend even the gospel. Sin threatens to poison our imagination against the body (and against bodies, especially bodies marked by age or ability or skin pigmentation) as baggage to be discarded on the way to life in the Spirit. Paul rejects this Sin-twisted imagining: The Spirit of Christ gives "life to our mortal bodies." Personal and social bodies are integral to working out our salvation!

Free us, Jesus, to see your saving body in the bodies of others.
Amen.

Jesus, the Rabbi of the People, sits in a boat to teach the standing-room only crowd. In this gesture he evokes the history of God's covenant faithfulness to Israel and poses as the new covenant, the new ark of salvation. His go-to teaching style is the parable, a story set in the milieu of the people and delivered in language they easily grasp.

This parable has to do with farming, a practice folks in that region understand as if their very lives depend upon it. (Imagine!) They know that the harvest requires receptive soil. Rocky, thorny soil bodes ill, and good soil bodes well. Easy! But not so fast. What kind of farmer scatters precious seed where it has little chance to grow? Why would Jesus counsel poor agricultural practices? Are we sure he's even talking about farming?

Jesus used parables to put hearers in familiar situations only to shake up their expectations and tweak their sensibilities. Jesus also taught in parables to communicate, if indirectly, something about his reign and his gospel mission.

He often deliberately provoked members of the religious establishment who thought that they already had a lock on God's favor. In the words of Emily Dickinson, Jesus tells the truth but tells it slant.

All of that and more is in play in this parable. Jesus' strong polling numbers are sliding as the risks of following him become clearer. Hearers find themselves living in houses divided by his inversions of assumptions about what a family is. Authorities who'd fancied themselves stewards of privately-held, perpetually fertile soil simmer red-faced because Jesus said their harvest has gone to the birds. Still others cling to the hope that an abundant harvest is coming and that they might be among its fruits, despite the current lack of evidence.

Harvest us too, Lord Jesus, even as we have scattered ourselves to the winds. Amen.

After Jesus shares his parable, after he sows this mystery of imagination and wonder, he gathers his disciples for a private tutorial. Readers find themselves wondering at this point too, though perhaps not exactly as the parable intends. Specifically, we wonder how Jesus' parable, which is by design infinitely fathomable, could be corralled with such exacting resolution at the debriefing. We thought parables by their nature could not be pinned down.

One possible explanation is that the parable's interpretation actually belongs to Matthew and his local church. The Great Gospel Giveaway isn't going as planned. Folks aren't decamping the synagogue in droves for the church, and no one even has a clue how to reach the Gentiles—not that there are many in town. What's more, many early adopters, baptized in passionate fervor for Jesus, seem to be drifting away. And then there's the constant threat of Rome.

The small-group meeting uses Jesus' parable to explain these tough times for the church. Like farming, evangelism and discipleship are unpredictable. But because much of the growth that God gives occurs underground and remains shrouded in mystery, hope is not lost. Perseverance will be rewarded with surpassing abundance—one of Matthew's favorite tropes.

With the present-day church enduring its own tough times, our first instinct may be to read the parable's explanation to our comfort. God will ensure this harvest! Because God has proven surprisingly subversive in this text and others, however, and because the nature of parable is to disrupt, we should hear it as challenge as well. Maybe Christians have fallen among the rocks and thorns. Or perhaps the parable calls us away from our field to its rocky margins to attend to bodies marked by suffering and to hope together for God's harvest.

Surprise us anew with your saving work, O astonishing God! Amen.

Beloved Children of God

JULY 17–23, 2023 • IRA STAN CAMPBELL

SCRIPTURE OVERVIEW: As God promised land and descendants to Abraham, in the reading from Genesis God confirms these same promises to Abraham's grandson Jacob. The psalmist meditates on and takes comfort in the fact that God knows everything and is everywhere. He asks God to search his heart and reveal if there are sins away from which he needs to turn. The Romans passage continues Paul's reflection on the life in the Spirit. Because we are children of God, we cry out with confidence that God will hear and answer. Jesus tells a parable in Matthew concerning the final judgment. He says that the wicked will be taken first, then the righteous will be gathered together.

QUESTIONS AND SUGGESTIONS FOR REFLECTION

- Read Genesis 28:10-19a. When has God quietly been at work in your life? How do these experiences help you recognize God's presence with you in ordinary days?
- Read Psalm 139:1-12, 23-24. God already knows us completely. What is holding you back from inviting God to search your heart?
- Read Romans 8:12-25. Consider the ways you already resemble God. In what ways do you wish to be transformed to resemble God more fully?
- Read Matthew 13:24-30, 36-43. Reflect on a time when you were frustrated by God's inaction in the face of injustice. In hindsight, how was God at work?

Served as a hospital chaplain in Nashville, TN, for twenty years and as a chaplain in the Army Reserves and Air National Guard for a total of thirty years.

My father was an insurance agent, so he was well aware of automobile accidents. Years before I started driving, he began saying to me, "Son, you have to be especially careful while driving in the rain because the roads get slick and that's when you are most likely to have a wreck." One week after getting my driver's license, I was driving home in a light rain and had a wreck in front of my high school. I ran back to the coach's office to call my dad. With a trembling voice, I told him about the wreck. "Is everyone okay?" he asked. "Yes, sir," I answered. "Son," he replied calmly. "Don't worry about it; this kind of thing happens all the time." I had feared a harsh reaction from my dad, but he responded with understanding and kindness.

"How do I perceive God?" is an important spiritual question worthy of our contemplation. Do I see God as a harsh taskmaster who punishes my failures? Or do I see God as a parent who loves and forgives me even when I fail to live up to Jesus' example? People of faith tend to fall somewhere between these two views of God. As for me, a spiritual transformation occurred in my life when I moved away from seeing God as a taskmaster and began viewing God as a loving parent.

Henri Nouwen, in his writings about our belovedness in the eyes of God, encourages us to rest in the grace of God and to resist the temptation to "fall back into fear." As today's scripture reminds us, the Holy Spirit bears witness with our spirit that we are "children of God," and as Henri Nouwen would say, *beloved* children of God.

Loving God, help me to rest in your grace today and to see myself and others as your beloved children. Amen.

A shift in my spiritual perspective occurred when I began to see all situations or places as potentially holy. From this viewpoint, walking the streets of Jerusalem or along the shores of Galilee is no more holy than strolling the paved boulevards of Birmingham or the red-clay back roads of Alabama. I can experience God's holiness on a mountain trail as easily as I can in a stained-glass cathedral. Even so, certain places hold special meaning for us for one reason or another. It might be the grounds of a youth camp where we powerfully felt God's presence or call on our lives. Some people consider Selma, Montgomery, and the Edmund Pettus Bridge as sacred ground because of their rich history in the Civil Rights Movement. When a particular place has personal spiritual significance to us, we naturally want to mark the spot in some way so we can return there for a time of remembrance and renewal.

Jacob marked the spot of his dream by setting up his stone pillow as a pillar and pouring oil on the top of it. Interestingly, he called the place *Bethel*, which means "House of God." I find this story encouraging because an ordinary plot of ground became a holy place for Jacob and his descendants.

Perhaps a meaningful time of reflection would be to think about places that are sacred or holy to us. Why is this place so special to us? How can we mark this spot literally or figuratively? What are some ways to share this experience with others that would encourage them in their spiritual journey?

Holy God, thank you for the places where I especially felt your presence. Help me to recall these times and to find strength for my journey in these remembrances. Amen.

When I was a hospital chaplain, I often visited people who were suffering through illness or loss. Sometimes, patients would say, "Well, there must be a reason for this." I usually thought to myself, "Well, things happen, and we try to make sense of it." I didn't actually say those words because it wouldn't have been appropriate in most cases. Suffering people don't need philosophical answers or spiritual platitudes; they need a listening ear and a compassionate, supportive presence.

Compassion literally means "to suffer with," which counters our natural human tendency to avoid painful situations. In my early years as a hospital chaplain, I felt inadequate to help patients or family members in their grief since my life had been relatively free of suffering and loss. When I told this to my supervisor, she assured me that suffering eventually comes to everyone—and she was right.

Suffering comes in many forms. For some, it is an acute or chronic illness. For others, it is the loss of a loved one. People can even grieve the loss of hopes and dreams, such as a couple that is not able to have children, or a child who can't participate in sports because of a medical condition. Instead of simply feeling sorry for people in these situations, we can show them compassion by being mindful of their circumstances and listening empathetically if they choose to share their struggles with us. These compassionate actions exemplify genuine care and concern.

In today's scripture, Paul accepts suffering as an inevitable part of life and does not offer an easy answer for it. Instead, this passage encourages us to remember in the midst of suffering that we are children of God and to wait in patience for the promised redemption.

Compassionate God, in times of suffering, help me to remember your promise of redemption. Amen.

Years ago, some friends and I hiked to the summit of Mount Whitney in California's Sierra Nevada mountains. I realized after finishing this hike that I had been so focused on making it to the top that I didn't notice the beauty of God's handiwork all along the trail. Thinking about this experience makes me wonder how often I miss the joy of God's presence because of my busy life or fruitless worry.

On Jacob's journey from Beer-sheba to Haran, he has a similar "aha" moment. He stops for the night and sleeps under the stars by using a stone for a pillow. This doesn't sound too comfortable, but the rock becomes meaningful later on in the story. He dreams about a ladder ascending to heaven, and in the dream, God tells Jacob that his descendants will spread across the earth and receive blessings. When Jacob awakes, he emphatically proclaims, "Surely the LORD is in this place—and I did not know it!"

Jacob's experience reminds me of a friend's comment, "I don't want to ever go camping again!" When I asked why, he replied, "Because I did enough camping in the Army to last a lifetime." He didn't have to explain. I understood what he meant since I spent eight years in the Army Reserves. Even so, we can still enjoy the outdoors if we are mindful of God's presence. One of my best memories involves camping with friends on the California Coast. We had a lovely view of the Pacific from our campsite and enjoyed campfire-roasted tacos as the sun set into the ocean. It is one of life's simple pleasures to sleep out under the stars, marvel at the beauty and grace of nature, and to feel blessed by sharing the experience with friends. Blessings truly await us when we realize the Lord is with us wherever we go.

Ever-present God, as we travel life's journey, open our eyes to your presence. Amen.

Beloved Children of God

Can we pray the words of the psalmist? *Search me, O God, and know my heart.*

This prayer involves an element of risk. It may bring to light some things about our lives that we have not previously acknowledged or confessed. As beloved children of God, however, we can trust God to search the far corners of our hearts without fear of condemnation. The Holy Spirit will reveal areas of our lives that aren't leading us in the way everlasting, and by God's grace, we can then make any needed changes.

Praying this prayer also means that we can't hide anything from God. I heard about a couple who welcomed a friend into their home for an overnight visit with the familiar words, "Our house is your house, so make yourself at home." When the couple returned from work the next day, they found their guest in the upstairs office going through their personal files. "What are you doing?" they asked. "I'm just doing as you said, 'Our house is your house.' I'm just making myself at home." "Yes," they replied, "but we didn't mean that!"

This story causes me to wonder if I am ever like the hospitable couple when I ask God to search my heart. What do I mean when I pray this prayer? Do I really want God to search every room of my heart, or do I want to keep some things hidden from God?

Perhaps a meaningful time of reflection would be to imagine ourselves in a conversation with Jesus—like the one he had with the woman at the well (John 4:4-18). We imagine ourselves as thirsting for living water as the woman did, but are we willing to hear what Jesus might say to us upon peering into our hearts? If so, let us pray with the psalmist.

Search me, O God, and know my heart. Amen.

On March 18, 1958, Thomas Merton was on a rare excursion away from his monastery to run some errands in downtown Louisville, Kentucky. While standing at the corner of Fourth and Walnut, he had an epiphany where he suddenly realized that although he was a monk, he was no different from all the other people he saw on the street. He described this experience by saying that everyone was walking around shining like the sun.

When Jesus explains the parable of the weeds to his disciples, he clearly indicates that the children of the kingdom are like good seeds that grow and produce wheat, while people who do evil are like weeds that grow alongside the wheat. Anyone who has ever tended a garden knows that weeds, if left alone, are invasive and create a nuisance for the good plants. The parable's instruction to let the weeds be until harvest time sounds counterproductive—and it is certainly not good news for the companies that produce and sell weedkillers!

As children of God, we can easily become discouraged by all the evil that surrounds and pervades our lives. We may, at times, even wonder why God allows sinful people to wreak havoc and cause so much suffering and chaos around the world. There are no easy answers to such questions, but this parable does remind us that a day of reckoning is coming for evildoers. On that day, as the concluding verse from today's scripture reminds us, the righteous will shine like the sun in God's kingdom. Until then, let us find encouragement from Merton's revelation. When the weeds of sinfulness seek to choke and entangle our lives, by God's grace, we can persevere and shine like the sun.

Gracious God, help us to remember that we are your good seeds—and thus, may we grow and produce the fruit of your Spirit in our lives. Amen.

I remember a Dan Fogelberg concert I went to in the seventies when I was fifteen years old. Most memorable about that night was the encore. Thousands of young people stood and illuminated the darkness with their BIC lighters and sang along to the chorus of the song "There's a Place in the World for a Gambler."

There's a light in the depths of your darkness.
Let it shine, oh, let it shine.

The following Sunday, I had an epiphany in the morning worship service. When the music director invited everyone to stand and sing a hymn, I looked around and noticed hardly anyone was singing, including myself. Since the "Let it shine" moment from the concert was still fresh in my mind, the irony was obvious to me. Suddenly, for the first time in my young life, I understood why we sing in church. Surely, I thought to myself, one of the reasons we worship God with songs of praise is because the Light of the World has come into the world and the darkness has not overcome it. I began to sing the words of the hymn and decided from that day forward, I would always lift my voice with songs of praise—in gratitude and in awe of God's marvelous light.

Today's scripture reminds and assures us of God's inescapable light and presence. God knows us completely, including our words before we speak them, all our comings and goings, and even when darkness seems to envelop us. In the most difficult times, we can find comfort by remembering that God is always aware of our circumstances. As God's beloved children, we can trust God to lead us through our darkest valleys.

Glorious God, shine your light into the dark times of my life so that I may find hope in your presence and continually seek your guidance. Amen.

God Is Doing More

JULY 24–30, 2023 • LEANNA K. FULLER

SCRIPTURE OVERVIEW: Jacob has tricked his brother out of his birthright and has tricked his blind father into blessing him instead of his older brother. This week the trickster is tricked, and his desire to marry Rachel will cost him dearly. The psalmist reflects on the faithfulness of God. God has made a covenant with Abraham, Isaac, and Jacob, and the author is confident that God will honor that covenant. Paul builds upon his argument to the Romans about the power of the Spirit. The Spirit helps us pray to connect with God, and nothing can separate us from the love of God. Jesus continues to teach about the kingdom of God using parables. Finding our way into the kingdom is worth far more than anything else.

QUESTIONS AND SUGGESTIONS FOR REFLECTION

- Read Genesis 29:15-28. How does a wise faith help you discern between differing loves?
- Read Psalm 105:1-11, 45b. How is your faith journey an extension of God's covenants with Abraham, Isaac, and Jacob?
- Read Romans 8:26-39. How have you experienced prayer as an opening of yourself to God's Spirit rather than a petition for yourself or others?
- Read Matthew 13:31-33, 44-52. How are you growing in Christ? If your faith has become stagnant, what "sorting" might help you to continue to grow toward proficiency in being Christlike?

Ordained in the United Church of Christ; Professor of Pastoral Care at Pittsburgh Theological Seminary in Pittsburgh, PA; active member of Trinity UCC in Dorseyville, PA.

The story of Jacob, Leah, and Rachel is a disturbing one. From our current historical vantage point, it's easy to read this passage and see only antiquated customs that treat women more like property than people. It's tempting to just skip over this story and conclude that it has no real relevance for contemporary faith.

But what if we were to read this passage from the perspective of Leah and Rachel? Instead of focusing on Jacob as the main character in the story, what might happen if we pondered questions like, "Did Leah even want to marry Jacob?" or "How did Rachel feel about Laban tricking her beloved into marrying her older sister?" or "What did Rachel see in someone who could not tell her from her sister?"

Leah and Rachel must have had thoughts and feelings about what was happening to them, even if those are not recorded in the biblical text. Imagining ourselves in Leah's or Rachel's place can help us to remember a vital truth: God's love and care extend to everyone—even those who aren't recognized by human structures as noteworthy. In fact, the witness of our scriptures is that God has special concern for those who are overlooked or forgotten, or who seem to appear as peripheral characters in someone else's story.

Listening for the unrecorded voices of Leah and Rachel in this text reminds us that even in Bible passages we know so well, there is always a richer story to be told. God is always doing more in a particular situation than we are able to grasp at first. Today, God is calling us to broaden our imagination so that we can discern the deeper truths God wants to share with us.

Gracious God, ignite our imagination so that we may grasp your truth more fully. Help us to listen closely to those who have been overlooked and to embrace what they have to teach us. Amen.

Yesterday's reflection noted that it can be hard to find meaning in some of the stories of the Bible. The account of Jacob marrying Leah and then Rachel can make it seem as though these women had no agency in their lives or that they were minor characters in a story centered on someone more important.

But when we read Genesis 29 alongside Psalm 105, we are reminded of the particular purpose the stories of the patriarchs served in ancient Israel: to remind all the people of Israel of their identity as God's chosen ones. The psalmist exhorts hearers to "remember the wondrous works" (CEB) God has done, addressing these words to "you who are the offspring of Abraham, his servant, and the children of Jacob, his chosen ones" (CEB). In this way, the psalmist emphasizes the connection between Israel's chosenness and God's goodness and faithfulness.

Indeed, throughout the Bible, the names of Abraham, Isaac, and Jacob are frequently used to signify Israel's status as the chosen people of God. These ancestors of the faith are symbols and examples of how God's purposes can be accomplished through God's flawed, scheming, all-too-human people.

No one would suggest that these men were the only figures through whom God has worked. Leah and Rachel and countless others were God's people too. They too were part of the covenant that God established with Israel; God was doing more to work through their lives than we will ever know.

Reading Genesis 29 together with Psalm 105 reveals that God's embrace includes everyone, even those whose names have now been forgotten. These texts remind us that God works through all of God's people: Abraham, Isaac, and Jacob, Leah and Rachel, and even you and me.

Remind us, O God, of your steadfast love and faithfulness, which stretch across so many generations. Thank you for working through all our lives to accomplish your purposes. Amen.

God Is Doing More   249

Scholars sometimes categorize Psalm 105 as a "historical psalm," which emphasizes the history of the relationship between God and the people of Israel. The psalm begins with a short song of praise in which hearers are exhorted to give thanks to God and to remember all God's marvelous works—including the establishment of God's justice.

Yet given that the Israelites had experienced so much oppression for so long, it may have been challenging for them to believe that God's justice would really come to pass. This may be why the psalmist begins describing God's covenants with Abraham, Isaac, and Jacob. The psalmist reminds the people that through these covenants, God has been faithful to them in the past and has promised be faithful to them into the future.

Today, we may feel like the people of Israel when we see injustice all around us, and things don't seem to be getting better. Sometimes we get discouraged and feel like God no longer cares about the kind of justice the psalmist sang about so long ago. But this passage from Psalm 105 reminds us that even when God's people experienced intense suffering and despair, they were still able to praise God's goodness and tell of God's wondrous works.

God is always doing more than we know to bring about justice in the world. But this does not mean that we should just sit back and wait for God to act, as if we have no part in ushering in God's reign. We give praise and honor to God by participating in the work God is already doing all around us.

God of justice, thank you for your care and compassion for all of creation. Help us to remember your faithfulness to us in the past and to rest in your promises for the future. Amen.

Here's a true confession: I am terrible at growing things. I struggle to keep a single house plant alive, and I've never dared to try tending a whole garden. I just don't seem to have the knack for coaxing life from seed and soil. My lack of a green thumb gives me a slightly different perspective than most on the parable of the mustard seed. Traditional interpretations of this parable focus on the fact that such a tiny seed can produce such a large plant—so large that it's more like a tree.

But when I read this parable, I'm struck less by the size of the mustard plant and more by the wondrous fact that plants can emerge from seeds at all. Part of my difficulty in growing things is that I'm too impatient to put in the effort needed to nurture plants, not knowing if what I'm doing is going to work or not. When I don't see results right away, I get discouraged and want to give up.

Today's parable reminds us that the kingdom of heaven is not subject to our force of will or our desire for control. It's more like a seed that was planted long ago and has been growing at its own pace, hidden under the earth. It arrives as a tender shoot, emerging from the ground just when we thought nothing could grow there. When our own efforts fail, we must remember that God is always doing more than we can see. God's will and purpose are always growing, and in God's time, we will be invited to join in the work God has for us to do.

Nurturing God, help us notice the signs of your kingdom emerging all around us. Open our hearts to accept your invitation to join in your work. Amen.

God Is Doing More   251

The first two parables in today's passage are familiar. Most of us have heard about the treasure hidden in the field and the precious pearl. But the parable about separating good fish from bad catches us off guard. It feels jarring to go from two parables emphasizing wonder and joy to one that ends with people weeping and grinding their teeth. So what do we make of these parables? The first two are distinct in theme and tone from the third, yet all three aim to describe the kingdom of heaven. What connections can we find among these parables to help us understand why Jesus told them to his followers?

Reading these parables together, I am struck by the theme of discernment that's present in all of them. In each case, people are confronted with a decision: whether to sell everything to buy the field or the pearl; whether a fish is good or bad. Perhaps in telling these stories to his followers, Jesus was showing them that pursuing the kingdom of heaven involves discerning what's most important and then acting accordingly.

These parables invite us to examine our lives closely and ask what God is calling us to do. Some situations may require us to make sacrifices to obtain a hidden treasure or precious pearl. Others may lead us to contemplate what dimensions of our lives are life-giving or death-dealing so that we can pursue what is good and turn away from paths that lead to destruction. Through these parables, we are reminded that everyday decisions are opportunities for us to join the work God is already doing and to bring our lives more in line with God's will.

God of wisdom, in each situation we face, help us discern where you are leading us. Grant us courage to make the choices that will bring us closer to your kingdom. Amen.

Everything happens for a reason." That's what well-meaning people often say when things go terribly wrong in someone else's life: the loss of a job, the end of a relationship, or even the death of a loved one. Sometimes it feels easier to accept that something bad has happened if there is a reason behind it, even if we can't perceive what that reason might be.

Today's passage is frequently cited as biblical support for the idea that everything happens for a reason—especially the part of verse 28 that says, "We know that God works all things together for good for the ones who love God" (CEB). But saying that God works all things together for good is quite different from saying that God engineers tragic events in human lives in order to accomplish a greater purpose.

Our faith teaches us that God's will is always at work, leading us toward the kingdom of heaven on earth. But our faith also teaches that first and foremost, God is love, and God never willingly harms God's children. Theologically, we can affirm that God can work through terrible situations to bring good out of them, without assuming that God makes awful things happen just to teach us a lesson.

In this text we hear the good news that God is always with us in our suffering. Even in circumstances that feel completely hopeless, God is doing more than we know to sustain us. God's Spirit intercedes for us when we find it hard to pray. God pleads for us, helps us in our weakness, and finds ways to bring good out of the most difficult situations. Thanks be to God.

We are grateful, O God, for your comforting presence that bears us up when we don't even know how to pray. Remind us today that no matter what we face in life, you are with us. Amen.

God Is Doing More   253

Yesterday's reflection emphasized that God does not cause bad things to happen. Instead, God finds ways to bring good out of difficult circumstances and is always with us in our suffering. Today's passage is a variation on the same theme: Though we may face troubles of all kinds—danger, famine, nakedness, distress—God's love is constant, always working to bring about God's will for our lives and for the world. Putting these two passages together shows us that the way God works things together for good is through God's love. God's love is the power that brings good out of evil and can never be defeated.

On the night my son was born and was placed in my arms for the first time, I was overcome with a feeling I'd never experienced before. It was a feeling of intense love, to be sure. But it was more specific than that. In that instant, I was overwhelmed with the knowledge that I would give my life to protect this child, and that nothing could ever make me stop loving him. When I read this passage from Romans 8, I'm reminded of that December night and my sudden awareness that my love for my son was unbreakable.

God's love for us is like that, but it is even more powerful and everlasting than we can imagine. It is so broad and so deep that nothing in all of creation—not even death—can bring it to an end. God's love is all around us, even when our circumstances are so dire that we can't see or feel it. God is always doing more than we know to surround us with love and to remind us that in life and in death, we belong to God.

Eternal God, thank you for your promise that nothing can separate us from your love. Inspire us to find ways to share your boundless love with everyone we meet. Amen.

Wrestling with Abundance

JULY 31–AUGUST 6, 2023 • ANGELA DENKER

SCRIPTURE OVERVIEW: Jacob is attacked one night by an unknown assailant and wrestles with him until morning. We discover that the assailant comes from God, so Jacob is given a new name, Israel. The psalmist is feeling unjustly accused and cries out to God. He is confident that he would be vindicated if all the facts were known. In Romans, Paul deals with difficult theological issues. He states that he would sacrifice his own soul if his fellow Israelites would accept Christ. Jesus teaches a crowd that is growing hungry, and his disciples are trying to figure out how to feed them. They see only what they lack, while Jesus asks them what they have. This story is a lesson about offering God what we have and trusting God.

QUESTIONS AND SUGGESTIONS FOR REFLECTION

- Read Genesis 32:22-31. When have you been forced to wrestle with yourself or your self-identity? How did this struggle reveal a blessing?
- Read Psalm 17:1-7, 15. When have you felt the need to serve as your own advocate before God? How has this experience affirmed your trust in God?
- Read Romans 9:1-5. When have you experienced Paul's anguish that others do not accept what you have come to know in your faith, whether by conversion, denominational change, education, or encounter with God? How do you continue to be in relationship with such family or friends?
- Read Matthew 14:13-31. When have you trusted God to do the seemingly impossible?

Lutheran pastor and veteran journalist who has written for many publications, including *Sports Illustrated*, *The Washington Post*, and *FORTUNE* magazine; her book, *Red State Christians: Understanding the Voters Who Elected Donald Trump*, was the 2019 Silver Foreword Indies award-winner for political and social sciences.

One of my best friends from seminary is a wrestling coach. Before studying to be a pastor, he worked as a nuclear engineer for the Navy and was a championship wrestler himself. Aaron views life as a daily grind. I first met him in Greek class, where he sat in the front row and called out every answer.

"Who does this guy think he is?" I scoffed.

Then I met Aaron in the seminary gym, and we started talking over curls and squats. I was impressed with his honesty and tenacity. He reminded me of the engineers I used to play pick-up basketball with in college.

A few months later, Aaron confessed that he was thinking about leaving seminary. He was a college wrestling coach and had decades of experience in engineering. How could he throw all that away?

We walked up and down the hills of the seminary neighborhood, sharing our struggles and worries and hopes. Ultimately, we both decided to stick it out. A decade later, Aaron and I have both served multiple congregations, while he has continued to serve the Navy and work with wrestlers on the side, maintaining his strict workout regimen. Even when we've had tough conversations, Aaron has never ceased to inspire me. He reminds me that contrarianism—or wrestling—is a vital part of growth in our faith. He has shown me that serving the church often looks different than full-time ministry, and that's OK.

Jacob's wrestling with God—and refusing to let go despite the pain—reminds me of Aaron and of all of my loved ones whose greatest strength lies not in ease but in resilience. As you wrestle with the struggles of your life and faith's unanswerable questions, may you follow the lead of Aaron and of Jacob and remain tied to God even in the midst of great pain.

God, grant me patience and resilience and hope that my wrestling will lead to deeper faith in you. Amen.

I have never competed in a wrestling match, donned a singlet, or even successfully learned one wrestling hold, despite the fact that my dad competed as a high school wrestler and told me tales of practicing to make weight with garbage bags over his head in a sweaty weight room.

Wrestling is not for the faint of heart. And so the Genesis story of Jacob wrestling with God lays bare in a rare way the closeness and physical intimacy that Jacob experiences with God. In the world of faith before Christ, Jacob's experience with God is notable for the ways in which God participates in humanity's pain, struggle, and redemption through his wrestling match with Jacob.

Notice that the wrestling match does not end with one crowned champion's fist raised in the air and the defeated wrestler collapsed on the other end of the ring. Instead this match ends with the wrestlers knowing one another in a deeper and more profound way, by the sharing of their names and identities. God's chosen method of closeness to Jacob and his family was through wrestling, through pain and struggle and gritty physical work.

Jacob emerges with a new name—an identity grounded in his relationship to the God with whom he wrestled and communicated. He also emerges with a limp. Because growth in faith and closeness to God in this world do not mean we are shielded from pain. Instead we go on, knowing that even in our limping we are carried by a God who draws nearer to us every single day.

God, grant me the confidence to know that when I struggle, you are committed to struggling beside me. Help me move from struggle into peace, knowing that my identity is grounded in your love for me. Amen.

The Psalms provide a manual of sorts for how to pray. Spoiler alert: There is no one right way to pray, so long as your direct address to God is authentic, honest, and full of genuine feeling.

Many are apprehensive about praying out loud, in front of others, or even just praying at all. We've watched too many examples of overly pious or practiced prayers. We've imagined that prayer must be pre-written and "holy sounding."

But read some psalms. They are raw. They often begin in a beseeching tone that reminds me of my five-year-old son when I have waited too long to respond to one of his many requests.

"Hear me, O God!"

Yet isn't this plea what we all desire deep down? Human beings need food, water, shelter, clothing—and love and affirmation. As parents and caregivers know all too well, babies cry not just for physical reasons, like a diaper change, milk, or even a sore belly. Sometimes they cry merely to be recognized and acknowledged. I read recently that human beings are the only species to cry real tears for non-physical reasons. The same report found that people were more empathetic after seeing images of people crying tears.

At its most powerful, the book of Psalms is a brilliant representation of the human desire to be connected to God. The psalms are a raging cry against a culture of heartless, cold individualism because the psalms demand emotional connection and response.

"Hear a just cause, O Lord; attend to my cry; . . . I call upon you, for you will answer me, O God."

God, grant me the courage to approach you with honesty and rawness, knowing that you hear my prayer. Amen.

Paul speaks from a place of "great sorrow and unceasing anguish" as he realizes that his commitment to the truth of the gospel has separated him from his own people and from who he used to be before he came to faith in Jesus. Despite his pain and grief, Paul holds fast to hope and righteousness for his people. He is certain that God's covenants and promises to the people of Israel will not fail, *and* he trusts that the truth of Christ is for everyone.

Paul wishes that he could somehow be sacrificed in order that "his people" could know, or could remember, their adoption as children of God. Because of that adoption, they should rejoice in the gifts God has given them—the Covenant, the law, the fact that from them has come the Messiah. Imagine wanting to remind a friend or family member how blessed they are to have God's unconditional love, God's forgiveness, grace from which they can never be separated—only to have them turn away from these great gifts of God! That frustration might be something like what Paul felt as he wrote to his friends at the church in Rome.

This passage from Romans 9 follows Paul's powerful, reassuring words concerning God's Holy Spirit, who is our constant companion—instilling hope within our spirits and praying for us when we are too weary to pray. Surely, Paul wonders, How can my people Israel not immerse themselves in these great promises of God? But in the end, Paul's faith tells him that God's promises will not fail because doubt and unbelief ultimately cannot stand against God's truth and will.

God, encourage me to speak the truth as Paul does in his letter to the Romans, worrying not about how my words will be received by the world but about how closely I am sticking to your truth in Christ. Amen.

Wrestling with Abundance

For the apostle Paul, following Jesus meant cutting himself off from all he had known prior to his conversion on the road to Damascus.

As he writes in his letter to the Romans, Paul's choice caused him a great deal of pain and angst. Imagine how his family and friends responded when he joined a new faith, leaving his home to travel and face persecution for following a man they believed was betraying their faith.

Paul's choice cost him a great deal personally. He goes so far as to say he wishes he were "accursed, and cut off from Christ for the sake of my own people."

As an apostle to the Gentiles, Paul spent most of his post-conversion life as a stranger in a strange land. He was separated from his family and friends, who viewed him as a betrayer and apostate. In the lands of the Gentiles, he faced scorn and ridicule for his Jewish heritage.

Not only this, but Paul spent much of his ministry in chains and under threat of persecution, eventually being martyred for his work for the gospel.

He never could have known how his letters would become immortal, stretching around the globe for millennia, influencing generations to "know Christ, and him crucified" (1 Cor. 2:2).

Like Paul, some of us may be called to be cut off from our loved ones because of our faith in Jesus and our desire to follow him no matter the cost. In doing so, may we know that, though the road ahead is not easy, we are in good company. We should travel this path with great humility, prayerfulness, and love, with respect for what lies behind and in front of us.

God, you call each of us to places unknown. Give us patience, courage, and connection to other weary travelers, so we can continue to follow you. Amen.

Have you lived your life according to the ethos of "never enough"?

Many of us have. In some ways, it is true. We go to bed feeling there is always more we could have done with our day. There are always more chores to be done, more dishes to clean, more floors to scrub.

You may have experienced the crushing toll of "never enough" as you've attempted to create a household budget in a period of economic and financial instability.

You may have felt powerless and small in a world with such big problems: climate change, inequity, hunger, injustice, pandemic. In view of problems so insurmountable, the feeling of "never enough" is natural.

Jesus' story of the feeding of the five thousand steps into a world dominated by "never enough" and shakes our convictions to their core. For though we live in a world dominated by scarcity, we worship a God of abundance.

For this God, what is seen cannot limit what can be. With love and faith and a little sharing at the outset, a small boy's lunch of loaves and fishes fed a hillside of hungry people with much left over.

Bear in mind, many of these same people continued to struggle with hunger and stability long after they had lunch with Jesus on the hillside. God does not promise an Abundance Plan. What God does give us is enough for today, enough abundance for everyone to go on until tomorrow. The power of this story is not only the miracle but also the way it shakes our preconceived notions about how God's provision works.

God, help me see beyond a world of scarcity and trust your abundance. Amen.

Wrestling with Abundance

At the height of his ministry, Jesus travels throughout Galilee sharing the gospel of love, peace, and justice with all sorts of people. It won't be long before the crowds will turn on Jesus and shout "Crucify him!" But at this moment they are rapturous to follow Jesus and receive miracles, healing, and new life.

After he transforms a small boy's lunch into a filling meal for thousands, Jesus seeks a time of refreshment alone. He needs prayer and communion with God to continue to share with others and avoid burnout.

But very quickly after his time alone in prayer, Jesus returns to his disciples in an unexpected way. Knowing that their boat is being battered by the waves and the disciples are imperiled, Jesus allowed his compassion for his loved ones to win out over his need for self-preservation, as God's compassion always does.

He returns to his disciples in their moment of need, defying laws of nature to walk to them on top of the water.

Instead of seeing Jesus, the disciples—who are overwhelmed by fear—imagine that a ghost is coming toward them. This is relatable, isn't it? In moments of stress and fear, even a source of love and relief is often wrongly perceived. We need to break down our own walls of fear and resentment in order to see the blessings of God coming toward us, often in unexpected ways.

Jesus does not scold the disciples out of frustration and anger. After all, he has just given up his peaceful time to come to them and help them. Instead, he responds with patient and encouraging words: "Take heart, it is I; do not be afraid."

God, grant me confidence to know that you do not respond to my fear with words that would shame me. Instead, you respond first with love and compassion. Help me respond with the same love to others. Amen.

The Greatness of God's Faithfulness

AUGUST 7–13, 2023 • SHARON WILLIAMS

SCRIPTURE OVERVIEW: The strange dynamics in the history of Abraham's family continue in Genesis. This week his great-grandson Joseph is sold into slavery by his jealous brothers. God will ultimately use this for good, as we read in Psalm 105, but in Joseph's time, there clearly is significant dysfunction. Perhaps the story brings encouragement to those of us who also have challenging family dynamics. Paul emphasizes in Romans that every person is welcome to call on the name of the Lord and be saved, but it falls to us to offer them the good news. How can they believe if they never hear? In the Gospel reading, Peter learns a valuable lesson about trust. He initially shows great faith, but he falters when he allows himself to be distracted by the waves.

QUESTIONS AND SUGGESTIONS FOR REFLECTION

- Read Genesis 37:1-4, 12-28. In the face of cruelty, how do you continue to believe in God's dream of unity for us all?
- Read Psalm 105:1-6, 16-22, 45b. When has a glimpse of God absorbed your pain?
- Read Romans 10:5-15. When have you witnessed Christian violence against persons of other faiths? How does your faith compel you to proclaim God's love for all—"no exceptions"? What does this look like for you?
- Read Matthew 14:22-33. When have you struggled to trust Jesus through life's trials? How has Jesus revealed his presence and companionship anyway?

Elder in the Indiana Conference of The United Methodist Church appointed as Associate Director of Mission, Service, and Justice in the Missouri Conference.

Holding a beloved position in one's family can come at a hefty price, and the upside does not automatically outweigh the downside. Today's passage introduces the account of Jacob and his family. However, the immediate narrative focus is that Joseph's father loves him the most, and consequently his brothers are jealous of and hate Joseph. So they sell him into slavery and tell their father he is dead.

Growing up with older siblings, I witnessed countless teenage squabbles. There is nothing unusual about siblings being unkind to one another from time to time. Nor is it uncommon for younger children to be pretentious tattletales like Joseph. Indeed, I was one! The rivalries and jealousy and bad behavior are relatable, but the extreme actions are not. Thankfully it is unthinkable from my experience for the pettiness to rise to such a level of hatred or violence seen in Genesis 37. And it is hard to believe that Joseph could not restrain himself just a bit and stop needling his brothers, but he could not.

This story of misconduct is a tragic example of the worst that can happen to a family when people are made to feel unloved, and jealousy goes unchecked. It is a stunning picture of the potential for unimaginable evil in the face of so much imaginative good. It is hard to imagine a less promising beginning to "the story of the family of Jacob"—the children of Israel—but God works to make a family. God doesn't just choose Joseph or just his brothers or just his father; God chooses them all. This story reminds us that somewhere between the best and the worst, the ups and downs, the good and the bad, is an unseen work that has yet to be told.

Dear God, help us remember that you can use our lives for good no matter the loss. Amen.

At my undergraduate reunion, an alumna I had not seen since graduation said that seeing me reminded her of a song I had sung. I didn't remember singing it, but her recollection of it was persuasive and reminiscent of music's influence on my life.

Music has been a lifeline for me and has tethered me to my faith. Still, I had not considered how much music can be a sustaining force for good when it seems that life is not. My college friend and I had both experienced suffering—her battle with an autoimmune disorder and mine with infertility. It resonated that grace and gratitude can take longer to rise when life is cruel, but this memory of singing set the tone for long-awaited greetings.

As such, the triumphant tone of Psalm 105 is instructive. Life's cruelty to Joseph is not lost on the psalmist. The psalm begins and ends on a high note, bookending Jacob's family tragedy with singing, encouragement, and praise—because Joseph's rise from the prison to the palace had proved redemptive. His brothers' attempt to get rid of the family dreamer was successful for a while, but it did not kill Joseph, his dream, or the family. Their descendants sing praises to God.

Looking back, my friend and I could not ignore our disappointments with life's setbacks and missed opportunities, but this undeniably grace-filled memory of music was a bold note and an important precursor to praise. I located the track and sang along to the chorus a bit while we celebrated the unexpected grace of this R&B throwback. In that moment, all our judgments about what might have been were suspended. My heart sang as we turned down the volume on life's testing so that thanksgiving could rise to meet the present testimonies and even welcome those to come.

Lord, when life's testing would dull our senses to the familiar rhythms of grace, help us remember to keep singing. Amen.

The Greatness of God's Faithfulness   265

When I was a seminarian, I was part of a church-planting team in North Philadelphia that understood incarnational ministry as doing life with people on their terms. Before we had the language of de-colonizing the church, we demonstrated de-centering Whiteness. We prioritized immigrant, diaspora, and indigenous cultural groups in our community and in our core team. We named the church, Iglesia Del Barrio, "church of the neighborhood," and together we became residents of the church's neighborhood and served with our neighbors in improving the quality of life for families in the community.

We held many different worldviews, but we also held key values in common that brought us closer to the realness of the beloved community—the kind Paul envisioned in this passage— than any of us could have imagined. It is a community where all are welcome to receive faith in Christ and whose circle of friends is bigger than we know.

When the same Lord is Lord of all, it is hard to subscribe to values that elevate dividing walls of difference. Of course, the limitations of this were tested as we grew in faith-relationship with our team members and our neighbors. But our struggles to live this out perfectly do not make it untrue.

That season of immersion into multiethnic ministry lasted less than a decade, but it remains core to my spiritual DNA. Not everyone in that Philadelphia neighborhood wanted to hear the message of faith in Christ that we attempted to share, but we could see the devastating effects of the injustices and exclusionary practices so many from this community experienced. We knew in our hearts that we were called to proclaim the good news that the same Lord is Lord of all.

Jesus, help us to make the most of opportunities to share the gift of universal love with all who desire to experience kinship in this new family. Amen.

For many people, "blood is thicker than water" describes the depth of their family ties, often set within highly hierarchical structures that are expected to be preserved even when they promote domestic dysfunction. Long before Jesus challenged the wisdom of unchecked family loyalties and called for a new way of seeing such relationships (see Matthew 12), the story of Joseph and the cost of family jealousy highlighted some of the faulty assumptions that are instilled in families.

Joseph was among the younger siblings of his family and was a devoted helper. He is described not only as responsible for tending his family's flocks but also as a special assistant to his father, Jacob. Studies of family caregiving have contributed much to the conversation about how helpers in families can be empowered to explore healthier ways of establishing support for themselves while taking on caregiving responsibilities, especially as adult caregivers to aging or elderly parents. But the reality is that differentiating oneself for the sake of one's self-care while also balancing the bonds of kinship is difficult.

I became a helper and key caregiver to my family for a season of my adult life. As a younger sibling who often felt like an outsider amongst siblings, despite my benefiting from parental preference, I accepted this role readily. I had something to prove, but so did God—in preparing me for pastoral ministry. Serving my family through the disappointing experiences of betrayals inspired a journey outward that led me, as it had led Joseph, to unexpected places of grace and favor. Thankfully, my departure from the familial nest was not as harmful a push out as Joseph's tragic experience. Still, it was the Spirit's way of teaching me that sometimes the only way to grow is to go.

Lord, give us wisdom not only to see but to do something about the harmful effects of assumptions and roles that keep us from growing. Amen.

I received one of the biggest ministry lessons of my life when my mother died. Arriving at her hospice bedside just a few hours before our final goodbyes, I quickly realized I needed to push pause on my own grief while the needs of executing my mom's will, arranging funeral services, caring for grief-stricken family, and celebrating her life took precedence. I'd spent almost two decades perfecting my bedside manner as a pastor and accompanying families in their bereavement journeys, but nothing but prayer could prepare me to sit on that front pew.

Death is disruptive even when it is expected. Skilled pastors anticipate grief's stages in other people, but when the grief is your own, it is painfully unpredictable. When Jesus "went up the mountain by himself to pray," he'd already tried once. He'd been given the news of John the Baptist's death and burial, and this first attempt, presumably intended for his time to mourn, was unsuccessful because of his compassion for the crowd (see Matthew 14:12-13).

As life-giving as ministry is, it is rarely convenient. In times of crisis, it is common for ministers and caregivers to go to great lengths to extend help and healing to others—sometimes at great expense to themselves. The crowd numbered more than five thousand and needed help. Jesus fed them, dismissed them, and even sent the disciples on ahead to meet up with Jesus a little later so he could finally retire for prayer.

What a relief to know that our sacrifices made on others' behalf will be rewarded! Deferring his own care to care for others might have caused Jesus a difficult delay, but the care he needed was ultimately not denied.

Help us, Lord, to trust that the power and provision of prayer are accessible and enough in our times of crisis. Amen.

Some storms in life are predictable, but many are not—failing health, global threats, relational discord, and dysfunctional leadership. I broke off an engagement many years ago because I was unwilling to risk the hazards of a cross-racial marriage. The winds of chaos from constant communication clashes and disconnects drawn from differing worldviews were telltale signs. I could not imagine navigating these difficulties well, so I got out before we got in, and I was grateful.

Sidestepping storms is one thing, but weathering them is another. Not every approaching storm can (or even should) be avoided. Far from the safety of the shore they had left at Jesus' behest, the disciples are in a storm they could not avoid and did not predict. They are way off course. When it looks like they will not make it through the storm, Jesus shows up walking on the water toward them. Exhausted and afraid, the disciples' disorientation and doubt come through in distressing cries. They mistake Jesus for a ghost until his words comfort them, "Take heart, it is I; do not be afraid."

Fear was reasonable; Jesus does not keep the disciples from the storm. But he does not leave them alone in it either. Faith rises when Jesus is present. Just as Jesus stepped into the storm with the disciples, we can count on Jesus to be with us through our difficulties—enabling us to face our fear with faith. We are not able to control the storms of life, but neither do we need to get caught up in fearing them. Christ's presence empowers us to turn up the volume of our faith and turn down the volume of our fear. In this way, we imitate Jesus as Peter does later in the text, by practicing being released from fear so that we begin to trust God in faith.

Lord, when we go through stormy situations in life, help us to de-center our fear and center our faith on you. Amen.

The Greatness of God's Faithfulness

Paul's call for preachers culminates in the passage from Isaiah, "How beautiful are the feet of those who bring good news!" Feet represented the effort to find new people and spread the good news. One preacher I know sees it this way: Our future is in our metaphorical feet. We must share with our words and our actions the message, "Everyone who calls upon the name of the Lord shall be saved." But the reality is that in our increasingly post-Christian and polarized society, the opportunity for faith to be made alive with each risk-taking step is difficult. Yet the hope I see resonates from a childhood lesson.

As a young girl, I loved shoe-shopping with my mom. Something about getting my feet measured, walking around in new shoes to break them in, and seeing my mother's smile when the size fit just right was good news. Aside from lessons about investing in quality brands, I was taught to trust that the best shoes for me were the ones that fit. And I've got good-looking feet to show for it, mostly due to "hard-wired" genetics but also because of valuing my feet and the shoes that I put them in.

When I connect the dots to my mother's teaching and the stories she and my auntie shared about the miles they walked to school in hand-me-down shoes—often in disrepair, worn to the soles giving way—I get it. Some might have thought I was just pridefully showing my new shoes. But the real message from my mother was about the livable wages my parents were able to earn, something withheld from their mothers who were both maids. I can imagine the privilege of a mother's love and the practical way she was empowered to share the good news with her daughter. With each memory, I celebrate my mom's message and God's promise of a future that she knew even then was in my feet.

Jesus, give us the confidence to carry a message of good news to those who might listen and receive it. Amen.

God's Mercy and Forgiveness

AUGUST 14–20, 2023 • R. SIDWELL MOKGOTHU

SCRIPTURE OVERVIEW: Joseph has risen to a high position in Egypt, and now his brothers come searching for food in a time of famine. He reveals his true identity and reinterprets their evil intentions as being part of God's plan. Sometimes we too are granted perspective to see God's working in difficult times. The psalmist rejoices when God's people are living in unity, as Joseph and his brothers were after their reunion. In Romans, Paul declares that his people are not rejected by the merciful God, for God's promises are unchanging. In Matthew, Jesus teaches that God looks on the inside, not the outside. Thus, what you take into your body is less important than what comes from your heart, and God does not favor one ethnic group over another.

QUESTIONS AND SUGGESTIONS FOR REFLECTION
- Read Genesis 45:1-15. When have you experienced God's grace in forgiving or being forgiven? How were those needing forgiveness still held responsible for their actions?
- Read Psalm 133. How has God called you to live in unity with those different from you? How do you receive God's abundant blessing through such unity?
- Read Romans 11:1-2a, 29-32. How does the eternal mercy of God's gifts and callings sustain you when it seems like God has rejected God's people?
- Read Matthew 15:10-28. When have you, like the Canaanite woman, felt like you had to insist that Jesus come closer? How did your faith change or grow from this experience?

———————

District Bishop of the Methodist Church of Southern Africa—Pretoria.

Many criminal justice systems of the world have been transformed from using punitive prisons to preferring a correctional and rehabilitative approach. Whereas the penal system is retributive in nature, the correctional is restorative and is based on the belief that offenders have the intrinsic human capacity to change. Restorative justice creates safe space and opportunities for perpetrators to seek mutual healing. In Africa forgiveness is based on the philosophy and spirituality of *Ubuntu*. Ubuntu (meaning "humanness") is about human beings appreciating the image of God in one another.

Today's text describes restorative justice happening in the Egyptian palace where Joseph is meeting with his brothers. This victim of human trafficking is meeting with the brothers who sold him to strangers who were passing through their land. Now Joseph is in a position of authority and privilege as chief of staff in Pharaoh's palace, and they are powerless beggars in search of food. Joseph could take this opportunity to settle scores and seek revenge. His brothers are vulnerable, fragile, and at his mercy. He instead takes the moral high ground and applies restorative justice that leads to forgiveness and reconciliation.

Christians are beneficiaries and custodians of forgiveness and reconciliation. The Lord Jesus Christ taught in many ways the importance and essence of forgiveness, setting as a virtue the high standard of forgiving enemies seventy-seven times (see Matthew 18:21-22). Christ modeled this forgiveness and reconciliation on the cross of Calvary while the perpetrators were torturing and killing him: "Father, forgive them; for they do not know what they are doing" (Luke 23:34).

Lord Jesus, may the power of your spirit restore us and our adversaries to lasting forgiveness, reconciliation, and healing. Amen.

Many artists collect leftover or discarded materials like glass, cowhide, bones, and scrap metals to make their art. They take materials ordinarily treated as waste to create something new and beautiful. They restore beauty to what is thought to be unworthy.

A remnant is a small group of people who, like the leftovers that become beautiful artifacts, are preserved to survive a destructive crisis and form the basis for rebuilding. They are a small fragment that escapes catastrophe. Noah and his family were taken into the ark as God's loyal remnant to save the world. Like a tiny mustard seed, the remnant is small but can grow large. They are a group of people left to serve, please, and honor God.

This is what the brothers of Joseph are, the family that bears the promise given to Abraham (see Genesis 12:2-3). Joseph forgives and puts aside their historical differences, hurts, and grudges. He instructs them to return home to pick up their father, Jacob, and the reason is clear: "God sent me before you to preserve for you a remnant on earth, and to keep alive for you many survivors." There are seven long years of severe famine that are coming when many are going to die. The only hope is in migrating to Egypt, which has gathered and stored adequate reserves of food during the previous seven years of plenty.

The world is in a moral crisis where evil manifests itself in almost every sector of society. The good news is that God is at work to save and preserve remnants for salvation. The church is a group of those called out to spread the redemptive love of God.

O God, we pray for a remnant church saved and preserved for the salvation of your creation. Amen.

We are living in a divided, fragmented, and broken world. The divisions are sometimes between private individuals—siblings, colleagues, family—and sometimes public and corporate groups—communities and nations. The divisions may be personal, tribal, racial, or national. Some are deeply complex with inter-generational pain and trauma. Paul observed how conflicts and divisions in the Corinthian church were like a cancer eating the very soul of the congregation.

Today's reading is a short, prayerful song for unity. The psalmist observed that this harmony is a good and right thing: "How very good and pleasant it is when kindred live together." Unity is a blessing like the precious anointing oil running down the beard of Aaron.

Unity is not a luxury but a gospel imperative that we as the church and followers of Christ must live, preach, and promote. This oneness is one of the paramount values that Jesus prayed: "That they may all be one . . . so that the world may believe you have sent me" (John 17:21). Living together is not just convenient tolerance and political correctness. It is authentic relationship based on living together and acceptance of the "other." Like justice, peace, and reconciliation, unity is hard yet necessary work. Christian unity is more than just reuniting two siblings. It is for the human kindred and the *oikoumene*—the household of God that is the whole of creation.

Unity is at the heart of the African concept of community. An African proverb counsels: "If you want to walk quickly, walk alone. If you want to walk far, walk together." The inclusiveness of community is about more than celebrating those who are here. It is about being conscious of missing "little ones of God"—the poor, the vulnerable and marginalized.

Holy Trinity, be our sacred model of unity. Amen.

Manufacturing and factory shops have to reject their products that do not meet quality standards. These goods are inspected to identify faults and flaws. Those who are well trained in quality control can pick up even the minutest of mistakes. If for example the products are clothes, the defects could be poor stitching or the wrong color dye. Manufacturers and retailers will not want to sacrifice their reputation by offering low-quality merchandise. They get rid of the goods by destroying them or selling them as seconds.

Paul writes to the Roman congregation to reflect on the status of Israel as God's people, now that Israel has rejected God's teachings. Israel has, by any possible spiritual standards, failed the examination. Israel has disobeyed God and, like the Prodigal Son, is "no longer worthy" to be called God's nation. It is against this backdrop that Paul asks, "Has God rejected his people?" He answers, "By no means. . . . God has not rejected his people whom he foreknew." This is the elect nation that God appointed as a model of God's plan of salvation. God is the Creator, not a manufacturer. Accepting flawed merchandise reflects poorly on a manufacturer. But that is not the relationship God has with creation. God's goodness is shown in love, steadfastness, forgiveness, and redemption.

Are we not ourselves like Israel? Have we not constantly failed to live up to God's expectations of what it means to be God's people and Christ's disciples as Christians? We have, through our inequities, disobeyed God's law and are worthy only of rejection. Yet God has chosen not to disqualify and reject us. We are exhibits of God's forgiveness.

Loving God, thank you for the gift of your forgiveness. Amen.

The scriptures are full of instances where Jesus clashed publicly with the Pharisees. The Pharisees were an important cohort of the Jewish religio-legal system who emphasized the importance of rules and rituals concerning purification and defilement for all Jews, not just the priests.

As important as the law was in guiding the nation, Jesus said that the Pharisees had become rigid and legalistic. Saul was a prominent example of this pharisaic passion. He was a genuine, circumcised Hebrew of Hebrews (see Philippians 3:5) but was concerned more with the outward appearance than the spirit of the law. Jesus criticized Pharisees like Saul for ignoring spiritual matters of justice and mercy.

Today's biblical text is one of those instances where Jesus has called the crowds to teach against and repudiate rigidity regarding non-Kosher food. The disciples informed him about how offended the Pharisees were by his teachings. Jesus says it is not what goes into the mouth—the food we eat—but what comes out of the mouth—what we believe and say—that can make us unfit to participate in communal worship (the meaning of *defile* in this context). Jesus shifts the focus to what comes from the heart.

Today there are many Christians who are obsessed with matters of rigid religion. We are experts of our church's polity and are ready to defend that with our lives, yet we are less concerned with discipleship and spiritual formation. Jesus calls us to deepen our faith and spirituality beyond the legalism that has brought much division and hurt to our churches.

Lord Jesus, fill our hearts and mouths with life-giving words. Amen.

Some Christians who gather for Holy Communion regularly confess with the liturgical words of the Anglican Prayer of Humble Access: "We are not worthy so much as to gather up the crumbs under your table; but you are the same Lord whose character is always to have mercy." The gathered believers acknowledge their sinfulness and unworthiness. This prayer is said like a sacramental password of humility that grants the unmerited community of faith permission to partake of this holy mystery. The key to their participation lies in the character of the Lord Jesus Christ, who is the host of this sacrament.

It is that mercy that Paul taught the church in Rome. No one merits God's love, but all receive it. God's mercy is the forgiveness that saves us from the wrath—the anger and deserved punishment from God. It is the character of mercy that changes our status from sinners to saints. We have fallen but keep receiving forgiveness.

We are fallen and sinful creatures. Yet God extends mercy to us. The scriptures tell us time and again that God's mercy endures forever. God's mercy does not expire but is forever available to all. This mercy is the steadfast and limitless saving love of God that is available to eternity. Even generations yet to be born have that mercy paid forward for them. They are shareholders of this great mysterious gift.

Merciful God, may your enduring mercy be upon leaders of governments, organizations, and all who have the power to transform and heal this world. Amen.

God's Mercy and Forgiveness

Today's text presents Jesus in an unfamiliar area of Gentiles where he meets with a local Canaanite woman. The woman addresses Jesus as Lord and Son of David, and she asks for help for her daughter who is tormented by a demon. Jesus and the disciples respond in an uncharacteristically prejudicial and discriminatory way. Jesus first ignores her and later compares her to a dog not worthy of his help. The woman demonstrates resilient faith and disarms Christ with soft power by kneeling and persistently asking for help.

Those of us who have experienced racial discrimination have struggled with Christ's attitude in this conversation. We have been treated as less than human by people who have failed to see the image of God in us. Jesus' intention is not clear. Is this an intersection of ethnicity and patriarchy? If so, why is this response so different from the one to the Samaritan woman at the well? A comforting suggestion is that Jesus was merely testing the woman.

The story of the Canaanite woman testifies to the power of resilient faith against discrimination. Those who stand against injustice and discrimination anywhere in the world can share how their faith has carried them through and brought them freedom and healing. Whatever the answers to the speculations, Jesus finally responds in a way that we have come to know as Christlike: "Woman, great is your faith! Let it be done for you as you wish." We also hear that her daughter was instantly healed.

Liberator Christ, we ask for the gift of resilient faith against whatever odds people over the world face. Amen.

Claim God's Deliverance

AUGUST 21–27, 2023 • MARTIN WILES

SCRIPTURE OVERVIEW: Exodus now introduces a painful turn in the story of God's people. The Israelites are forced into slavery; yet amid this dark time, a baby boy, Moses, is born. God has already begun the story of their deliverance. The psalmist recognizes that the Israelites would be overwhelmed and swept away without the help of the Maker of heaven and earth. Paul gives the Romans two specific instructions: First, they should be changed so that they follow God's ways, not the world's. Second, they must understand that they all need one another. Each child of God has a part to play in the overall body of Christ. In a famous passage in Matthew, Peter makes the basic Christian confession: Jesus is the Messiah, the Christ, the Son of God.

QUESTIONS AND SUGGESTIONS FOR REFLECTION

- Read Exodus 1:8–2:10. How can you serve in a priestly role?
- Read Psalm 124. Reflect on the many ways God has blessed you and your community. Consider writing your own song of ascent.
- Read Romans 12:1-8. What part of yourself are you holding back from God? How can you bring your whole self to your faith?
- Read Matthew 16:13-20. Why is it important to fully understand Christ's identity before witnessing to Christ's mission?

Pastor of Buffalo Baptist Church, McCormick, SC; managing editor for *Christian Devotions*; senior editor for *Inspire a Fire;* author of six books; a loved child of God.

Believers the world over experience oppression of one sort or another. Where Christianity is illegal, they risk imprisonment or death. Even in countries that legally protect the free exercise of religion, oppression still can and does take place. It comes through peer pressure, emotional attacks, and physical assaults.

In this passage, fear drove the oppression. A new king to whom Joseph meant nothing ascended to the throne of Egypt. Perhaps this new king knew nothing of Joseph's story, or maybe he did know the account but felt no personal connection to Joseph. Either way, he feared that Joseph's descendants would join with Egypt's enemies and rise up against the Egyptians.

Fear led the king to enslave the Israelites. But he went even further. He issued a murderous edict to the Hebrew midwives to kill all the male babies. When they disobeyed, he commanded that all male babies were to be thrown into the river.

Nowhere does the Bible instruct us to intentionally do things that would make others fear and hate us. We should carry a message of love and forgiveness. Yet our message must denounce sin in all its forms, and this part of our message will naturally draw persecution.

Jesus' short ministry brought various types of persecution: emotional, spiritual, and physical. Ours may too. Jesus said all who choose to follow him will be persecuted, as he was. Oppression for our faith isn't enjoyable, but it identifies us with Jesus. During times of oppression, God promises to walk beside us and give us the strength to endure. As God used the Hebrew midwives to deliver Moses, so God will deliver us from those who attack us because of our faith.

Dear God, help me trust in you when I am oppressed for my faith. Amen.

God had a purpose for Moses and quite famously told him exactly what it was. Long before Moses had his encounter with God at the Burning Bush, however, God had a purpose and a calling for Moses' mother and sister that was less dramatic and direct but was every bit as important to God's plan to liberate the Hebrew people from slavery in Egypt. Instead of telling Moses' mother with words what to do, God directed her with her love for her son.

When Moses was born, God's people had toiled in slavery for four hundred years, but recently the situation had gotten even worse when the king ordered the murder of all the Hebrew baby boys. Moses' mother loved her son and refused to follow that horrific law. When she could no longer hide him, she made a boat from a papyrus basket, put him in the Nile, and bet correctly that the Egyptian women who would find a baby wouldn't obey the law either. Through God's miraculous direction and the machinations of Moses' mother and sister, Moses ended up back at home, and Pharaoh paid Moses' mother to raise the future liberator of the Hebrew people.

God used the courageous acts of Moses' mother and sister to begin delivering the Hebrew people from slavery. They played out their purpose so Moses could later fulfill his. Although evil surrounded them, with God's guidance they resisted evil and overcame it.

Maybe our call isn't as clear or miraculous as Moses', but surely, we can do God's will—as did Moses' mother and sister and even the daughters of Pharaoh—by listening to our hearts and acting out of love. When we do, God will show us the path forward.

When your purpose seems obscured from my eyes, Lord, open them so that I see your plan. Amen.

Claim God's Deliverance

Which side we're on matters. Who can forget physical education classes where team captains selected teammates for a game? They wanted peers who were quick, agile, strong, and popular. Those who didn't fit those categories knew they would be among the last to be picked.

Among the many pagan gods available, David chose the one true God for his team. Scholars believe David's defeat of the Philistines provides the background for this psalm (see 2 Samuel 5:17-25).

After the people anointed David as king of all Israel, the Philistines mobilized their forces to battle Israel. To his credit, David consulted the Lord and asked if he should fight them. God told him to proceed. David obeyed and experienced victory—being careful to attribute his success to God. He named the place of his victory Baal-perazim, which means "the Lord who bursts through."

But the Philistines did not forget their defeat and humiliation. Later, they mustered their forces again. As before, David consulted the Lord. This time the Lord told him not to attack them head-on but from behind. The sound of marching feet in the balsam trees would be David's sign that the Lord marched before him. David listened, heard, moved ahead, and once again soundly defeated his enemies.

Sometimes, the odds seem stacked against us—whether because of a spiritual battle or unpleasant circumstances not of our own making. But a way out always exists because God will not leave or forsake us when the trials of life attack us from all sides. God marches ahead of us and will lead us to victory. God showed David the way to triumph and will do the same for us.

Undefeatable God, I thank you that no forces of evil or untoward circumstances of life can defeat me. Amen.

The word *sacrifice* normally has negative connotations. As a verb, sacrificing entails giving something up. If I want to lose weight, I must give up some unhealthy foods I enjoy.

As a noun, a *sacrifice* is a thing. The Old Testament is filled with examples of sacrifices—from animals to grain offerings. In pagan ceremonies, the sacrifice could be a person.

Paul changes the idea of a sacrifice by telling us we are living sacrifices. Under the old sacrificial system, sacrifices didn't live but were slain on an altar. Believers, however, are living sacrifices. We sacrifice (verb) ourselves by giving ourselves to our heavenly Father through a faith relationship with Jesus Christ. Thereafter, we become a living sacrifice (noun) for God. We put ourselves on the altar but then get up and do what a sacrifice is designed to do.

Paul even tells us how to be a living sacrifice through a two-step process: We avoid conforming to the world, and we renew or transform our minds daily.

The "world" is not the physical planet but rather the system of thoughts and actions that run contrary to God's principles and commands. If we conform to the world, we'll find ourselves disobeying God. We win our spiritual battles—we are transformed—by renewing our minds, which means changing how we think. Since actions follow thoughts, we must think about those things that are pure, honest, true, just, and good. When we follow Paul's directives, we will experience spiritual victory.

Merciful God, I ask for spiritual victories over sinful thoughts and actions. Amen.

Self-esteem is a hot topic. Some have too much of it, thinking more of themselves than they should, which leads to a prideful attitude. But others do not have enough self-esteem. Depression can follow . . . even suicide. Low self-esteem affects relationships, employment, and finances.

Paul tells us not to think we are better than we are but rather to evaluate ourselves honestly. A good example of a person who lived hundreds of years before Paul but could have used Paul's advice was King Nebuchadnezzar of Babylon. Legend says he built the Hanging Gardens of Babylon, one of the Seven Wonders of the Ancient World. For forty-three years, he reigned, but pride over his accomplishments led to his downfall. The prophet Daniel delivered God's sentence on Nebuchadnezzar: He would live with the wild animals until he recognized God as sovereign over all kingdoms. To Nebuchadnezzar's credit, he finally did.

Instead of thinking too much of ourselves, Paul tells us to measure ourselves by the faith God gives us. Apart from Christ, we can do nothing, but we can do all things through Christ—and only through him. In our own power, we will make a mess every time. In our natural state, we are sinners in need of a savior; we are not people who can do enough good for God to accept us on our merit.

As a part of the church—Christ's body—we assume our positions according to where Christ places us. Regardless of how God gifts us, none of us has any reason to boast . . . to let pride ruin us . . . to have elevated self-esteem. Christ is responsible for everything we have and are. Through prayer and the study of God's word, we can discover our place and our gifts. And whatever we accomplish by using our gifts, we should give all the honor and glory to God, the giver of our gifts.

Holy God, thank you for who I am in a relationship with you. Amen.

Christ's body, the church, has many parts, all arranged according to God's wisdom. Through the Spirit, God gives believers diverse gifts for the work of the kingdom. Even when we possess the same gifts, we use them differently because we have different personalities and circumstances.

No scripture passage—this one included—contains all the spiritual gifts. However, the ones Paul mentions hold immense importance for God's people.

The gift of *prophecy* contains two elements. As seen in the Old and New Testaments, prophets sometimes predicted future events. In fact, a prophet's prediction coming true was the mark of a true prophet. The other element entailed explaining God's revelation.

Serving, encouraging, and *showing kindness* define themselves and are probably gifts all believers have, whether or not they use them. Jesus demonstrated by washing his disciples' feet and in many other ways that he wants us to serve others. Every person we meet needs encouragement, and we can always find a way to do kind acts for others.

If we do not have the gift of *leading*, we will find out soon enough when we are placed in a leadership position. And *giving* is encouraged throughout the Bible by example and direct instruction. As God has given to us, we need to give back to God and others. Only by doing so can we enjoy life to the fullest and carry out God's will for our lives.

Almighty God, give me opportunities to use my gifts to serve you. Amen.

Those who are in bondage long for deliverance. Our bondage can be emotional, relational, physical, or spiritual.

Jesus once asked his disciples who people said he was. Their answers included John the Baptist, Elijah, or one of the other prophets. Impetuous Peter said, "You are the Messiah, the Son of the living God." Jesus commended Peter for his answer.

Jesus then told Peter that upon that rock he will build his church. Christians have debated the meaning of *rock*, proposing that it could refer to Jesus' work on the cross, Peter as the first great leader of the church in Jerusalem, or Peter's confession of faith. Regardless of our answer, we must conclude the same as Peter did to enter a relationship with Christ.

The keys to the kingdom of heaven are issued to those who agree with Peter's conclusion. But what are the keys? Believers have debated this also. Some say they represent believers' authority to carry out church discipline, legislation, and administration. Later interpretations of what Jesus meant by "keys" relate to Christians' authority to offer the forgiveness of sin that Jesus himself offers—thereby bringing people into the kingdom of heaven. Based on the Great Commission that Jesus later gave to all believers—and based upon what Jesus did on the cross—we have the privilege of offering forgiveness to others.

God gives us the wonderful opportunity of telling others how they can experience deliverance from spiritual bondage that then leads to being free indeed.

Give me the courage, O God, to announce your deliverance to all people. Amen.

Trust in Action

AUGUST 28–SEPTEMBER 3, 2023 • CATHERINE KELSEY

SCRIPTURE OVERVIEW: Moses has fled Egypt and is living in the desert, where God calls him to return and free the Israelites. Moses resists, but God does not relent. In many of the Psalms, the psalmist reviews God's record of faithfulness. Psalm 105 is no different and highlights the calling of Moses. In Romans, Paul addresses practical ethical concerns. How should we treat those who treat us poorly? We should never repay evil for evil, but instead should bless those who harm us. This goes against our natural instincts, yet the gospel is countercultural and calls us to a higher standard. In Matthew, Peter has just had a tremendous moment in declaring his faith in Christ. Now he stumbles in failing to understand that Jesus' path to glory will pass through suffering.

QUESTIONS AND SUGGESTIONS FOR REFLECTION

- Read Exodus 3:1-15. What sacred encounter might have been your burning bush? How did you know God's presence was with you in the encounter?
- Read Psalm 105:1-6, 23-26, 45b. How does obedience to God shape your life? Recall an instance where your obedience to God's call or teachings made a difference.
- Read Romans 12:9-21. When has working toward a common goal helped you better love your family, friends, or community?
- Read Matthew 16:21-28. When have you had to trust God and accept that you "have no idea how God works"? How did your trust help you through the situation?

Dean of the Chapel and Spiritual Formation and faculty member of Iliff School of Theology in Denver, CO; elder in The United Methodist Church; teaches Methodist history, doctrine, and polity.

When Moses took his flock beyond the wilderness and came to Horeb, the mountain of God, he had come to a location between two places where people have been known to meet God—the wilderness on one side and the mountain on the other. He was not likely to be in that place by accident. In a season of uncertainty and lament, Moses brought himself into a place of encounter and then paid attention. He might have been able to hear the voice in some other place. But here every fiber of his being had to be alert. Here he would see and hear. By putting himself in that place, he trusted that Someone would give him direction.

At first, Moses said only three words: "Here I am." There was trust in those words. Without knowing what could possibly come next or who was calling his name, he looked and listened. And he heard three important things: First, the one who spoke was known to his ancestors. Second, the one who spoke was paying attention to the lament of Moses' enslaved kin. Third, the one who spoke was sending Moses to bring the people out of enslavement.

It is easy to think that this story is a one-time event about a singular hero. Could it also be a description of where we put ourselves each day as we pray? Our prayer becomes a place of encounter, so all our senses are attentive. Then, like Moses, we listen and hear: First, that the One who speaks to us is the God of our ancestor Jesus Christ. Second, that the One who speaks is paying attention to the lament of our earthly kin. Third, that the One who speaks has something for us to do today in response.

Here I am, Holy One. You have my attention because I trust you. Help me to trust you even more. Amen.

These verses are a major turning point in Matthew's account of Jesus. They are sandwiched between two statements that Jesus is in fact the Messiah. Just before it, his disciples say out loud, "You are the Messiah, the Son of the living God" (Matt. 16:13-20). And just after, Peter, James, and John witness the Transfiguration of Jesus and hear a divine voice say, "This is my Son, the Beloved; with him I am well pleased; listen to him!" (Matt. 17:1-8). In these two acknowledgments, heaven and earth agree.

But what it means to be the Messiah is so unexpected that it might be missed if it were not surrounded by those acclamations. Jesus the Messiah, Jesus the Christ, must go to Jerusalem, suffer, be killed, and be raised on the third day. The way God is going to do the saving is definitively not the way humans would do it. Just ask any Caesar, president, or CEO. This is a different use of power.

We know what follows. We know Jesus was right and Peter was wrong about how the power was going to work. Yet just like Peter, our minds slide easily to human ways. Our trusting grasp of divine ways loosens, and our choices begin to look less and less consistent with the reign of God and more and more like the reign of the cultures we live in and cherish. But keep your eyes on Peter, and trust that Jesus loves you just as completely as he loved Peter. Even after rebuking Peter, Jesus invites him to the mountaintop. The divine way of using power consistently serves holy love.

Here I am, Saving God. You have my attention because I trust you. Help me trust you more, especially when you confound my expectations. Amen.

Jesus says, "If any want to become my followers, let them deny themselves and take up their cross and follow me." It is easy to minimize or trivialize this invitation, as if a cross were a burden we might carry for a while. The only time persons carried their cross in the Roman Empire was on the way to their execution. The condemned person had a few hours left to live at that point. Cross-carrying put one into liminal time between life and death, heaven and earth.

Jesus is explicit that a change will occur: "Those who lose their life for my sake will find it." We could get sidetracked pondering what life we might lose and what life we might find. But Jesus' declaration invites us to think about something else instead: *What does it mean to trust Jesus?*

Does it mean trusting enough to let go of what we know, our lives as they are, in order to be "found" in a different kind of life? Moses, taking his flock beyond the wilderness to Mt. Horeb, found himself in a place where his life as a shepherd ended and his life as a prophet began. Where do we go to lose and then to find our lives? We go to prayer.

Prayer can put us in a place where we practice trusting Jesus. Not just trusting that what we ask for will be granted, but also trusting that the One who invites us to lose our lives for his sake will find our lives for us. Our attentive, listening time in prayer is practice for the bigger moments of losing and finding. Those moments will surprise us just as surely as Jesus' death and resurrection surprised the first disciples.

Here I am, God who resurrects. You have my attention because I trust you. Help me trust you in the loss of my familiar life so that I am ready to be found in yours. Amen.

Moses has placed himself at the edge of a wilderness that was also the edge of the holy mountain—both places where one might meet God. But that doesn't mean that Moses is trusting God completely. As he receives a divine task ("I will send you to Pharaoh") he tries twice to get some leverage with God, first a sign and then a name. A sign would show the Hebrews that Moses and his God could be trusted because of God's power. A name would allow Moses to summon God when needed. But God does not give in to Moses' lack of trust.

The sign "that it is I who sent you" will appear after the Hebrews have left Egypt, not before! Having first trusted that God was leading them through Moses, they will look back from their arrival at Mt. Horeb and see that God had, in fact, been leading.

Not wanting to argue that this sign wouldn't help him get people to follow him, Moses asks for God's name. Surely, he expects a concrete name like El Shaddai, "God of the mountain," a name that would locate and characterize who this is. Instead, the name doesn't fit with how we think about past, present, and future: "I AM WHO I AM" but also "I AM WHAT I AM" and also "I WILL BE WHAT I WILL BE." Moses learns no more than he could already say: "The God of your ancestors . . . has sent me to you." Moses must decide whether to do what he is charged to do.

In our prayer time, we can notice when thoughts and desires arise that are like those of Moses. When we notice, we can choose to ask for greater trust and call on the name of the One who sees and responds.

Here I am, God-who-won't-be-pinned-down. You have my attention because I trust you. In this moment, help me to trust you more. Amen.

In today's reading, it sounds as though the apostle Paul is set-ting high expectations for what members of the body of Christ should strive to do daily as we live our faith. But back in 12:1 Paul set the context for those expectations. He said that "the mer-cies of God" make it possible to love genuinely, hate evil, and hold fast to good. Therefore, what appears to be a list of things we must accomplish on our own turns out not to be that at all. Rather, we can expect these results to emerge as we trust God to work in us.

This trust in God's mercies is essential. Notice Paul's injunc-tion to "let" love be genuine. We cooperate with God's mercies; we let God use us. This also suggests we can block God from using us.

Perhaps Paul listed these specific actions because he knew that they are what members of the body of Christ frequently block. *Love. Hold fast. Show honor. Be enthusiastic. Be on fire. Rejoice. Be patient. Persevere. Contribute. Extend hospitality.* When these actions are not showing up in our day-to-day lives, we can try to fix the problem ourselves. Or we can ponder the possibility that they are getting blocked, perhaps by our unstated fears. We know that the antidote to fear is reaching out to trust again the mercies of God. Our trust lets God do all these things in us and through us. So we begin again by asking for greater trust, espe-cially when trusting is hard.

Here I am, God of mercy. You have my attention because I trust you. Please address my fear. Help me in everyday moments to trust you more. Amen.

Bless those who persecute you." The Common English Bible translation says, "those who harass you." In our day-to-day lives we might recognize feeling harassed. Blessing others while being harassed by them is not easy, and the apostle Paul knew it. He wrote more than one letter to faith communities that were not treating each other well. Even when living as members of the one body of Christ, we have trouble with each other. Harassment happens. In this passage, Paul suggests that we should do the opposite of our first inclination when relations are toxic. Do not repay evil for evil. Try humility. Do not be overcome by evil, but overcome evil with good. Turn to God and seek God's response.

When we are in the midst of the stress of harassment, and particularly when we are facing evil, our prayer can make space for God to move us beyond our first inclination. This is especially true if we are listening for how the Holy Spirit directs our attention to new possibilities.

Fights happen within the faith community. Perhaps they can become times to practice turning to prayer and discovering the capacity to bless under stress. Perhaps the practice can prepare us to bless during more difficult fights in more public times and places. Perhaps, once we have experienced good overcoming evil in our smaller circle of faith, we can be bold to trust God to use good to overcome global evil. That kind of active trust takes practice.

Here I am, God who blesses. You have my attention because I trust you. I cannot imagine how good can overcome evil. Help me imagine what you know is possible. And use me to help it become reality. Amen.

Trust in Action   293

Sunday is for joy! This passage tells us to praise God by remembering all the things God has done. The psalm recalls specific stories in detail so that their memory continues to evoke joy: the covenant with Abraham, delivery from famine, escape from bondage in Egypt. Remembering and celebrating what God has done strengthens our trust and gives us courage. So we finish this week by pausing to remember in prayer specific events.

Our immediate ancestors also found themselves in confusing and stressful times. Peoples were divided against peoples. Leaders did not seem up to the task. The threat of the end of the world as we know it was held in human hands. But God remained faithful through wars and famine and smaller evils, guiding people to overcome evil with good in unexpected ways. Give thanks for God's faithfulness to your ancestors.

Remember how God chose to come in person into human life. Tell in your own words the story that you love the most about Jesus. Recall what his willingness to take up his cross means to you. Feel again the amazement that his death was not the end of the story. Marvel that the power of death is broken. Give thanks for the faithfulness of Jesus Christ.

Finally, remember your day yesterday. Beginning with waking up, where and how was the Holy Spirit giving you life? Can you recognize how the Spirit was present in the interactions you had? Where were the small signs that the Holy Spirit is actively transforming your community? Give thanks for the ever-present faithfulness of the Holy Spirit.

Here I am, Holy Trinity. You have my attention because I trust you. Thank you for helping me remember how trustworthy you are. Thank you for moving my trust into active joy! Amen.

The Embodiment of Faith

SEPTEMBER 4–10, 2023 • LEE CATOE

SCRIPTURE OVERVIEW: We move forward in the story of Moses to the climax in Egypt, the tenth plague. God tells the Israelites to prepare for the terrible night to come and establishes the feast of Passover. It is to be an eternal reminder of what God has done for the people. The psalmist praises God for faithfulness and victory, including overthrowing those who would oppress them. Egypt is not mentioned specifically, yet the Passover represents just such a situation. Paul echoes Jesus in summarizing much of the Law in one simple commandment: Love your neighbor as yourself. Jesus provides practical teaching on handling disagreements. Our first responsibility is to go to the other party privately and then include others only as necessary. Gossip and social media are not the ways to handle our disputes.

QUESTIONS AND SUGGESTIONS FOR REFLECTION

- Read Exodus 12:1-14. How has the story of Passover shaped your faith?
- Read Psalm 149. How has God called you to seek freedom from oppression for yourself or others through praise and through action?
- Read Romans 13:8-14. What does it mean to consider love a driving force rather than a warm feeling? How does this understanding change the way you act toward yourself and your neighbors?
- Read Matthew 18:15-20. When have you participated in or witnessed true reconciliation? How did you see compassion at work?

Ordained minister in the Presbyterian Church (USA) and editor of *Unbound*, a digital publishing platform that speaks to the intersections of faith and justice; co-host of the webcast *Just Talk Live: A Faith and Justice Talk Show* and co-host of *A Matter of Faith: A Presby Podcast*; lives in Washington, DC, with his husband and their beagle.

Every year I find myself experiencing moments of passing: seasons, loved ones, celestial bodies, relationships. Marking these moments has manifested in the literal marking of my own body. Tattoos are sprinkled over my arms reminding me of my beloved dog, my dad's time of cancer, my ordination, and my friendships. Once a year, I make the journey to my tattoo artist—this has become my ritual of passing, my marking of time.

The people of God tattoo their homes as God passes over, sparing their firstborns' lives. They mark this event through the rituals and traditions that surround food and the time of Passover, cementing a journey of remembering and passing. Much like the Hebrews, we find ways to capture moments that remind us of God's mystery and omnipotence. And during this time of marking, we use the bodies that God has given us.

Our bodies, formed and shaped by the Creator, express our faith by how we move, what we create, how we look, or what we consume. Our bodies mark a moment when God formed, shaped, and named each one of us in God's image. As we pass through time, our bodies change and adapt, continuing the process of remembering and marking.

As God passes over, above, through, and within us, may we pause and give thanks to the wonder that is our embodiment. May we remember those moments of passing. And may we open ourselves to the beauty of others, for we are all wonderfully made in God's image.

Holy Creator, remind us of your love manifest in the embodiment of Christ. Open our hearts to see ourselves as your good creation. Guide us in the path of justice and peace, so that all may live into their true abundance. Amen.

Even great singers have performance anxiety sometimes. Behind the safety of the walls of a studio, their voices are unhindered and soar with melody and harmony. But when the crowds show up and the stage lights are on, some performers freeze while fear creeps into their hearts, scared of the judgment of others. They hold back, worried that they will be judged and found wanting by the audience.

This fear is often felt just moments before singers open their mouths to release their God-given talents. If they press on, however, that fear disappears as they feel that they are doing what they are called to do. Singing out into the universe and to God gives them a spiritual release. When the singer is really good, the audience feels the divine connection as well.

The psalmist proclaims that we all are to sing out even when it is hard to do—and even when we aren't good at singing. Maybe we don't need to be alone on a stage singing to an audience, but we are all called to join in the assembly of the faithful in singing to the Lord. Singing creates spaces of vulnerability and accountability. Because God is a God of the weary, we are to sing out in the name of justice. Our throats may close, our stomachs may churn, and our minds may tell us that singing is not such a good idea. But in singing to God we find our moments of calling.

How are we singing out to God? What is holding us back, giving us stage fright? May we ask ourselves these questions through our journeys on the stages of discipleship.

God of the song, open our hearts and our voices to sing praises to you. We sing the melodies of justice and peace. May we harmonize with our siblings in Christ as we walk with one another in equity and humbleness. Amen.

The popular children's television show *Mister Rogers' Neighborhood* created a space where everyone felt like a neighbor. Fred Rogers walked with us as we entered his home and his make-believe world where he showed us that it is possible to truly love our neighbors. He even invited us to be his neighbor with his famous song, "Won't You Be My Neighbor?"

What many people do not know is that Mister Rogers was an ordained Presbyterian minister. The foundation of his morals and faith was expressed by the words of Paul and the words of Christ, "Love your neighbor." Fred instilled in his young viewers that very foundational basis of Christianity through television without ever claiming to be a pastor.

We can't all be Mister Rogers, and not all of us are called to be ordained; but we are all called to be ministers. Where can we embody the call to love our neighbors? How do we begin to create a world where people do no wrong to their neighbors because love purposely harms no one?

That calling is not easy, and creating a new world is some of the hardest work there is. Yet using our imaginations and embodiment to spread the love of God to each of our neighbors, no matter our differences, is the true calling of God.

May we always have the kind of childlike faith that Mister Rogers had—a faith that sees the image of God in each person we meet and invites them into a space of neighborly love. May we also look within ourselves for those moments where love is hard and ask ourselves why.

God of the ones we call neighbors, keep us open to your likeness in all humanity. Open our hearts to receive the presence of others, and keep us grounded in your calling to love. Amen.

Food is my favorite thing in the world. My earliest memories of my grandmother are connected with biscuits baking, collards bubbling on the stove, and big egg-filled breakfasts that we'd eat on the weekends. Sometimes when I find myself thinking about her, I can smell these aromas.

I imagine the smells of the Passover meal filling the air as the Hebrew people answered the calling from God, preparing the lamb and making sure to eat it all as the Passover approached. Families would gather to make sure everything was in place. Can you smell it? Can you imagine the conversations? The joy? The fear? Everything that comes when families get together?

Centuries have passed and meals are still being prepared with families surrounding one another creating memories that our bodies will hold in strange and beautiful ways. We will magically hear a loved one's voice though it isn't there anymore. We will catch a glimpse of them even though they are gone. But the thread that weaves through these memories is our body, its relationship with food, and how all of that connects us.

Throughout this week, notice when you sense the presence of your ancestors. Live into that moment because that is God working through the world to remind you of our connectedness. May those embodied times give you joy, peace, and hope.

O God, you are the God of the harvest. Remind us of your presence among us and the presence of those we love. Amen.

The Embodiment of Faith

Reds and yellows, oranges and pinks all come to together in an array of beauty as the leaves change colors in autumn. Each leaf adds a shade and a shadow. This natural art leads us to admire God's creation, opening us to the presence of God in the world.

The effect of the fall leaves can be overpowering, a beauty far beyond that of the sum of the individual leaves, giving us a glimpse of God. We see the plans behind leaves doing exactly what they were made to do.

Much like the changing leaves, people gathering together can display the Spirit at work. But the first part of today's reading shows that just being assembled in a group is not what we are talking about here. Sharing space is a beginning—Jesus shows it as a first step in possibly addressing disagreements and dissensions—but it is not the end. The beautiful leaves are all changing together with the seasons so there can eventually be new life. When we gather together in Jesus' name, we see the Spirit at work in every color, ethnicity, and expression working toward a new world.

Jesus proclaims that where two or three are gathered in his name, he is there among them. Jesus is in our moments of listening to music together in concerts, sharing our stories, eating dinners, and attending festivals. What a gift that is! The gift is that God is among our relationships and our connections.

As the leaves fall and gather in piles, and as we feel the presence of God among us, may we move and act with our God-given bodies to find community. It is in those moments that we truly see each other.

God who is the creator of all, remind us of our human instinct to be together. Create in our hearts the longing to find connections even when it is hard to do. Amen.

The beauty of music is not only the sound or the beat but the human interaction with whatever is making the sound. A tambourine needs hands to make the cymbals hit each other. A lyre needs fingers to pluck the strings.

The psalmist proclaims that we are to create new music for the Lord with our talents, and we are to do so with joy! That creation involves us in an immense and intentional way. What new songs are we creating in our world? What new ways are we working together to make new sounds and melodies? Are we creating new songs with new words that invite all God's people into the band or the choir?

Too often, however, our new music is centered only on the praise of God, telling God how worthy and marvelous God is. And that is surely true. But the new music of our day must sing out justice, love, peace, and hope. The new instruments of our time are created by the hands and minds of those who have been ignored, shunned, or forgotten. And the newly formed assembly of the faithful opens us up to a vibrating kingdom of God that encompasses all into a heavenly choir and band of immense diversity. God delights when we praise with creation and with one another.

So, let us look at our world and invite those people who are missing from the choir. May our music be ever new because God's Spirit is always moving. May this new music accompany us in our work for the kingdom of God.

Gracious God, make us instruments of love. Guide us to be bearers of justice. Be our conductor as we make a joyful noise to you. Amen.

Paul tells us that we are to put on the armor of light. I can't help but wonder what that would be like. What would that armor look like in a physical form? Would it be blindingly bright or just shiny? How would it feel? Would it be hot? Would it be heavy like armor or weightless like light?

Paul's metaphor is compelling and naturally leads to science-fiction inspired imagining, but Paul tells us right in the passage what it looks and feels like to put on the armor of light. When we put on this armor, our posture changes. How we interact with people changes. We smile as someone passes by, and we say hello to someone who needs human interaction. We live honorably and love one another. This armor creates action as we dispel the darkness of oppression and suffering. This armor is not just a metaphor; it is physical and real.

The new armor holds us to God's amazing assurance that love will win over darkness. But it is up to us to find ways to shine that light. How are we letting this light shine? Are we stuck perpetuating darkness in the forms of oppression? Or are we ready to move into action to bring forth a new day?

If we are ready for a new day, we must be ready for the hard work of light. It is a work that will shine, change us, and, yes, make us seem different in action and appearance. Let us get ready in the light and do the work of God.

God of light, shine upon us your love. Illumine our hearts to do the work you call us to do. Amen.

Parting the Waters

SEPTEMBER 11–17, 2023 • SUSAN M. HUDSON

SCRIPTURE OVERVIEW: Again this week, Exodus tells a story about Moses that is retold in the psalm. The angel of the Lord protects the Israelites and allows them to cross the sea on dry ground, but their enemies are swept away. The psalmist recalls this glorious event. The forces of nature tremble and bow before the presence of God, and the people are delivered. Paul recognizes that there are matters of personal preference or conscience that are not hard and fast rules. Some will feel freedom in areas that others do not, and we are not to judge each other for these differences. Jesus tells a parable in Matthew that highlights the danger of hypocrisy. We who have been forgiven so generously by God have no right to judge others for minor offenses.

QUESTIONS AND SUGGESTIONS FOR REFLECTION

- Read Exodus 14:19-31. When has the path of faith seemed risky? How have you trusted God and others' wisdom along the way?
- Read Psalm 114. How do you see God's hand at work in creation? Spend some time in nature. What is God saying?
- Read Romans 14:1-12. When have you recognized something as more important than your being right? How has that recognition shaped your faith?
- Read Matthew 18:21-35. How do you recognize your own wounds—or those you have inflicted on others—in this parable? How might this parable help you to repair these wounds or the relationships attached to the wounds?

Minister of Word and Sacrament in the Presbyterian Church (USA); served with her husband and family as a mission co-worker in South Korea, Pakistan, and India; recently published her memoir, *Spirited Voyager: A Memoir of Motherhood, Mission and Ministry* (Xulon); completed the Spiritual Guidance Program through Shalem Institute.

In our scripture passage for today, the Red Sea separated Moses and the Israelites from freedom. The Egyptians were chasing them even though Pharaoh had given them permission to leave. The people of Israel were complaining and terrified, but God told Moses in the verses right before this text that God was ready to show both Israel and Egypt that God would defend God's people. The Lord's words to Moses were these: "The LORD will fight for you, and you have only to keep still."

God's angel had been in front of God's people but moved behind them to be a barrier between the Israelites and the pursuing Egyptians. Then God invited Moses to lift up his staff and stretch out his hand over the sea to divide it. The people of Israel crossed the sea on dry land. The water formed a wall for them on their right and on their left. The Lord invited Moses to stretch out his hand over the sea one more time, so that the water would come back upon the Egyptians and not one remained alive.

This act of God to defend God's people was miraculous. All of creation is in God's hands, and it was God who orchestrated the deliverance of the Israelites. The winds and waves obeyed. It was not the Israelite's good behavior, positive attitude, or acts of righteousness that parted the waters for them that day. God simply wanted them to be still and wait for God's timing and God's purpose to be fulfilled by the Creator of all things.

Lord, teach me to keep still while you provide a way where there is no way. Instill trust in me that exceeds imagination! Amen.

It can be difficult to decide to leave a place we have grown accustomed to—even if it is an unhealthy place—in order to make our dreams come true. The internal and external obstacles we must face to find freedom are much larger than we are. That was true for Moses and the Israelite people as they departed Egypt on short notice. Moses had no idea what he was getting into with God. His initial response was that he did not have the qualifications or skills to be the leader of God's people.

Have you ever been nudged by God to do something that no one else understood or to leave a place on very short notice? Let us ponder this call to depart. How is God inviting us to stretch? How is God inviting us to enter an unknown place with only a few possessions? We often gloss over how difficult it must have been for the Israelites to walk between those walls of water. They knew that was not how the sea was supposed to work. Perhaps an important but often overlooked part of the "parting of the waters" is being willing to enter into an unknown future that God is preparing for us.

Moses was not told what getting to the Promised Land would look like. He had to depart in the darkness of night, trusting God's light to lead him. Moses and the children of Israel ended up wandering for forty years in a desert before it was God's time for them to enter the Promised Land. Sometimes it is best if we do not know the future but simply live in the present, trusting that God has us, holds us, and leads us wherever we go.

Lord, please meet us where we are. Help us trust that you will part the waters before us and will keep our feet on dry ground. Amen.

Sometimes God shows up in amazing ways in the deserts of our lives. Psalm 114 talks about how all of creation responded to God's presence at the time of the Exodus. The writer refers to two acts of God on their behalf. First, the Lord parted the Red Sea under Moses' leadership. Then, when Joshua was preparing to enter Jericho, the Jordan River turned back. All of creation responds to God's presence, as this psalm joyously portrays.

If God can show up in all of creation, we can trust God to show up for us also. The deliverance of Israel was not expected. It came as a gracious answer to many years of prayer and cries for help. Did God abandon God's people? *Heavens, no!* Will God abandon us? *Absolutely not!*

Sometimes we feel unheard. How do we respond? Do we ramp up our prayers? One Sunday morning I was on my way to church, but I did not feel energized or worthy to be God's servant in the pulpit. As I was driving, I cried out: "I need you now, Lord. Please give me a sign that you are here." In minutes I received a call canceling an evening meeting: my first God-wink. When I arrived at church, I got my second God-wink when I opened a book by Joyce Rupp called *Prayer Seeds* to a poem that spoke to the core of my being. The third God-wink was a solo sung in church by Vessa Morales, "Just Give Me Jesus." In those three moments, I knew that God had heard me. God turned the rock in my heart into a pool of water, the flint into a flowing stream.

Lord, only you can turn a rock into a pool of water or part the waters so that we can pass on dry land. Hear our prayer today for your powerful intervention in our lives. Amen.

Sometimes we want God to part the waters when God is calming the seas. The passage from Romans is urging us not to judge anyone, regardless of what decisions they make. Let those who eat meat and those who are vegetarians be respectful of each other. Some observe special days; others do not. Our task is to show respect for all people, regardless of religious, political, economic, emotional, or psychological differences.

The essential teaching in this scripture is that we are not on this earth to please ourselves but to give ourselves to others and honor to Jesus Christ. We know from the scriptures we have studied all week that God alone is the judge. We are arrogant to think we can judge how other people serve God. We were put on earth to give honor to Jesus Christ, who identified himself with the least and the lost.

Jesus submitted to God to the point of dying on a cross. He was sinless and did not deserve his punishment, but his way of living threatened the powerful people who controlled society. The powers of our world put Jesus to death. But in the end, Jesus will judge the living and the dead. Paul writes: "As I live, says the Lord, every knee shall bow to me, and every tongue shall give praise to God." We are accountable only to God, so let us take a few moments to offer ourselves to this One who loves us unconditionally.

Lord Jesus Christ, have mercy on me and on us. Help us to see the beauty and the presence of God in everyone we meet. May your love radiate in and through us all. To God be the glory! Amen!

What is forgiveness? We regularly pray some form of these words in the Lord's Prayer: "Forgive us our trespasses, as we forgive those who trespass against us." What is the measure of forgiveness we are asking to receive? We are asking for God to use the same measure on us that we use in forgiving others. But that's a dangerous petition. In Matthew's Gospel, Jesus speaks these words: "For if you forgive others their trespasses, your heavenly Father will also forgive you; but if you do not forgive others, neither will your Father forgive your trespasses." Some theologians have said that's the only part of the prayer Jesus felt he had to "editorialize on." I think Jesus was saying, in our vernacular, "Be careful what you ask for."

Matthew 18 tells of Peter's asking how many times Christians should forgive another member of the church. "Seven times?" Jesus answered, "Not seven times, but, I tell you, seventy-seven times." In other words, we should stop counting how many sins have been committed against us. Just forgive.

Forgiveness is liberating for the person who sinned against us, and it is also liberating for us. Let's quit counting! In Matthew 18, Jesus tells a story of a servant who has his debts forgiven but will not in turn forgive his debtors. Therefore the forgiveness of his own debts was rescinded.

When we are forgiven for our failures and shortcomings, does that allow forgiveness to overflow into all our relationships? Can we offer that "living water" of loving forgiveness to our spouses, children, siblings, friends, and enemies? Can God use that forgiveness to part the waters of division and disrespect among us?

Lord, please grant us the ability to let go and let you forgive others abundantly so that we too can be forgiven for our times of disobedience to your will. Amen.

Sisters and brothers in Christ, how is God leading us out of a place where we are caught or stuck? Moses' words to Pharaoh were to "let [God's] people go" (Exod. 5:1). If you feel trapped in a routine that does not bring grace to your life, how can you walk away from it or welcome a healthy intervention to address the situation? In whom can you confide? My prayer is that the story of the Exodus will encourage each of us to assess where we are, how we are, and where God is leading us.

As a mother of three daughters, my deepest desire has always been to protect them and to set a good example of trusting God, while also using all of my God-given gifts to glorify God wherever I am. Each of us must walk our own path, listening to God's voice and moving forward when the moment is right.

God empowered Moses to pick up his staff and command the waters to be parted. What is your "staff"? What instrument has God placed in your hands to initiate change or work miracles in your world? I love to write. It has been a great privilege to create devotional words for the Upper Room.

I think of the choral director at the church I am serving. He invited me to come hear the students at his university. I was riveted by how his hands led the entire choral ensemble to grow quiet or to surge into harmonic and uplifting melodies. Each student held nothing back! The director's hands were like Moses' staff inviting the presence of God to be expressed through beautiful songs of praise.

The purpose for all of our lives is to embody Christ in the world. What does that look like for you?

Lord, may we be your instruments of praise, anointing your creation with God-given joy! Amen.

Parting the Waters

In Exodus, God parted the waters of the Red Sea to provide a way for God's people to cross over safely. According to the writer of Psalm 114, Judah became God's "sanctuary" when they left behind their Egyptian oppressors. God wants us to be God's sanctuary also, a place where the presence of God is felt, honored, heard, and obeyed. It does not matter whether we are living in a foreign country or still in the place where we were born; God wants our full and undivided attention.

God definitely got the attention of Moses and Israel. What will it take to get our attention? Do we need to see spectacular miracles, or can we see God's everyday miracles of welcoming the holy presence of our Lord and Savior Jesus Christ into our hearts, thoughts, and actions. Psalm 114 is a song of praise based on God's deliverance. Let us compose a song of praise for our time.

Dance, beloved earth, in the presence of your Creator. We long for you, O God, to come and guide our lives—reconciling families, neighbors, churches, and nations. You want every person, animal, and plant in your kingdom to radiate and reflect your goodness and love for all creation. God of love, part the waters of our resistance to your will. Protect our vulnerability when we are weak. Teach us to join hands with all who are different so that we may become one family. Inspire us to do a circle dance, where none is excluded and all are welcome. Let the drums of heaven begin to thunder and the birds begin to sing as your family sways rhythmically to the music of unconditional acceptance. Lord, you are not aloof. The winds and waves obey you! May we fling open our hearts to receive your loving-kindness and mercy. Amen.

Divine Provision

SEPTEMBER 18–24, 2023 • BARBARA BROWN TAYLOR

SCRIPTURE OVERVIEW: The psalmist recounts many of God's glorious deeds. The escape from Egypt features prominently, including the Exodus story we are reading this week. God knows that the people need food and provides both meat and bread. Unfortunately, the people do not have the perspective of the psalmist, so God's miraculous provision does not stop their grumbling. In Philippians, Paul reflects on Christian suffering. Although he would rather be with the Lord, he endures suffering so that he may help others. Other believers should expect to suffer as well. Jesus tells a parable about a landowner. No matter what time the workers go out, they are all equally paid. Likewise, those who follow Jesus their entire lives and those who meet the Lord late in life will partake equally in glory.

QUESTIONS AND SUGGESTIONS FOR REFLECTION

• Read Exodus 16:2-15. When have you been confident of God's love and presence? When have you been uncertain?

• Read Psalm 105:1-6, 37-45. When do you smooth over the "bumps" in the stories of your family, your church, or your faith? When is it important to recount the complaining or mistakes along the way?

• Read Philippians 1:21-30. When has the "good news to the poor" challenged you? When you feel challenged by it, how do you seek to live "worthy of the gospel"?

• Read Matthew 20:1-16. How does Jesus' idea of equality surprise you? How might a posture of generosity change your concept of fairness?

––––––––––

Episcopal priest in the Diocese of Atlanta and author of many books.

Though the people's life in Egypt was bad, the bread was good. Pharaoh's royal kitchen produced fifty-seven different kinds of bread. Native emmer wheat was so valuable it was kept in vaults and used as currency. Rich or poor, Egyptians used the same word for the bread they made from it: *'aish*, they called it, the Egyptian word for *life*.

Six weeks into the wilderness, the Israelites missed all that life back in Egypt. They weren't stoic about it, either. They complained bitterly to Moses and Aaron (the closest they had to clergy) about their raw deal. If God meant to kill them, why not do it back in Egypt, after a big bowl of stew and all the *'aish* they could eat? Even condemned prisoners got a last meal.

God responded by raining bread from heaven—one kind, not the kind the people had in mind, but bread all the same— along with directions about when and how much to gather each day. "In that way I will test them," God said, "whether they will follow my instruction or not." But what was the crux of the test? Gathering the manna? Not gathering it on the sabbath? Dividing it fairly?

"All of the above" is the safest answer, but leaving the question open is the best way to find your place in the story. When you imagine heading out in the morning to gather your daily manna, what strikes you as the hardest part?

Enough is where I hit the wall. Based on my closets, cupboards, and drawers, *enough* is not a measure I understand. Or it's not a measure I trust, even when it comes straight from the Lord. *Excess* is my standard measure: fifty-seven kinds of bread, when only one is necessary for life.

Sustaining God, give us this day our daily bread and forgive us our excesses, for your manna diet is all we need on the way from bondage to freedom. Amen.

No one has parsed Exodus more carefully than the Jews whose story it tells. Rabbinical literature is full of best guesses about the meaning of each detail. Cherished legends fill the gaps between what is said and what is not, like the one about how manna tasted different to everyone who ate it. To babies it tasted like mother's milk; to the old like honey wafers; to heathens like bitter linseed oil. God provided for all according to their need.

The Jewish Publication Society's *Tanakh* version of the Bible reminds me that the same thing can happen with language. Take the Hebrew word *kavod* for instance, which the NRSV translates in today's reading as "glory." That's a good flavor—one most Christian Bibles use—though *kavod* can also mean *reverence, honor, respect,* or *significance* depending on who translates it. The *Tanakh* surprises by choosing the English word "Presence" instead. (Why choose an honorific when you can choose the Honoree?) In the morning, Moses and Aaron tell the people they shall see the "Presence of the LORD."

But what is it, exactly, that they shall see? According to the French medieval rabbi Rashi, the most obvious answer is *manna*. When they wake up in the morning, the people will see manna lying on the ground for the first time; that is the form in which they will see the Lord. To Abraham and Sarah, the Lord came in the form of three strangers (see Genesis 18:1-2). To Moses, the Lord came in the form of a burning bush (see Exodus 3:4). To the Israelites, the Lord came in the form of manna. God provides for all according to their need.

The beauty of this particular interpretation is how it relieves us of any further anxiety about where God has gone. Is there bread on your plate today? Behold the Presence of the LORD.

Open our eyes, Holy Shape-Shifter, to all the forms in which you come to us. Amen.

Divine Provision

This psalm praises God for giving the land of other nations to Israel, lending fuel to the long-burning fire between Israel and Palestine—but that gift is just one in a long list of reasons to bless the Lord for assuring the survival of Abraham's offspring. Bread from heaven is also on the list, along with quail cutlets, gushing water from a rock, and the twin pillars of cloud and fire that guided the people through the wilderness. Read as a whole, the psalm presents a condensed version of salvation history from Abraham to Moses.

But its purpose is not to educate. Its purpose is to keep the habit of praise alive through all the tight spots of a precarious existence. Whether it is an individual life in the red zone, a family life, or the life of a whole congregation, the *Tanakh* translation of the psalm offers ten imperatives in its first five verses: Praise the Lord; call on his name; proclaim his deeds; sing praises to him; speak of his wondrous acts; exult in his holy name; let those who seek the Lord rejoice; turn to the Lord; seek his presence constantly; remember the wonders he has done.

This echoes the good advice to count your blessings in an intentional way—writing them down in a gratitude journal at night, sending thank-you notes to people who offered a hand in a hard time, or making a timeline of your life and marking the passages where manna rained from heaven for you. But it also kicks the advice up a notch by raising the volume. Instead of writing something down, why not exult out loud for a change? Instead of making a list, how about making some noise? Even if you scare the cat, the psalmist seems to think there's Someone Else listening who might enjoy your performance a lot.

Open our lips, O Lord, and our mouths shall proclaim your praise. Amen.

Paul is in prison. He does not say where, but the church in Philippi has been good to him. A member of the congregation named Epaphroditus has come with gifts and is now returning home with this letter in his pocket. Paul wants the Philippians not to worry about him. Whatever happens, living is Christ for him, and dying is gain. What does he have to lose?

Many of us assume that Paul is weighing life and death because he is facing execution, but that seems not to be the case. He uses the words "prefer" and "desire," employing concepts that show up in ancient dialogues about suicide. Whether he does that for rhetorical effect or because he is really thinking about ending his life, Paul decides against it. Why? Because he believes that staying in life is more necessary for the Philippians, even if departing life is more desirable for him.

This is an unexpected entry in the list of divine provisions we are counting this week. Manna and quail are obvious additions to it; so are the practices of praise commended by the psalmist. Today, thanks to the strong connection between Paul and the Philippians, the divine provision of tender relationships enters the list at number one. The needs of the saints in Christ Jesus who are in Philippi take precedence over Paul's desire to depart and be with Christ. The connective tissue of Christian community tethers him to this life even when dying is gain for him.

As unsettling as it may be to overhear Paul's thinking about all of this, his decision gives "necessity" a whole new meaning. What the saints need from him is "more necessary" than what he prefers for himself. Their love of him is what keeps him in life.

May we never forget those who love us, Christ Jesus, or how their need of us gives us life. Amen.

Philippi was a Roman military colony, which helps explain the military language here. Paul worked hard to use the language of the people to whom he wrote. If more Christians could read the New Testament in Greek, we might benefit from Paul's use of a word at verse 27 that shows up nowhere else in his letters: *politeuomai*, translated variously as "live your life," "conduct yourself," or "live together."

Since the root word is *polis*, the Greek word for city, what has gone missing from English translations is the deep connection between how we live our lives and the communities in which we live them. A more literal translation of verse 27 might begin, "Conduct your citizenship in a way that is worthy of the good news of Christ."

The net effect of this change is the way it puts believers in relationship with one another. We are not owners of private lots in a gospel subdivision where the good news means anything we say it means on our own property. Instead, we are citizens of a divine commonwealth that depends heavily on us to uphold its reputation. Whether Paul is with the Philippians in person or hearing about them from a distance, he is counting on them to conduct their citizenship in unity—standing firm in one spirit, striving together with one mind—which will not only distinguish them from their opponents but will serve as evidence of their salvation as well.

This is God's doing, he says, a gift that includes the twin privileges of believing in Christ and suffering with him. The mention of opponents makes it sound like they are the problem with our unity, but of course they are not. Our unity is one of God's provisions that we have rebuffed all by ourselves.

Strengthen us to do what unity requires of us, Christ Jesus, as we remember what it costs you to stay in unity with us. Amen.

Today's parable is so familiar to church-going Christians that it seldom receives a fresh hearing. Once you know the punchline, the story is just the vehicle for getting there. But if you park the punchline for a moment, other details have a chance to emerge.

The first is that the kingdom of heaven is not likened to a vineyard but to its owner. Early in the morning, he's not at home drinking his first cup of coffee. He's already at the marketplace, hiring day laborers to work his land and agreeing to their usual wage. From this we learn that the kingdom of heaven has everything to do with the local economy, the labor force, and how much they are paid.

If you have hired day laborers yourself, you know how hard it is to see so many people lined up hoping for work. Some lean down to look in your car and make eye contact, while others drop their heads so they don't have to watch you judge them. It's not like they can afford to be choosy. They are there to be chosen, not to choose.

The kingdom of heaven opens when the landowner nods at some of them. *You, you,* and *you.* However hard the work, this is good news. Tonight their families will eat. Not a lot but enough: a manna meal.

Inexplicably, the landowner returns to the marketplace four more times that day. Is it because there's more work than he thought or because he loves how people's faces change when he hires them? Since this is the kingdom of heaven we are talking about, the answer is *both.* There is always more work to do, and being chosen by this landowner is reason to rejoice. An honest day's work for a fair wage is proof of heaven, even before the punchline arrives.

Dear Divine Landowner, help us do all our work as if we are doing it for you. Amen.

Jesus never calls the landowner "God" and neither should we. Like every parable, this one does its best work when it's not locked down ahead of time, no matter how many times we have heard it. Every detail of the story would have been familiar to its first listeners, allowing them to walk around in it before being told what it was *supposed* to mean. Today we join them by hanging out in the middle of the story for a change.

The most noticeable difference between the landowner's first visit to the marketplace and the second one is the pay he offers the laborers. First thing in the morning, he agrees on the usual daily wage, which was probably a Roman *denarius* (the same coin soldiers in the army were paid). It was enough to feed a family of four for a few days but not enough for a full week. A day laborer would have to be hired two or three times a week in order to make ends meet, praying not to fall ill or be injured.

When the landowner goes back to market later in the morning, he cuts a different deal with the second shift. He will pay them whatever is right, he says, and they go with him, either because he seems like a trustworthy person or because anything he ends up paying them is better than the nothing they will earn by standing there.

Which deal sounds better to you? It's a good question, especially since the kingdom of heaven is likened to this landowner. Would you prefer an agreed-on reward for your labor or one dependent on the character of your employer? You don't get to choose, of course. Only the landowner gets to choose. So turn the question around: Which deal sounds more like the kingdom of heaven to you?

I know the right answer, Lord. Now help me act on it by going with you. Amen.

Who's In Charge?

SEPTEMBER 25–OCTOBER 1, 2023 • BRIAN R. BODT

SCRIPTURE OVERVIEW: For the second time this year, we read the story of the Israelites complaining in the desert about their lack of water, only to see God provide a miraculous spring. The psalmist reminds the people of the many powerful deeds performed by the Lord, including leading them through the sea out of Egypt and providing them water from the rock. Paul emphasizes to the Philippians the need for humility and unity. In quoting the earliest known Christian hymn, Paul encourages them with the example of Christ, who gives up all his rights for the sake of others. In back-to-back encounters with religious leaders, Jesus evades an attempt to trap him in his words and then teaches that true obedience is shown not by our speech but by our actions.

QUESTIONS AND SUGGESTIONS FOR REFLECTION

- Read Exodus 17:1-7. When have you tried to "do it all"? How can admitting your limitations help you lead?
- Read Psalm 78:1-4, 12-16. Recall times when you have known God's presence. How might remembering and retelling these stories shape your faith?
- Read Philippians 2:1-13. How does your life speak of God's love for you and for all humanity?
- Read Matthew 21:23-32. How have you created your idea of Jesus in your own image? What would change if you found your identity in Jesus rather than creating Jesus' identity from your own?

Retired United Methodist pastor staying in love with God; blessed in human loves by his wife, Carol Galloway, their children and grandchildren; skis, runs, and plays with big and small trains; worships at the Cheshire (CT) United Methodist Church and the Greenfield Hill Congregational Church, Fairfield, CT.

Who's in charge?" Explicitly or implicitly, it's a question asked in households, businesses, government, and churches. As ministry moves into the heart of fall program activity and nominating committees prepare their slates for 2024, pastors and people could do far worse than asking, "How do you lead and what constitutes good leadership?"

The religious leaders in Jerusalem asked that very question: "By what authority are you doing these things?" By now Jesus' ministry had long challenged the status quo (see Matthew 7:28) and was in direct conflict with institutional religious authority. It is not a stretch to imagine that the authorities were threatened by the Palm Sunday throngs that had shouted "Hosanna!" (O save!) only the day before. Was that a joyous spiritual acclamation alone or a cry of political defiance to their Roman occupiers? Only the crowds knew, but the authorities weren't taking any chances. "By what authority are you doing these things, and who gave you this authority?"

Jesus didn't defend his teaching or his popularity. By answering the question with a question about John's baptism, he got to his challengers' hearts: What is the source of true authority? The authority Jesus' critics knew was externally conferred. But Jesus spoke of an authority that was internally discerned from an intimate relationship with God. Jesus not only turned the political tables on his questioners; he reminded them of the long succession of prophets sent by God but rejected by people. He challenged them to rethink the very source of their authority.

What is the source of your authority? What constitutes good leadership? How does Jesus' authority challenge you?

Lord Jesus, grant me the assurance of your presence that I may see the authority that comes from you. Challenge me to use my authority to bring glory to you. Amen.

Y ou're not the boss of me!" Most of us have said or been told this expression of desired autonomy. Part of maturing personally and spiritually is self-differentiation. If we are not tethered to an external authority—a parent, the church, or God—then who are we?

It is a potent brew when all three authorities are in play! An important part of the discernment of my call was exploring the shadow side of my mother's spiritual influence. As Susanna Wesley influenced her sons John and Charles, my mother cultivated my God-given spirituality while also instilling a love for Jesus and the church. Without her influence it is unlikely I would have responded to God's call.

Yet she also made no secret that I should aspire to be like her father and brother, both Methodist clergy. Was my call from God, or was it a misplaced desire to be a "good son"? Her influence in and beyond the local church made me wonder if I could be my own person in ministry. Part of resolving these tensions meant moving to another part of the country. I honored the past by living in the present.

Exousia—the New Testament Greek word for authority—means "out of that which is one's very own." True authority comes from integrating human and divine influences while being attentive to each. Jesus was clearly shaped by his religious tradition; his frequent use of scripture testifies to that. Still, there was something more: an attention to God's special blessing and a fidelity to God's unique call of him. When the tradition and God's call conflicted, he knew which to choose.

Who is the boss of you? Which boss do you choose?

O God, thank you for all the influences that help me respond to your call on my life. Help me to cultivate always those that honor you. Amen.

Who's In Charge?

W hat shall I do with this people?" Most of us have said that. Is there anyone who hasn't at least thought it? Pastors, congregations, parents, children, leaders, and followers: What shall I do with those who don't "get it" or "get me"?

I feel for Moses. Since the dramatic crossing of the Red Sea and the triumphant song of victory, there's been persistent testing of his authority (and patience) and finding fault with his leadership. One would think that liberating the people from Pharaoh's slavery and saving them from Pharaoh's army by leading them unharmed through the sea would erase any doubt that God had chosen Moses to lead them. But no. You can almost hear Moses' fear of insurrection and death.

Still, I also feel for the people. They can't survive without food and water. When people are about to die of thirst, they start to think that Moses and God hadn't thought through the whole escape plan.

It turns out that God did have a plan, or at least God has last-minute solutions. God is faithful to Moses and works through him to save the people and show them that they should trust Moses. There is little evidence that the people see themselves in partnership with Moses and God, or that Moses sees the people as capable of being partners in their own liberation. Some humility would have been required for either of these relationships, but humility seems to have been in shorter supply than water or food.

How do we see ourselves, particularly in times of trial or struggle? Do we lean only on those whose authority we perceive, or do we humbly claim our own authority?

O God, help us just for today to put aside our testing and finding fault, whether of others or of you. Amen.

I don't want you and him making all the decisions." So I snapped a church leader at me about the trustee chair, after our trustees adopted a security measure in the wake of several church shootings. A security professional recommended securing an often-used and equally often unsecured rear door. We adopted a six-week trial to see how people would adjust to the change. The irony was that for five and a half years I had demonstrated collaborative leadership. Rarely were decisions made unilaterally, especially given the church conflicts I had inherited. This decision was also collaborative. It simply didn't please the critic.

Leaders sometimes make hard and unpopular decisions. Moses led the people in the wilderness, yet the springs were dry. The people became fearful and angry, and Moses and the Lord were tested ("Massah") and criticized ("Meribah") until the Lord intervened. The crisis intervention came when Moses followed God's direction and took the elders of Israel with him to the sacred mountain (Horeb/Sinai) and used the staff that had earlier proved that God had appeared to Moses (see Exodus 4:1-17). There God through Moses provided water for the Israelites and proved that God was with them and spoke directly to Moses.

Is God's action in this story normative for other conflicts? Perhaps. It is worth considering these steps where authority is challenged and pride outweighs humility. Gather trusted leaders. Identify tools you have previously found effective that may work in this situation. Go to the place—literal or metaphorical— where the challenge can be met. Above all, seek God's guidance. God will surely guide all who earnestly seek direction.

O God, when I lead, help me seek you. When I follow, help me seek you. Help me do the best I can and believe that others are doing the same. Amen.

Who's In Charge?   323

"What have you done for me lately?" We live in a time— thus ever it was—where the "now" triumphs over the "then." Certainly life moves forward. Living today and not yesterday is part of the Divine mind (see Isaiah 43:18-19). Yet forgetting or ignoring past challenges, defeats, and victories, will lead those seeking faith to fall into the trap of the Athenians who would "spend their time in nothing but telling or hearing something new" (see Acts 17:21).

This psalm is one of a group of psalms (also including 105, 106, 135, 136) that were used at the major festivals and recite the history of God's dealings with Israel. Verses 15-16 speak directly to God's action in Exodus 17:6.

Yet this recitation is not simple, particularly in the face of current trials and challenges. Unlike financial securities, where "past performance does not guarantee future results," recalling God's past activity reminds us that God has been faithful, is faithful, and will be faithful. The psalm reminds us that we worship because God is God and we are not. As Fred Craddock so tenderly expressed it, "A mother does not put a ribbon in her daughter's hair to make her pretty, but because she is."

Trusting and remaining faithful to God requires large help-ings of humility, giving up our tendency to domesticate God and make God's authority subordinate to our own. Consider two questions: How much of our fidelity to God is based solely on receiving God's favor? How are we also faithful to God's author-ity in times of trial?

O God, I worship you today as Lord of my life. Grant me humility as I remember your past faithfulness and discern your yearning for me. Amen.

In humility regard others as better than yourselves." Church leaders praise "servant-leadership," and nowhere is its tension and cost clearer than in Philippians 2. Verse 3 in particular is a tall order!

The challenge is particularly stark in light of, at this writing in early 2022, Russia's invasion of Ukraine. One can immediately think of other examples—all forms of abuse, capitalism without regulation, some sports and entertainment venues and, sadly, church—where "humility" becomes the doorway for exploitation.

Paul is not naive. He is a prisoner of the Roman Empire for his proclamation of the gospel. Yet his appeal to the church at Philippi, where there has been conflict, is to "be of the same mind, having the same love." Eighteen centuries later John Wesley echoed the same message: "Though we cannot think alike, may we not love alike? May we not be of one heart, though we are not of one opinion? Without all doubt, we may. "

Authority is balanced by humility, with Jesus as the prototype for a sacrificial humility rooted in love. The One whose authority was equal with God did not exploit that for his own glory but loved us to our redemption. Self-emptying was possible because Jesus knew who he was and to whom he belonged.

Jesus' followers know that self-awareness and inner strength are required for this kind of humility. So did Paul, who exhorts each of us to "work out [our] own salvation with fear and trembling." Paul knew better than to think we could save ourselves. If we could, we would not need a Savior. Rather, he reminds us that we are responsible for our role and attitude in salvation, which requires a strong dose of humility.

Lord Jesus Christ, you loved us even to death on a cross. Help me to love like you, in a spirit of humility that knows myself as a beloved child of God. Amen.

Who's In Charge?

Jesus Christ is Lord." Wow. WOW! THAT'S who's in charge! Prose is inadequate for such an overwhelming, awesome affirmation! Paul recites an early hymn to convey the magnificence of Christ's Lordship. Today hymns like "At the Name of Jesus" and "He Is Lord" help us wrap our hearts and minds around the authority of Christ's Lordship expressed in humility.

Paul says, "Let the same mind be in you that was in Christ Jesus." On this World Communion Sunday, we remember "that we, receiving these thy creatures of bread and wine . . . may be partakers of the divine nature through him." That "divine nature" is Christ's sacrificial love, mystically conveyed in this meal by which we thank God for this gift of love, accessible through the man and Savior, Jesus.

World Communion Sunday is also an opportunity to seek Christian unity in the midst of our diversity. Protestants who celebrate Communion monthly or quarterly can practice humility today by remembering that *every* Sunday is World Communion Sunday for nearly two-thirds of the world's Christians. The elements of bread and wine recall the manna and water so desperately sought and so providentially provided in the wilderness, and they are a source of spiritual sustenance today.

The Lord, Founder of the Feast, wants nothing more than that our hearts lift praise and glory to God's name. As a traditional hymn says, "The peace of Christ makes fresh my heart, a fountain ever springing! / All things are mine since I am his! How can I keep from singing?"

O Jesus, grant me the faith to call you "Lord" and the conviction to live as if you are, truly, the Lord of my life; to the glory of your holy name. Amen.

Did you know that you can enjoy
The Upper Room Disciplines
in multiple formats—digital or print?

The Upper Room Disciplines is available in both regular and enlarged print, but are you aware that it is also available in digital formats? Read *Disciplines* on your phone, computer, or e-reader. Whatever your preference, we have it for you today.

The Upper Room Disciplines is available in a variety of formats:
- Print (regular-print and enlarged-print versions)
- E-book
- Digital subscriptions (website and app)

For more information, visit bookstore.upperroom.org or call 800.972.0433.

What is a standing order option?

A standing order allows you to automatically receive your copy of *Disciplines* each year as soon as it is available. Take the worry out of remembering to place your order.

Need to make changes to your account?

Call Customer Service at 800.972.0433 or email us at customerassistance@upperroom.org. Customer service representatives are available to help you with any updates.

Authentic Discipleship

OCTOBER 2–8, 2023 • MARIA DIXON HALL

SCRIPTURE OVERVIEW: A common theme this week is the danger of self-absorption. When we are young, we may struggle to understand the importance of rules because we think that our individual freedom is the highest good. God gives the Israelites commandments to guide their relationships with God and others. These laws will help them thrive because God knows what is best for us. The psalmist understands this: The laws of the Lord are good and sweet. Self-absorption might also lead to pride. Paul shows that a true understanding of the gospel means laying aside our rights in the knowledge that God will reward us. In a parable about the rejection of the prophets and Jesus, servants seek to seize a vineyard for themselves, unwisely ignoring that the owner will eventually reclaim what is his.

QUESTIONS AND SUGGESTIONS FOR REFLECTION

- Read Exodus 20:1-4, 7-9, 12-20. Recall your earliest experiences with the Ten Commandments. How do they continue to shape your understanding of God's expectations?
- Read Psalm 19. How does the natural world call you to follow God?
- Read Philippians 3:4b-14. Whom do you emulate? What would it mean for you to emulate Christ in life and in death?
- Read Matthew 21:33-46. When have you participated in or witnessed the rejection of one who could be God in disguise? How might things be different if you had recognized that person as a potential cornerstone of your community?

Chief Diversity Officer and Associate Professor of Communication for Southern Methodist University, Dallas, TX; ordained deacon in the North Texas Annual Conference of The United Methodist Church.

No authentic relationship can begin without a proper introduction. Who are you? What kind of relationship do you want? What do you want from me? These are the foundations of an authentic relationship. As much as we would like to define the relationship's terms on our own, we must listen to the other person's answers.

Today's text finds the children of Israel awaiting their first meeting with God. For three days, they had consecrated themselves and waited at the foot of Mount Sinai as Moses had instructed them. No doubt, the people anxiously anticipated a face-to-face encounter with the God of Abraham, Isaac, and Jacob, who had guided them through the waters of the Red Sea and quenched their desert thirst with water from a rock. No more clouds during the day or fires at night, no more mediation from Moses. Today would be the day that God would meet the chosen people of Israel in the ultimate act of betrothal.

Descending upon the mountain with fire and smoke, God arrives like a triumphant bridegroom preparing to sign an eternal covenant with his beloved. Then the whole camp trembles in anticipation of a royal introduction.

Yet just like the day when God met Moses through a burning bush, God introduces God's self simply as "I am," the one who brought them out of slavery. With this introduction, God offers the people of Israel a statement of timeless relevance and history—words that signify creator, protector, lover, healer, and savior. Moreover, God's introduction of *I am* clarifies that theirs will be a relationship of infinite possibility—limited only by their willingness to accept the gift of unconditional love.

Today, Great I Am, prepare my heart to meet you anew. Show me how I have limited your love in my life, and extend to me the opportunity to come to you authentically in love. Amen.

During Snowpocalypse 2021, much of Texas was under several inches of snow and ice. Our power grid collapsed, and many of us were literally frozen in place. Without electricity, water, or natural gas, a whole new reality dawned on us. What we thought was so important only twenty-four hours earlier—Zoom, Netflix, jobs, and Wi-Fi—paled in comparison with our need for the basics of life.

When contemporary readers of today's text envision this part of God's introduction to the people of Israel, it strikes them as quite nonsensical. After all, who would make a fish or a piece of wood their god?

However, each day we are surrounded by gods of our own creation. We define ourselves by the title of our jobs, the ZIP Code of our homes, the praise of other people, or the accomplishments of our children. Our vacations are more lavish yet less restful. Our tables are more bountiful yet less filling. Texts and emails abound yet leave us craving real connection. The promises to spend more time with God fall by the wayside in the face of the pings of texts and the schedule of soccer games. We chase a dream of elusive joy that gets further and further out of reach no matter what new trinket we obtain.

God's warning to have no other gods is rooted in a simple reality: The created can never create the Creator. We will never have an authentic relationship or authentic joy disconnected from God. Every attempt to do so will leave us empty, overwhelmed, and dissatisfied. There is nothing wrong with family, jobs, service, or fun. But when we allow them to define us or become a measuring stick of our success, they will disappoint us every time.

Gracious God, remind us that we can never be fulfilled apart from you. Recalibrate our affections, and revive within us a genuine desire for only you. Amen.

Authentic Discipleship

My husband and I spent days arguing what to name our new puppy. A beautiful fawn-colored American Staffordshire Terrier from a long line of grand champions, our dog needed a name that would properly represent who he would be in our family. My husband wanted to name him Hamlet because the dog looked contemplative. But I wanted him to have a name worthy of his birth, our family, and our faith. So in the end, we named our new family member Thatcher (after Margaret) Stewart (after Maria) Wesley (after John and Charles) Hall.

Names are important. I believe they are both symbolic and prophetic. We spend considerable time telling our children not to embarrass the family name. Many of us spend tremendous amounts of money to wear clothes, buy cars, or attend schools because of a name. The way we speak someone's name tells a lot about how we feel about them and their relationship with us.

Therefore, is it any wonder that God would care so much about God's name? Our text today is an essential reminder of the sacredness of God's name. To hold something sacred is to revere it and honor it as distinctive and without equal.

How we speak our Creator's name reveals our true understanding of God's character and identity. To toss it out as a curse or indication of frustration indicates that at our core, we hold very little distinction between the One who loves, cares, and provides for us and the guy who struck out in the ninth inning with the bases loaded. So think about your conversations today, and reflect on your use of God's name.

Throughout history, O Lord, your authentic disciples have used your name to set captives free, give the blind sight, and feed the hungry. Your name is excellent, and there is none like it in the world. Remind me each day to keep it holy. Amen.

My passion is wildlife photography. Over the years I have learned you can't force nature to give you a great picture. The animals and the light follow their own schedules and are not interested in making a good picture. I have lots of favorite photos, but the one that moves me most is the one I call "Daybreak."

As the morning was breaking atop Mount Nebo, I was fortunate to capture the sun as it rose to reveal the Dead Sea and Israel in the distance. On that cold December morning, I felt a kinship with Moses and David, who must also have been awed by the beauty of God's creation.

Psalm 19 provides authentic disciples with insight into how we can learn from God. The psalmist praises two sources for our instruction: Creation and God's word. Never in competition, the heavens, earth, seas, and God's word work together to teach us about God's essential nature.

Too often we busy ourselves with our destination rather than the pathways that take us there. We decry the rained-out ballgame, the snow-covered streets, or the brightness of the morning sun during our commute. Instead we should look up into the vastness of the sky. Feel the autumn breeze blow across our skin while we are being warmed by the midday sun. Stand before a tree and ask how it knew when it was time to bud. Each speaks volumes about God's power, attention to detail, and engineering prowess without saying a word. Apple trees bear apples, and the ocean does not suddenly depart and head for the mountains. Each is a perfectly obedient reflection of its creator.

Elohim, you are a master builder. Your creation testifies to your glory. Let me bask in your artistic prowess, appreciating every detail under your skies. Allow me to reflect the earth's beauty in each beat of my heart and word from my lips. Amen.

When was the last time you read a map? I mean one of those paper maps that our parents used to buy at gas stations and could never be properly refolded. My dad used those maps during my childhood and would study them before every road trip so he would know every cutoff, side highway, and cultural site to make the trip a learning experience.

In today's reading, David explores the second element of how God instructs authentic disciples in their earthly journey. Each verse in our study today tells us something that God's word provides us in our quest to live a disciple's life: revival, wisdom, enlightenment, warning and counsel, and reward.

When illuminated by the Holy Spirit, God's word provides a perfect road map for our lives. There are no shortcuts in authentic discipleship, but there are plenty of pitfalls. So many things deplete our souls before we even put our shoes on to begin the day. Concerns about family, finances, health, or the state of the world can leave us barren of the fruit that testifies to the world of the bounty of living for Christ—diminishing our witness and undermining the Great Commission. Our willingness to immerse ourselves in God's word, in full reflection rather than in a "done that, check it off" manner, plants seeds that yield fruit for the world. Grab your map and get to living!

Gracious God, make your word like the sweetest honey to my weary soul. Strengthen my resolve and testimony to walk among those who scoff at our faith. Make me a bountiful table of your love for a hungry world. Amen.

At first glance, the texts for our study today may seem to have little to do with each other, but they speak of the same problem for those who seek to be authentic disciples of Christ: our inability to accept truthful correction.

After meeting God at Mount Sinai, the children of Israel were sure of one thing: They didn't want a repeat of the smoke, fire, and a voice like a trumpet. So they decided that meeting God for a weekly one-on-one was definitely off the list. They told Moses, "You speak to us, and we will hear; but let not God speak to us, lest we die." Were they going to die? No. But I bet it sure felt like it. Having God hold a mirror up to our behavior would undoubtedly feel like the end of the world. *Let us just hear from your messenger and we will get along just fine.*

Jesus' parable of the wicked tenants highlights what happens when the people get their way. When the landlord sends intermediaries to collect what the tenants owe him, the tenants prove that they don't respect or value the messengers and don't accept the message. Each time, when a servant shows up to take stock of the fruitfulness of the tenants, rather than listen and make an account, they choose to kill the messenger.

Our acceptance of God's truth-tellers in our lives is a mark of maturation as disciples. If your first response is to defend or attack, then you might want to ask yourself why. Many a bruised ego and insecure soul who had been praying for discernment has rejected the answer to prayer.

Lord, push me to hear your correction with open ears and a closed mouth. Remind me to treat your messengers as gifts from you for my growth and strengthening in your love. Amen.

What makes you credible? Why should people listen to you? Is it your age? Your business experience? Where you went to school? Your profession? I am ashamed to say it, but I have used my resume and awards to win arguments far too many times. Sometimes I feel the need to prove that I am worthy of having my voice heard at work, at home, and even when I am doing the work of Christ.

Yet Paul takes me and others to task by reminding us that these worldly accolades have no real meaning when we become authentic disciples of Christ. The source of our authority, power, and efforts can no longer be rooted in our human accomplishments. On the contrary, Paul says, "I regard everything as loss because of the surpassing value of knowing Christ Jesus my Lord." A loss? Seriously?

Everything? My degrees, my heritage, my connections, my 401(k)? Yes, Paul says, they are no longer your currency as a disciple. What the world values is of little importance to Christ.

When we commit to Christ, we renounce the gods of this world and serve the one true God. We cast off the jewels of ego and choose a crown of righteousness. Why? Because the very idea of being in Christ should be more compelling than all the riches of this present world. When we die, nothing will matter but our eternal works. So the most daring thing any of us can do is stand before the world and allow Christ and Christ alone to be the foundation of our lives.

Today, O Christ, I am choosing to renounce my power for yours. I will strive to forgo the rights offered by this world to pursue the simple and tremendous joy of being your authentic disciple. Amen.

RSVPing to God's Invitations

OCTOBER 9–15, 2023 • PETER M. WALLACE

SCRIPTURE OVERVIEW: The texts this week remind us of how quickly we can turn away from God. Even while Moses is on the mountain receiving the Ten Commandments—the first of which is not to worship any other gods—the people fashion an idol and begin to worship it. The psalmist refers to this story as evidence of how often the Israelites have gone astray, and yet God repeatedly has restored them. The parable in Matthew speaks of many who are invited to a banquet, yet they reject the invitation of the king. It is often read as a warning about turning our backs on God's gracious invitation. Paul encourages the Philippians to seek God with confidence in difficult situations and to focus their thoughts in ways that lead them closer to God.

QUESTIONS AND SUGGESTIONS FOR REFLECTION

- Read Exodus 32:1-14. When have you or your faith community gotten it wrong? When have you interceded with God on others' behalf?
- Read Psalm 106:1-6, 19-23. How has forgetting that you can be wrong hurt you or your faith community? How has admitting that you were wrong strengthened you or your faith community?
- Read Philippians 4:1-9. What issue or conflict has divided your faith community? How might Paul's urging to "be of the same mind in the Lord" help you work toward peace?
- Read Matthew 22:1-14. What work might you need to do to open your heart so you can resolve a conflict?

Episcopal priest and author or editor of fifteen books, including *The Passionate Jesus* and *Getting to Know Jesus (Again)*; executive producer and host of the ecumenical *Day1* radio/podcast program, accessible online at Day1.org.

THANKSGIVING DAY (CANADA)

The psalmist lovingly reveals God's gentle yet mighty care for creation. The earth yields all that we need because God visits it, waters it, and enriches it. God's life-giving water supports all growing things. God's strong hands softly work the earth, preparing it for fruit-bearing. God blesses the growth.

We are clay in God's hands, and God works in our lives in the same way God works the earth. God waters us with the Spirit of joy. God enriches us with every spiritual nourishment. The river of God's Spirit washes over us, cleansing us. God provides the bread of life, the necessities to sustain us.

God waters our spirit lavishly, works our hard edges, softens our hearts, showers us with peace, and blesses our growth. God crowns the year—and our whole lives—with a generous bounty.

How open are we to God's molding, pruning, and working of our hearts?

On this day of thanksgiving, spend a moment with these natural images. Acknowledge that God's grace abounds toward us, and that all we have and need comes from God's hand.

Then let's consider how we are caring for God's creation— the source of this provision—and what more we can do to join with others in that holy work. With our hand in God's, we can choose to accept the invitation to walk the path of God's generosity with fulsome gratitude. When we do, our life is full. We have all we need and more.

What can we do today to help ensure that the rest of the world, our siblings in God's creation, are able to express their thanksgiving for God's provision as well?

God of creation, my heart is full of thanksgiving for your abundant provision. Kindle in me a desire to join others in caring for your creation. Amen.

Moses meets with God on the mountain, but the Israelites in the valley below decide he is taking too long. Before you know it, they've convinced hapless Aaron to build a golden idol they can worship and sacrifice to—a god they can pretend is the one who delivered them from Egypt.

Then things get out of hand. With their gaudy yet powerless idol, God's people break God's first commandment—that God alone is God—and then only compound their disobedience.

Of course, God knows what's happening and is angered by the people's swift infidelity. God tells Moses, "Go down at once! Your people, whom you brought up out of the land of Egypt, have acted perversely." God seems to blame Moses for this unholy mess, calling them "your people."

That doesn't seem fair, and Moses flips the script, telling God they were "your people, whom you brought out of the land of Egypt with great power and with a mighty hand." *Touché.*

"And the Lord changed his mind." All it took was one person, Moses, to plead with God to spare the people.

So, can we change God's mind about our own situations? Our unanswered prayers, our unmet needs, our unfulfilled dreams? Theologians have argued about this for centuries, but let's not get bogged down with that question. Instead let's note that it's not about Moses being a model. It is better to realize, as this passage reveals, that God is a jealous God. God invites us to know, trust, and love God wholeheartedly. God wants us.

How deeply do we want God?

God of liberation, you set us free from our spiritual enslavement so we can worship and serve you. Give us strength to respond with wholehearted trust and enthusiastic faith. Amen.

The psalmist sings praise to the Lord and gives thanks because the Lord's steadfast love endures forever. But then the psalmist acknowledges a bitter truth: "Both we and our ancestors have sinned; we have committed iniquity, have done wickedly."

Case in point: The Israelites sinned by worshiping a gaudy idol—the story we read yesterday from Exodus. "They forgot God, their Savior." And God said they would be destroyed, but Moses stood in the breach and convinced God to turn away the well-deserved wrath.

It's one thing to admit that you've broken faith with God, as the Israelites did. It's another thing altogether to take responsibility for the entire group of which you're a part—and even those who came before you.

Neither confession is easy. It takes a humble heart, an honest mind, and an obedient spirit to acknowledge what's gone wrong and why. The psalmist admits that they are just as much sinners as their ancestors who literally rebelled against God. The psalmist doesn't blame the people's sin on those past acts or avoid their personal responsibility.

We can blame our family for our character flaws. We can point to the environment in which we grew up. We can even let ourselves off the hook simply with the excuse that we're faulty human beings.

But God invites us to take responsibility for those actions or words that have hurt ourselves or others, that move us away from God's ways, that stifle our servant heart. It's important to clean the slate with our loving and forgiving God through honest, meaningful prayer. Only then can we freely and fully express our praise for God's steadfast love.

God of forgiveness, help me to be honest about the ways I have hurt myself and others, the ways I have tripped up in my walk with you. Then fill me with your forgiving spirit, with your steadfast love, and with a heart full of pure praise. Amen.

Rejoice in the Lord always; again I will say, Rejoice." Beautiful words simply put yet so difficult to achieve. Perhaps that's why Paul has to repeat the invitation. But what does it mean?

Celebrate God. Acknowledge the Lord gladly. Express joy over God's presence!

Given all the graces God has showered us with, why is this so difficult? Because we get sidetracked by the pile of work that confronts us. The wandering child that worries us. The finances that trouble us. The ailing parent that concerns us. The lingering illness that scares us. The ever-present stress that keeps us captive. If only life would cooperate, it would be easy to "rejoice in the Lord always."

Paul's circumstances didn't stop him. After all, when he urged his fellow believers to revel joyfully in God, he was locked in a dark, damp prison cell. Paul knew stress and pain. So perhaps one's circumstances don't have to inhibit one's joy.

What if we simply tried to accept this invitation? What if, just for a moment, we set aside our worries, fears, concerns, pains, hardships, and circumstances and spent a moment in joyful praise? Praise God for the love and mercy lavished upon us. Glorify God for the salvation we have in Christ. Adore God for all the ways our prayers have been answered. Sing to the Lord and revel in God's presence. Do it just for a few minutes right now. And tomorrow for a few minutes more. Then for an hour or two early next week.

We have been invited to a joyful party that never ends. Let's RSVP. Before we know it, we'll be rejoicing in the Lord all day, every day, no matter where we are.

God of joy, thank you for your invitation to rejoice, to celebrate your presence in my life, even amid all the concerns and fears. I accept, and I will bring a guest or two with me. Amen.

RSVPing to God's Invitations   341

The mind can play terrible tricks at night, keeping itself wide awake in the dark. One after another, life's cares and concerns arise and demand attention, setting loose adrenaline to fight or flee—which only wakes us further, creating more worry that we aren't getting enough sleep.

In those moments, God whispers to us to stop fretting. "Do not worry about anything." Instead, pray. Pray about your concerns and worries. Oh, it can be a fine line between worrying over something and praying for something, can't it? Sometimes praying about something only causes more anxiety.

In those times I turn to meditative prayer like the Jesus Prayer of the Orthodox tradition: "Lord Jesus Christ, have mercy on me." Or the Lord's Prayer. Or any memorized prayer or psalm or scripture that moves my focus away from my worries and onto God. Before long, I drift away into peaceful sleep.

A wonderful thing happens when we accept God's invitation to lift our concerns into the holy presence and then let go of them, putting them wholly into God's hands. When we allow Christ to displace the worries at the core of our life, we experience true peace. We catch a glimpse of God's perfect will; we accept the reality that this divine peace guards our hearts and our minds in Christ Jesus. We settle down in the realization that God is working in and through every situation that worries us.

What we choose to focus on, and how we choose to focus on it, is up to us. God invites us to choose prayer. To choose a thankful heart. To choose Jesus at the core of our life. To choose peace.

God of peace, when my mind goes feverish with fear, pour your cool, calming, peaceful presence over me. Help me focus on Christ, who invites me to place my burdens in his strong hands. Help me choose to pray. Amen.

Jesus loved to tell stories. And it seems he often enjoyed confusing his listeners! His parables are designed to express a truth about God or the way of life to which God calls us. We may get tripped up by story details, which may or may not have relevance to the main point. It is best to try to discern Jesus' primary message with the help of the Spirit.

In this story a king who's planning a wedding banquet for his son is frustrated by the very few RSVPs he has received, and then he becomes enraged by the humiliating, cruel, and violent responses he does get. So he has the people who mistreated his servants obliterated. I doubt any of us have had the kind of reactions to our party invitations that the king did, but if we did, we too might be enraged. He finally sends his forces into the streets to invite anyone they can find, good or bad.

Jesus is telling his listeners that God has issued invitations to enjoy the divine presence in an eternal celebration, sending messengers time and again to make the offer clear. But the invitation has been repeatedly ignored, scorned, even killed over. It's saddening. Enraging. *Ridiculous!*

God can't seem to get enough of us, begging us all to come to the party. How do we respond? Take a moment today to contemplate all the divine summonses—God's glorious, gracious, generous invitations to live in the way of Jesus—that you have ignored, avoided, laughed at, shrugged off . . . or worse.

Open your heart instead to say yes to God's invitation. And join the party!

God of welcome, open my heart to the gracious invitations you send me—encouragements to love, to serve, to celebrate your presence. Invitations I so often toss aside because I'm busy, don't care, or fear them. Now, I accept them with pleasure. Amen.

The parable we pondered yesterday continues. The king's servants have invited anyone they could find to the banquet—good and bad folk filled the wedding hall. It would be nice if the story ended there, but Jesus persists.

"When the king came in to see the guests, he noticed a man there who was not wearing a wedding robe. And he said to him, 'Friend, how did you get in here without a wedding robe?' And he was speechless."

We might be speechless too! How is it fair for the king to demand proper attire when all sorts of riffraff have been invited at the last minute because the original guests refused to show? It gets worse: The man is bound hand and foot and thrown into the outer darkness where he will weep and gnash his teeth.

What is the moral of Jesus' story? It is that "Many are called, but few are chosen." Meditate on the distinction between being called and being chosen. It's all about our response.

The other guests knew that if they were to accept the king's invitation, they should dress and act the part. This man does not—he sees only a good time for free. You see, it can be tempting to take God's calling lightly—to assume that once we're at the party we can just stay as we are.

But no, we need to don a wedding robe—a symbol Jesus' listeners would have understood. In light of the king's gracious invitation, what is due in return is respectful, righteous obedience—an active, committed faith.

You've been invited. Are you dressed properly? Consider prayerfully what you're doing to broaden God's kingdom—to free the oppressed, heal the sick, comfort the brokenhearted, and make peace. That's your wedding robe.

God of our calling, may we respond to your extravagant invitation with a sober, heartfelt desire to wear the robe of righteous living as we follow our Savior in an active, living faith. Amen.

To Be Known

OCTOBER 16–22, 2023 • LYN PACE

SCRIPTURE OVERVIEW: Popular images often portray God as a passive grandfather figure. However, this is not the picture scripture provides. God's presence has a profound impact on the physical world. In Exodus, Moses feels insecure about the calling on his life and asks to see God's glory. God in part grants this request, but no one can experience the presence of God completely and live. The psalmist describes how God is exalted and how God's holiness shakes the earth itself. The New Testament readings explore different themes. Paul opens his letter to the Thessalonians by commending them for their faith and partnership in spreading the gospel. In Matthew, the Pharisees attempt to trap Jesus in his words, but he confounds their efforts.

QUESTIONS AND SUGGESTIONS FOR REFLECTION

- Read Exodus 33:12-23. When have you struggled to believe that God is with you? How did you find a sign of God's presence?
- Read Psalm 99. How has God heard your cry? How can you listen with God for the cries of others?
- Read 1 Thessalonians 1:1-10. When does your faith call you to live in a counter-cultural way? How do you show the world how to live?
- Read Matthew 22:15-22. You belong to God. How do you feel God's call on your life?

College chaplain at Oxford College of Emory University and an ordained United Methodist minister; has written for his local newspaper as well as a devotional app; enjoys running, reading, good food with friends, and Jimmy Buffett concerts; lives in Oxford, GA, with his spouse and ten-year-old.

It is good to be known. In my local coffee shop, Gina knows me. She has been working there since it opened more than five years ago and knows my name because my order is always the same. We have had conversations, shared laughs and a few tears too. If it is not too busy, she always has my coffee ready even before I check out at the front register.

How are you known? Perhaps you are known as a parent, child, or sibling; uncle or aunt; teammate or teacher; coach or student. Maybe you are the mayor, dean, server, minister, doctor, or paramedic. How are you known and who knows you?

Our readings this week are drawn together by the theme of "being known." They highlight the ways God knows us, how we are children of God.

In Exodus, Moses makes his third intercession on behalf of God's people, pleading for God to remain present along the journey to the Promised Land. As Moses asks whom God will send with him to assist with this journey, he seems to already know. He reminds God of God's previous promise: "I know you by name and think highly of you" (CEB).

God knows us by name and goes with us. When someone forgets our name or misspells it, or when we do not feel welcome—especially in places where we should—it is a gift that God still knows us by name. Being known by God also means being loved. That truth never goes away.

Today's text reveals a God who not only knows us by name but will bring us back to our true self by God's grace again and again. God says to Moses, "I'll do exactly what you've asked because you have my special approval, and I know you by name" (CEB).

How are you known in the world? Give thanks that you are known and loved by God!

Callings come in a variety of forms, and we see many ways of responding. Today's psalm reminds us of the calling Moses and Aaron responded to as priests. Samuel, which means "name of God" or "God heard," was also called by God. Samuel, the last of the ruling judges, anointed both Saul and David. The psalmist includes these leaders to describe the relationship between God and God's people.

When we were discerning names for our now ten-year-old, we knew we wanted a meaningful name. The middle name was easy, we both loved to laugh and hoped he would too. We chose Isaac, which from the biblical Hebrew means "he laughs." The first name was harder, but we finally landed on Samuel, which we had read meant "one called by God."

The other requirement for names was that they needed to translate into Spanish, the primary language spoken by my spouse's father and family who are all from Colombia. She wanted a name that would feel familiar to the family there and to my father-in-law, a professor of Hispanic studies at a college in South Carolina. This would help Sam feel more known to his South American family.

One of the icebreakers I use repeatedly with new students at the college is a name game. "Tell us what you know about your name." Most students give the meaning of their name or offer a story of how their parents chose it. It is always a revealing moment as we build relationships together.

Our names become markers of how we are known in the world. It is the name of God, though, that the psalmist says requires our attention. Magnify the Lord our God and bow low at God's holy mountain. Why? Because our God is holy and knows us by name.

What is the story of your name? Share that story with someone in your life today, and invite them to share too.

To Be Known

Many of Paul's letters follow a similar format, especially at the beginning. They open with a greeting to specific people or communities. Then Paul presents the thanksgiving portion of the letter, which allows him to reconnect as he remembers them and reminds them of their faith. This seems to be a way of drawing closer to the community even though they are geographically separated.

Paul follows his usual pattern in today's letter to the community at Thessalonica. Not only does he want them to know he remembers them, but he connects their mission to his own by giving thanks for their work of faith, labor of love, and steadfastness of hope in Jesus. "Brothers and sisters," he says, "you are loved by God, and we know that he has chosen you" (CEB). Again, our theme of "being known" is front and center.

Being known by God also means knowing that we are buoyed by the Holy Spirit on our faith journey. Paul reminds the community that the good news came to them not only in speech but with power and the Holy Spirit. Paul knows that his words to them have been influential, but he admits that his words alone cannot do the work of God. It is the ever-present Holy Spirit that helps them understand they are known by God. Despite their great suffering, the message of the good news came to them through the Holy Spirit "with joy."

The Thessalonians became imitators of the Lord and those who shared the good news with them. Because they were known by Paul and God, they became examples to other communities and helped this message of faith to ring out. They shared God's loving embrace widely, and Paul gives thanks for all of them constantly in his prayers.

Who will you remember today? Pray for them, write to them, and then visit them if you are able.

When everything shut down in March 2020, our seven-year-old's world completely changed. School moved home and online, soccer abruptly ended, and play dates with friends disappeared. His time with his parents increased, including many walks through our small town as we adjusted to the changes.

During this time of significant shifts, one of the highlights was an increase in handwritten letters he received. One of my students who had provided childcare before the pandemic wrote him a thoughtful note. His art teacher sent notes on cards with paintings by famous artists they had been studying. One of his best friends from school had his mom drop off notes to our mailbox with special Lego pieces in them. This exchange went on through much of the summer of 2020.

There was much to be celebrated in these letters, just as there is in Paul's letters. Our son had not been forgotten. The letters encouraged him to take time to write back, which meant he not only responded to the person but remembered them too. The ongoing exchange of letters and Lego pieces with his friend strengthened that relationship for later in-person meetings. All the letters reminded him that he mattered. He was known.

Paul reminds the Thessalonians that they have been chosen and are known, and because of this, they have also set an example to others through their faith. "The message about the Lord rang out from you. . . . The news about your faithfulness to God has spread so that we don't even need to mention it" (CEB). Just as they were known by God, so have they revealed to others that they are known by God too. This is the work of faith, labor of love, and strength of hope in our Lord Jesus Christ.

Write a letter to someone for whom you are grateful. Remind them of how/why they matter to you.

To Be Known

Once God commits to Moses to do what he has asked, Moses pleads, "Please show me your glorious presence" (CEB).

The back-and-forth dialogue between Moses and God before verse eighteen feels as if Moses has discerned his own purpose. God remains with him through his doubts, questions, and challenges. Moses presses God for clarity in his calling, especially on behalf of the people with whom he is called to minister and lead.

In the second half of the text, Moses is promised goodness, kindness, and compassion as God will pass in front of him. He will not see God's face, but he will experience God's glorious presence.

Irenaeus, bishop of Lyons in the second century, was one of the early leaders who expanded the reach of Christianity into the region now known as France. He is also remembered for teaching us that "the glory of God is humanity fully alive."

The response to God's passing in front of Moses or us, like Irenaeus says, is humanity fully alive. We are known fully and are called to know God, but we are finite creatures and cannot comprehend the totality and mystery of our God. Instead, we are called to live life fully alive, a reflection of God's own glory as it moves all around us and in the world.

Theologian and civil rights leader Howard Thurman once said that our task is to figure out what makes us come alive and then go do it. The world, he said, needs people that have come alive. If the glory of God is humanity fully alive, our task is to practice discernment so that we pay attention to the holy in our midst and respond to it. Then we will radiate God's glory as we move in the world.

What makes you come alive? If you need help with your discernment, ask God and then ask trusted friends.

They were plotting to entrap Jesus. The Pharisees sent their disciples to him and asked him a question about paying taxes to the emperor. As Jesus so often does, he used a question to foil the Pharisees' plot to trap him. We usually see this in his parables—how he flips the situation, causing us to look at familiar things from another angle.

Jesus does not use a parable here; instead he takes their question and responds with another, "Why are you putting me in a bind?" (CEB) He then asks who is on the coin. I especially like how Clarence Jordan, the founder of Koinonia Farm in Americus, Georgia, shapes this part of the text as he interprets it in his *Cotton Patch Gospel*. In Jordan's rendering, Jesus asks about a dollar bill, "Whose engraving is on it?"

An engraving conjures up the word image, and that reminds me of how important the idea of *image* is in the Christian faith. We are told early in Genesis that we are made in the image of God. Put another way, God is engraved on us. We are known.

The coin bears the image of the emperor or the government, and the things that belong to the emperor are just that, things. They are material. They are not permanent. They are lifeless coins that, though important and significant to everyday living, are not life.

But that which bears God's image—all human beings and, I would argue, all of God's creation—belongs to God. As one college chaplain colleague says, "We bear God's image—as the palm of God's hand bears ours."

Thank you, God, for creating us in your image. Help us treat ourselves and others as if this is true. Amen.

The implicit question in this exchange, "Whose engraving is this on the coin?" comes back to us as it did to those listening to Jesus. Just as it did when farmer and theologian Clarence Jordan reworded it for his community in the mid-1900s.

What belongs to God?

Is it everything?

Clarence Jordan's "God movement" was an experiment in responding to the world's materialism with intentional Christian community. Though they could not avoid relying on money and some material goods to live, they were able to create a community that responded to God's call on their lives, shared their resources, and supported one another in faith and formation. They believed that not only were they created in the image of God but that they belonged to God. They believed that humanity belonged to God, and this was demonstrated primarily through how they treated their neighbors. They paid White folks and Black folks the same wage and sat together at the same table for meals in South Georgia in the Jim Crow South. That was unheard of in those days, but it was not unheard of in the city of God.

They were discerning their life amid God's life. Jesus is helping us do the same in Matthew's Gospel. To know that we are known by God means to know that our neighbor is too. We may not be sure sometimes what to give to the emperor. It is always clear, though, what belongs to God.

For Christians, that clarity comes at the table where we are all invited to stretch out our vulnerable hands to receive the gifts of God. Why? Because we are people of God who bear God's image. It is engraved on us.

Let everything that has breath give thanks to God. Take a deep breath in, count to three, and let it go. Repeat as often as you need. Remember you are known.

Wandering and Wondering

OCTOBER 23–29, 2023 • SOPHIA AGTARAP

SCRIPTURE OVERVIEW: The end of Deuteronomy completes the story of the life of Moses. Although he led the people out of Egypt, he was not allowed to enter the Promised Land because he lost his temper in the desert. The difficult task of leading the people back to the land will fall to Joshua. The psalmist calls out to God for mercy because the people have been suffering as a result of their disobedience. Paul defends himself against the charge that he has been preaching out of a desire for fame or money; the approval he seeks comes only from God. Jesus has yet another confrontation with religious leaders attempting to trick him. He avoids their schemes and emphasizes that love of God and love of neighbor summarize the entire law.

QUESTIONS AND SUGGESTIONS FOR REFLECTION

- Read Deuteronomy 34:1-12. When has a leadership transition in your faith community been difficult for you? When has it been sacred?
- Read Psalm 90:1-6, 13-17. How do you make God your dwelling place?
- Read 1 Thessalonians 2:1-8. How can you strive to love those whom you have never met? How can you meet new people with love as siblings?
- Read Matthew 22:34-46. How do you wrestle with the Bible? When have your questions strengthened your faith or revealed something new?

A 1.5-generation Filipina American and intercultural communicator who values curiosity and wonder; serves as director of equity and language services for a school district in Washington state.

I am not much of a hiker, but the trails I have explored here in the Pacific Northwest have stirred in me wonder and awe. Reading the first verse of today's scripture passage, I wonder what that hike was like from the Plains of Moab to Mount Nebo facing Jericho. How steep was the slope? Was the path arid and dusty, or was it lush? Could Moses smell the Dead Sea as he made the ascent?

As the daughter of a United Methodist clergyperson, I have an interesting relationship with land and place. Having moved every few years, home for me was more about people than places. The more I learned about my parents' ancestral home in the Philippines, the more I felt a kinship to it, even though I had spent little time there.

The places that are named in this reading may not mean much to us today, but we should linger a bit in these initial verses. Read over the names of these places and look them up in an atlas or Google them. Imagine the expansiveness of the "whole land" that the Lord showed Moses and imagine what it would be like to experience these places.

Perhaps in this imagining, we might find ourselves wondering about the places where we live and move and have our being. Where is home for you? Whose land do you occupy? I, for example, live on the traditional homelands of the Puyallup and Coast Salish peoples. In our wondering and wandering, may we find ourselves more connected to the Lord who showed Moses "the whole land."

God of all people and places, stir in us curiosity and a sense of wonder for your people and the lands they call home. Amen.

In many ways, the COVID-19 pandemic led us into our own time of wilderness wandering and wondering. As we experienced the shutting down and reopening of our places of worship, work, school, social gathering—the ways we did life together—many of us began daydreaming about new possibilities. While navigating the realities and demands of life and grief in a pandemic, we have begun reassessing priorities and privileges, imagining other ways to organize our lives.

Sometimes, we find ourselves living as Moses was in an already-but-not-yet moment. We have caught glimpses of what life could be after experiencing a global pandemic and mourning loss in so many ways: new relationships, callings, and ways of being. Some of the various communities that held our intersecting identities have strengthened and shown promise of interacting in ways that we never before considered. Other communities have proven unhelpful, and we must leave them so we can progress. We have seen what is possible as we have adapted to new routines, let go of practices and habits that were not serving us, and allowed ourselves and our communities to experience life together a little differently.

We, like Moses, have helped shape some things into being that we will not see come to their fullness in our lifetime, but we have the gift of a clear vision of the destination.

What has God shown you? What visions and wonders and glimpses have you seen with your own eyes? How can you lend your prayers, presence, gifts, service, and witness to make the vision a reality?

God, meet us in the wilderness, in our wandering, and in our coming home. Amen.

As the daughter of a United Methodist pastor, the concept of home and dwelling has come to mean for me less about land and place and more about people. Our family immigrated to the United States when I was three years old, and my sense of home has since been formed by those people who came into my life—our lives—and not the structures and places where we lived.

Some of them were church members and neighbors, like Mrs. Gladys Hammer, who lived across the street from the parsonage and taught me all about her stone bird bath and how to care for it. Others are friends from elementary school I've recently reconnected with as adults. Still others are those friends I keep on speed dial for when there's something I need to process.

This passage from Psalm 90 invites us to think about our sense of home. What or who is home for someone in exile? For someone who has been displaced due to conflict and persecution? For those who have been rejected? For those who feel cut off from community and connection? I imagine the Israelites in their post-Exodus state of wandering and displacement must have felt some sense of kinship and connection to their ancestors, knowing that across generations, geographic spaces, and time, they found their home in God. God was and is and will be their refuge, their dwelling place.

As we experience wilderness moments in our lives—death of loved ones, loss of vocation or purpose, disconnection from community—we too are invited to remember God who has been our dwelling place for generations.

God who has always been and always will be, meet us in our wilderness moments, and help us remember your constancy and faithfulness from generation to generation. Amen.

I have a colleague who would end her emails with this invitation in her signature: *Make it count!* In a way, that is also the invitation to us in this portion of Psalm 90.

But what counts?

What are the contours of a life well lived? Of a life wisely lived? Is it a long life that is extended with exercise and good eating? Is it a life that was spent in service of others? Is it a life whose legacy continues in one's descendants?

I lived both inside and outside the United States and find it interesting how different societies approach life and death. In the United States, we try so hard to prolong life. We take supplements, buy skin-firming creams, dye our hair, and generally refuse to face the natural movement of our lives from birth to death.

The first funeral of a family member that I recall attending was my grandfather's. I was in elementary school, and his pneumonia progressed quickly during a visit to the Philippines. But what I remember most about his death was how we celebrated his life. As is customary, we held a wake at my mother's ancestral home for several days. That allowed family and friends from all over to make their way home. Live music, food, and stories about his kindness and generosity all punctuated the days leading up to the service and burial.

My grandfather, I believe, lived as a response to the petition, "Make the work of our hands last." I believe he petitioned to be filled every morning with God's faithful love so that his whole life was that of rejoicing and celebration.

Beloveds, as you seek the lines and curves, the practices and habits that define a life wisely lived, *make it count.*

God who calls us to work and rest, to wandering and wondering, stir in us a joy that sustains us all our days. Amen.

"They will know we are Christians by our love." I think about this line often and wonder what folks would think if they only had one interaction with me. Would they feel a sense of belonging? Would the interaction recognize their gifts and give them a sense of kinship? Would they be curious about the God I believe in and the Christ I follow because of the love and hospitality that I have shown?

As twenty-first century Christians, we may not think much about what it means to be an apostle of Christ. Many of us have places of worship, can attend our small groups without fear of persecution, and can get all the Christian literature we want—all great things. But what does a life of discipleship look like for those of us who are not personally or immediately the targets of opposition and injustice but live in an unjust world? What is discipleship when the dominant version of Christianity is individualistic and doesn't see the apostolic call as a call to community?

When I was growing up, our house was the place people gathered. Everyone from a friend of a friend who was passing through town and needed a place to stay to college friends who needed a home-cooked meal found our home to be a place to land.

In what ways are you accepting the call to use your whole self to share the gospel? How are your actions and words evidence of the love you have for God and neighbor?

"They will know we are Christians by our love." Or better yet, they will know we love God and neighbor by our love.

Nurturing God who calls us to embody "the gospel of God but also our own selves," test our hearts so that the love we experience from you will be poured out to our neighbors. Amen.

Throughout Matthew's Gospel, Jesus is perceived as a threat by the Pharisees. They confront him with question after question designed to stump and discredit him.

Jesus, of course, is well versed in scripture and continues to surprise and astonish them with his responses. When asked for the greatest commandment, Jesus quotes the first commandment from Moses: "You shall love the LORD your God with all your heart, and with all your soul, and with all your might" (Deut. 6:5). But Jesus doesn't leave it there. He includes love of neighbor, extending the love of God to those whom God loves.

When I think about the divisive times we are living in, I know that they are no more divided or acrimonious than anything people have experienced before. But today's reading is painful evidence that we keep missing the mark of loving God and those God loves.

A sentiment that has started appearing on yard signs, T-shirts, and bumper stickers over the last few years can be summed up like this: *Love your neighbor who doesn't look like you, think like you, love like you, speak like you, pray like you, vote like you.* It is unfortunate that many of us need Jesus' straightforward commandment clarified like this, but Christians have proven over and over again that we can read this story and not even consider loving the Pharisees.

God who invites, you have called us to love you and all those you love. Open up our senses so that we see you in all we encounter, from the grass that grows to our neighbor we pass on the street. Then we will be able love all that you have created with all our being. Amen.

In today's reading, Matthew presents a comic scene in which Jesus bests the religious experts and shows the limitations of any narrow, literal reading of scripture.

In the part we discussed yesterday, some Pharisees try to stump Jesus by asking him what the greatest commandment is. He astonishes them by not quite accepting their terms and offering two commandments that together sum up the entire law and the prophets, something they had not thought could be done. They are testing him on the letter of the law, but he answers with the spirit of the law.

The second part of the scene is even more interesting. Jesus turns the tables on the Pharisees and asks them a question they cannot answer about the Messiah, a topic they had been studying all their lives. Surely the Pharisees should have some explanation for why David would call his own descendant "Lord," but they don't. And the reason they don't is that the answer isn't in their scripture, where they think all answers are to be found. Interestingly, Jesus doesn't explain the riddle to them. He sends them off with a question that undermines their certainty. Maybe this led some of them—like Nicodemus—to seek the answer, but we can't know because Matthew doesn't tell us.

Matthew's concern is with his readers. He has set us up for this exchange from the very first verse: "An account of the genealogy of Jesus the Messiah, the son of David." We are in the exciting position of knowing more than the experts and seeing how Jesus is the unexpected Messiah who makes everything make sense. But we must not miss the cautionary tale here too: It is easy to become experts in our religion and forget that "everyone who loves is born of God and knows God" (1 John 4:7). We do not want to get so caught up in our rules and traditions that we can't see Jesus standing right in front of us as the answer.

God of wonder, invite us to curiosity as we learn what it means to love and serve you and those who you love. Amen.

Pressing Forward

OCTOBER 30–NOVEMBER 5, 2023 • KIMBERLY C. ORR

SCRIPTURE OVERVIEW: An overarching theme of the All Saints Day lectionary texts is "Keep pressing forward, despite observable challenges, because God is still at work among us." Joshua seeks to bolster the sojourner's faith by linking the present moment with the rescuing actions of God in the past. The psalm is a song of corporate thanksgiving, a deep inhalation and a collective sigh of relief from the those who were drowning in the dark waters of exile. In Thessalonians we read an apostolic plea to allow the word of God to continue its revelatory, good-news work among believers. And in Matthew we hear the charged opening of Jesus' final discourse, as he sharply warns against religious arrogance and hypocrisy that can hinder God's work of kingdom justice.

As we celebrate and remember "the great cloud of witnesses" who have preceded us in death, we are called to commit ourselves to navigating the faith-filled path that Jesus blazes before us (see Hebrews 12).

QUESTIONS AND SUGGESTIONS FOR REFLECTION

• Read Joshua 3:7-17. When have you had to trust leaders for the good of your community?

• Read Psalm 107:1-7, 33-37. Recall difficult times in your faith journey. How did you experience God's steadfast love through these times?

• Read 1 Thessalonians 2:9-13. What daily practices give you insight into God's word? How do you encourage others in their life of faith?

• Read Matthew 23:1-12. Do your leaders live what they preach? How do you strive to live the gospel?

Associate General Secretary of Discipleship Ministries of The United Methodist Church and Publisher of The Upper Room.

Psalm 107 opens with a Hebrew imperative, *hōdū*! ("Hey, everyone, let's give thanks!") Why? Because YHWH is good and faithful. How can I be sure that God is good? The fact that the congregation is standing there after the Exodus and the Exile shows that God faithfully led them out of their dead-end situation onto a "straight way, until they reached an inhabited town."

The opening of the psalm shows a people without direction or purpose, trying but failing to survive by their own wits. They have hemmed themselves into a no-win situation. Out of desperation, they cry out to the Lord, and before the verse can take a breath, God snatches them out of their box canyon and sets their feet on the path that leads to provision and life.

Choosing covenant faithlessness over faithfulness exposes the people of Israel to the dangers of the wasteland. Yet even amid their infidelity, God is still present among them. God provides manna and quail after the Exodus event (see Exodus 16:11-12), and later, the Lord even pulls up stakes and goes into exile with the people (see Ezekiel 10 and 11).

God's presence did not, however, prevent them from suffering the consequences of their choices. We can sense that a mature and robust faith is blooming within us when we are able to hold both of these realities in tension: God is with us and life is hard. Can we dare to walk away from our idols of Christian perfectionism and self-reliance? Can we risk—even when life is messy and we are in need—giving thanks for God's abiding presence among us?

Lord, you are good and your covenant love endures forever. Set our feet firmly on the path that leads to life. Increase our awareness of your abiding presence even when things may not go according to our plans or meet our expectations. Amen.

The interweaving of the impact of human choices with God's creating and un-creating activities is evident in today's passage. The psalmist briefly draws on imagery from the Noah story: "The LORD saw that the wickedness of humankind was great in the earth" and determined to "destroy them along with the earth" (Gen. 6:5, 13).

As image bearers of the Creator, we have a sacred duty as caretakers of all that God has created. Our actions and inaction are consequential. Either we live in harmony with God as creation's stewards (see Genesis 1:26-28; 2:15), or we do not. As the apostle Paul reminds us, "Creation waits with eager longing for the revealing of the children of God" (Rom. 8:19). We, my dear siblings in Christ, are these redeemed children of God for which creation is longing.

"The evil that human beings do" is not only about breaking the moral codes and the Ten Commandments; it is also about failing to keep the very first commandments ever issued to humanity (see Genesis 1:26-28). On balance, do we contribute to de-creation by exploiting and abusing the earth, or do we tend, keep, and guard it for the glory of God and the benefit of all? It is our responsibility as redeemed humanity to live so that the intentional stewardship of God's creation is evident in our lives.

As an aside, this evening—known as All Hallows Eve—has traditionally been spent in prayer and preparation for the celebration of All Saints Day. This Christian observance goes back more than 1300 years and is a perfect occasion to take account of how we have managed the earth for the sake of all its inhabitants.

Creator God, forgive us for too often living more in alignment with the forces of chaos than with stewardship for your creation. As we await the new heaven and earth, may we work to honor you and one another through reverent use of the resources you have left in our care. Amen.

All Saints Day

The distillation of Torah in the Sermon on the Mount recorded by Matthew portrays Jesus as the second Moses, seated on the mountainside, calling all earnest disciples into alignment with God's original design for humanity.

As we alluded to yesterday, the Creator intended from the beginning to cooperate with humanity in building out the earth and spreading abroad God's faithful nature. God's hope was subsequently focused on the people of Israel who received the call to be "priests to the nations" (Exod. 19:6). All who would follow Jesus have been summoned to rally around this same cause. The priestly attributes the church is bidden to embody are cataloged in our reading.

According to Jesus, to be *contented* (a better translation than "blessed") as a God-bearer derives from humility ("poor in spirit"), righteous suffering ("mourning" and "persecution"), not seeking personal advantage at the expense of others ("meekness"), being hungry for justice and ethical living ("righteousness"), showing mercy (like God), having a holistic commitment to truth ("pure in heart"), and being a conduit of wholeness and healing ("peacemaker").

Today, as we remember those who have preceded us in death—heroes of the faith and heroes of our lives who sought to exemplify these priestly characteristics—may we be encouraged by Jesus' imagery of comfort and a brighter tomorrow, while also keeping a clear-eyed perspective on what it means to be a citizen of God's kingdom here and now.

God of us all—those assembled in the great cloud of witnesses and those gathered on earth—today we remember those who have gone before us. May we live according to the teaching and example of Christ through the empowerment of the Holy Spirit. Amen.

Draw near and hear the words of the Lord your God" was the appeal from Joshua to the descendants of Israel as they stood along the banks of the Jordan at the edge of the Promised Land. In this moment, Joshua issued two imperatives, "draw near" and "hear," that focused the people's attention on YHWH's generative power and relational personhood rather than on the danger they were facing.

This was indeed a time of uncertainty for the Israelites. Their great leader Moses had recently died, and God had called Joshua to complete the mission of taking them across the Jordan River "into the land I am giving them" (Josh. 1:2). The people (and Joshua) needed reassurance that God was with them.

"Drawing near" and "hearing" are concepts that underpin the entirety of the Torah. In today's reading they evoke key, past events that signal God's faithful activity among the people. In particular, the liberated masses "drew near" to Moses at the base of Mount Sinai to receive the details of YHWH's covenant with them (see Exodus 34:32), and their foundational prayer is "Hear, O Israel: The Lord is our God, the Lord alone" (Deut. 6:4).

Where do we need to be reminded of God's presence and purpose today? Where do we need a renewal of our spiritual imagination? Draw near and listen.

Holy God, draw us near to hear your loving invitation to remember that your presence sustains us even in uncertain times. Amen.

While it is apparent that the intent of today's reading is to recall the Exodus through the Reed Sea (see Exodus 14:21-22), the attention-grabbing headline of the Jordan River crossing is Joshua's pronouncement, "By this you shall know that among you is the living God."

Not only is YHWH fulfilling covenant obligations by bringing the people called Israel into the long-promised land, but a physical representation of God's word and presence is walking ahead of them in the priesthood and the ark. This embodied word is re-creating and renewing a weary and disparate people as they ramble across yet another miraculously dry passageway.

From yesterday's reading we remember the call to "draw near and hear the words of the LORD your God." And what are these words? That God is awake and active, breathing new life into God's covenant people. As God walked with Adam and Eve in the Garden, so God walked with the people "during harvest season" into a land "flowing with milk and honey" (Exod. 3:8). Further, the genitive "your God" emphasizes God's loyal relationship with a people who have had to "sojourn in the wilderness" (see Numbers 14:33) for forty years to be purified and prepared for living in the land ahead of them.

This example of God's enduring presence among a less-than-faithful people should offer us hope. Contrary to how we may feel or what circumstances may imply, the fact is that YHWH remains committed to God's creational covenant with humanity. Thankfully, our foundation does not rest on shifting sands. As Jesus insists, "Everyone then that hears these words of mine and acts on them will be like a wise man who built his house on a rock" (Matt. 7:24).

Living God, you give us the words of life. Even when life is intolerable and we are tempted to abandon all faith and flee, your constancy brings us hope and contentment. Amen.

The opening of Jesus' final discourse in the Gospel of Matthew is a sharp warning against religious hubris. Jesus uses hyperbole to highlight the pretentiousness of a subset of the Jewish leadership. To be clear, the Pharisees of Jesus' day were not his mortal enemies. From the outset, Jesus acknowledges their authority and compliments their exposition of Torah. The issue at hand is *orthodoxy* (right belief) not producing *orthopraxy* (right doing). Hypocrisy and arrogance had become a seedbed for burdensome regulations that were choking out the tree of life, that is the Torah (see Proverbs 3:18). A life hidden in God was meant to be a wellspring of life, liberation, and joy—not a weight to carry. The presumption of religious superiority had blinded some Jewish leaders to the possibility of embracing the embodiment of YHWH standing right in front of them.

This gospel drama is being played out simultaneously on two stages in this passage. On a textual level, Jesus warns a group of his Jewish contemporaries to guard against exalting themselves. But we also see that the author of Matthew is using this story from Jesus' life to warn his Christian contemporaries that they are vulnerable to the same blindness and self-deceit that tempted the Pharisees.

We can certainly carry this scene forward into our own time by reaching back to God's warning to Cain, "Sin is lurking at the door; its desire is for you, but you must master it" (Gen. 4:7). Through the grace and presence of the Holy Spirit may we be strengthened to push back against the temptation to "be right in our own eyes and shrewd in our own sight" (Isa. 5:21).

God who searches the depth of our being, ground us firmly in your love for us, so that we may have the courage to face the truth of our failings. We long for you to mend our brokenness and restore us in humility. Amen.

Our week together closes with a victory chant, recorded for us by John of Patmos. He gives us a vision of the celestial throne room transformed into a coliseum abuzz with a diverse, exuberant crowd wildly waving palm branches like gladiatorial banners and shouting, "Salvation belongs to our God who is seated on the throne, and to the Lamb!" (Rev. 7:10).

This is no passive audience. The assembled saints have persevered through the horrors of life and death, persecution and disgrace. They are celebrating their ultimate victory won for them by their champion, the Lamb of God. The irony is, of course, that a lamb is a small and vulnerable sacrificial animal, and some of those depicted as shouting from the ramparts would have died for their faith on the fields of civic arenas, such as the Circus Maximus and the Circus of Nero.

This imagery is a satire of the parades and spectacles that were held for Roman emperors and politicians, but it is also a window into the inverse ethics of the kingdom of God. "Jesus said, 'Truly I tell you, there is no one who has left house or [family] or fields, for my sake and for the sake of the good news, who will not receive a hundredfold now in this age . . . and in the age to come eternal life. But many who are first will be last, and the last will be first'" (Mark 10:29-31). Jesus also said in our reading from yesterday, "The greatest among you will be your servant. For those who exalt themselves will be humbled, and those who humble themselves will be exalted" (Matt. 23:11-12, NIV).

May we this day join the great cloud of witnesses in their cele-bratory cheer, "We have been rescued by Jesus himself and not another, his work on our behalf is finished and he is seated on the throne of God, ever making intercession for us. We are beloved, and we are not alone. Amen."

Building Culture

NOVEMBER 6-12, 2023 • KELLER HAWKINS

SCRIPTURE OVERVIEW: Although God miraculously has brought the Israelites into the Promised Land, some continue to worship foreign gods. Joshua tells them that they must choose whom they will serve and warns of the dangers of unfaithfulness. After they declare that they will follow God, Joshua reminds them of the laws given by God. The psalmist affirms the importance of this kind of reminder; telling the story of God's faithfulness in the past encourages us in the present. The New Testament readings address Christ's return. The Thessalonians are concerned that those who have died might miss the final resurrection, but Paul assures them that this will not be the case. Jesus tells a parable to highlight the fact that his return will be unexpected, so we should always be ready.

QUESTIONS AND SUGGESTIONS FOR REFLECTION

- Read Joshua 24:1-3a, 14-25. We are prone to wander. When have you failed to keep promises you have made to God?
- Read Psalm 78:1-7. How do you put your hope in God? What are you doing to awaken faith in the next generation?
- Read 1 Thessalonians 4:13-18. How does the promise of the "coming of the Lord" provide hope when present authorities seem to have a stranglehold? How does the notion that the coming Lord will hold us all accountable encourage you?
- Read Matthew 25:1-13. How do you daily choose your faith? How do you keep awake?

Pastor, facilitator, and sexuality educator currently training to become a Licensed Marriage and Family Therapist (LMFT) and Licensed Clinical Pastoral Therapist (LCPT); lover of labyrinths, play, and good food; provisional deacon in the Tennessee-Western Kentucky Conference of The United Methodist Church.

Today's passage is an apt one to come right after All Saints Sunday. It is a comforting message, one that may allow us "not to grieve as others do who have no hope." Paul reminds us that this communion of saints is a real one, and one day we will be all together in Christ. Those who have come before us are not gone. These ancestral saints walk with us. We hold each other through time, and the saints become a part of us through Christ. Anyone who has lost a dear friend or spouse or family member knows this to be true.

So then the question for me becomes, "How shall we live?" In the face of death, we often cling to life even more. It is on occasions like All Saints when we have the opportunity to take stock of our own lives, our convictions, our commitments, and our communal practices. What do we want our lives to embody? What culture do we want to build? And how shall we do it?

Culture is communal embodied identity. It is cultivated with words and actions, thoughts and behaviors, theory and practice. As Christians, how do we build a culture centered on a God who does not let us go even in death? What are our shared rhythms? What are our commitments? How do we hold each other? How do we honor each other? How do we welcome, invite, and cherish? How might we build a culture where we grieve with hope? How might we build a culture where we encourage with conviction? How might we build a culture that honors the saints who have died, while also producing life in the here and now? And even further, how do we teach these things?

Boundless God, be with us as we grieve. Remind us that with grief comes hope, and with hope, new possibilities. Amen.

There is something sacred about the gathering of kin, whether it be around campfires or couches or tables full of food. Inevitably, stories are shared. Indeed, this is the heartbeat of our gatherings, is it not? Storytelling helps us remember who we are, where we've come from, who came before us. From this sacred act of remembering our stories, we are also invited to envision together who we want to become. This expands as we recall and retell our story with God and God's abiding relationship with us and our people. We are anchored in our divine relationship and moored by God's continued grace and love.

Storytelling is a key tool for building a communal embodied identity. In the final chapter of the book named for him, Joshua does just that with his people, God's people Israel. He gathers all the tribes together, "the elders of Israel, its leaders, judges, and officers" (CEB)—everyone. He reminds them of all that has come to pass, the struggles and the triumphs. And then he gives them a fierce charge: "Put aside the gods that your ancestors served . . . and serve the LORD" (CEB).

As we seek to build a God-centered culture, Joshua's appeal is a serious one for us. We are challenged to put away the givens—the things that have always been—and take stock. We are invited to think critically about our traditions, our practices, our monuments, our language, our names and nicknames. Are these things honoring who we are called to be? Are they representing all of us? Are they truly life-giving for all? Are we serving the Lord or other gods (like capitalism, pride, white supremacy, or ego)? I hear Joshua's directive speaking to us today: "Choose today whom you will serve" (CEB). May we have the courage to serve the Lord.

God, may we always remember that you are the author of our story. Embolden us to serve you well. Amen.

After hearing Joshua's words, the gathered community responds promptly that they do indeed choose to serve the Lord. They mirror Joshua's storytelling for themselves, recalling all the things that God has done and all the ways God has shown up for them. In this way, they acknowledge that it is not just Joshua who remembers these things; the whole community does too.

This back and forth reminds me of the call and response of liturgies and litanies we say in worship. The leader and the gathered community remember together the promises of God and the stories we've lived. We communally acknowledge when we have fallen short and when we have rebelled against the love of God. And we remind each other of God's grace.

This back-and-forth between Joshua and God's people is a harsh one. It almost seems like Joshua is testing their earnestness, perhaps because he knows full well that they have strayed in the past. But the people reply again with urgency that they will in fact serve the Lord. Joshua's reply—"You are witnesses against yourselves that you have chosen to serve the LORD" (CEB)—highlights the importance of accountability in commitment for building a culture of embodied identity focused on God.

I've found this to be especially true in my life. Saying I will do something is not the same as doing it. I need trusted friends and colleagues to hold me accountable to my convictions. I need my church community to be with me as we together speak our communal confession each week. I need my small group so I can share openly about my struggles and be encouraged. Building a culture set on God means building a culture of accountability, honesty, and trust.

Who builds this culture alongside you? Pray and give thanks that they are in your life today.

How do we teach our history? And whose stories are included? It is tempting to frame our history to hide all our mistakes and failings. But how we tell our histories affects the present and the future. What we choose to pass down and what we choose to hide when telling our communal stories is powerful. These details dictate narratives, build legacies, and shape values.

The psalmist knows these stakes. Psalm 78 is one of the longest in the Bible, totaling seventy-two verses. It is a liturgical psalm that is meant to teach and be used in public worship. The psalmist narrates God's redemptive action toward God's people, even as the Israelites' faith wavered time and time again. I find it refreshing to read the psalmist's commitment to telling the whole truth of the people's history. "We will not hide [these stories] from [our] descendants" (CEB), however difficult or disappointing they are. The psalmist tells these truths so the next generation won't be like the previous "rebellious, stubborn generation" (Ps. 78:8, CEB). Indeed, we must learn from the past so we can imagine our future with hope.

I am prompted here to remember the importance of the children in the next generation. They carry on the stories of who we were. And they have the precious option of living into the legacies of the past or changing the direction of the story. Are we teaching them well about where they have come from so they can step into the future with courage and faith? How are we doing this truthfully and completely? What is left out, and why? How might that affect those to come?

Dear God, may we face our past with courage, remember your wondrous works, and live into our future with our eyes set on you. Amen.

In college, I became enamored of learning our old family recipes. I would go to my Nana's house each break and learn to make one of our family's signature dishes. As is true with many old family recipes, there wasn't really a recipe. The cooks who made them over time knew them so well that they could feel them out, knowing exactly what was needed when. For this kind of learning, I needed to serve my apprenticeship. And so I did. Slowly but surely, I learned the way the dough should feel, the color the roux needed to be, the type of weather we need when we make divinity (a candy that when I have countlessly failed at making it, my Nana gracefully always blames the humidity).

Over the years, I've gotten better and better at making those recipes. My Nana still makes the best gumbo, but my chicken and dumplings gives hers a run for its money. But the real treasure is that I am passing along the tradition. Each time I go into the kitchen and make something from the family cookbook, I feel I am doing holy work—the soft kneading of biscuit dough, the sautéing of the veggies, the stirring of the caramel. This is a part of my culture that I am proud of, that I wanted to learn so I could pass it on. It excites me, energizes me, and gives me purpose.

When the psalmist talks about passing down our stories and wisdom to the next generation, I think about my moments in the kitchen with my Nana. The psalmist yearns for that next generation to "rise up and tell their children to put their hope in God" (CEB) not because they have to but because they want to. How might we live in a way that spurs our grandchildren to ask, "Can you teach me?"

God of wisdom, guide us to build cultures we are proud to pass on in your name. Amen.

Today's passage sits squarely within the eschatological section of the Gospel, in which the kingdom of heaven and the coming Son of Man are outlined through narratives and parables such as this one. The parable of the ten bridesmaids suggests the kingdom of heaven might not come "on time" or as expected, and the final line sums up the lesson: *Keep awake and alert.*

It is intriguing that this passage does not admonish the bridesmaids for sleeping. Rest and renewal seem to be a natural and expected part of this story. When there are delays and we get tired, we sleep. They are admonished instead for not preparing. The cautionary lesson of *Keep awake and alert* should then be taken less literally and more figuratively. Be aware of the long game, and watch for any events of disorientation or delay that might change the plans. Keep the faith, even when the outlook seems doubtful or bleak.

I am grateful for this story, even though the traditions of first-century Jewish wedding ceremonies are foreign and perplexing. The parable's theme of balancing rest and preparation have much to say to us today, particularly in contemplating resiliency as we explore what it means to build a culture set on God. If we are not building a culture prepared for the long game, we join the foolish bridesmaids without extra oil, caught off guard, desperate, and ultimately missing out on the celebration feast.

If we do build a culture with stamina and attentiveness, we will naturally allow ourselves to honor the gift of rest as an important component of our God-centered culture.

God who rested, ready our hearts and minds and bodies for the strength we need to build resiliency so that we can rest easy when we tire. Amen.

Building Culture 375

I think it notable that the backdrop for this Matthew parable is a wedding celebration, a significant event that binds families and communities together publicly. Rituals like weddings are a vital part of the fabric of cultures. They provide markers of time, growth, change, and maturity, while also providing space for reflection, commitment-making, and, most important, *joy*—preferably in the form of dancing! And anyone who has been involved in planning and preparing for a big celebration knows it is a labor of love that needs many helping hands.

Celebratory rituals like weddings mean so much because of all that it takes to get to that day. The intentional preparation and anticipation of the day makes it all the more momentous. The stories that have been lived, the relationships formed, the wisdom from elders, the hopes and fears confronted, things that have been and the things that are to come—all of these are present in these celebrations. We simultaneously honor and create our culture, our communal embodied identity, with words and songs and candles and feasts.

Rituals are holy moments where we collectively experience the already and the not yet. We celebrate what has already been, and we trust in the unknown that is to come. I celebrate my birthday, knowing there is no guarantee I will make it to my next one. I may experience moments of redemption and also know that the need for God's redemption is ongoing. How might we celebrate God's reign in the here and now and also engage in the continual task of co-creating God's eternal reign on earth? Both are possible. Both are necessary. Even though there is still work to be done, what culture-building might we celebrate today?

God of multitudes, inspire us to celebrate and yearn for more. May we be wise in our preparations and joy-filled in our rituals. Amen.

Awake, Alert, and Ready to Act

NOVEMBER 13–19, 2023 • CHANEQUA WALKER-BARNES

SCRIPTURE OVERVIEW: Like us, the Israelites struggle to be consistently faithful to God. God therefore allows a foreign king to rule them until the people come to their senses and cry out for help. The prophet Deborah gives instructions for the battle that will begin the deliverance of the people. The readings from Psalms and Zechariah demonstrate that this pattern of unfaithfulness and restoration has occurred frequently in the history of God's people. In Thessalonians, Paul echoes what Jesus says in last week's Gospel reading: We must always be prepared for the return of Christ because we do not know when it will occur. God gives us resources to use for the kingdom, and in Matthew Jesus indicates that God will ask for an account of how well we have used them.

QUESTIONS AND SUGGESTIONS FOR REFLECTION

- Read Judges 4:1-7. Who has been a judge—someone who helps you discern—in your life? How can you help others discern the way?
- Read Psalm 123. How do you focus on God through conflict and struggle?
- Read 1 Thessalonians 5:1-11. When have you encouraged someone in a time of darkness? When have you been the one in need of encouragement?
- Read Matthew 25:14-30. What would change if you considered your dreams and desires to be from God? What first step can you take to enact your desires?

_____

Professor of Practical Theology and Pastoral Counseling at Columbia Theological Seminary in Decatur, GA, and an ecumenical minister with Baptist and United Methodist roots.

Stay woke" is a common phrase these days, a cultural call to arms designed to galvanize people's attention to social and political issues. Wikipedia traces its etymology to African American vernacular English, but while that is true of its current popularization, followers of Christ recognize its scriptural heritage. "Stay awake," Paul wrote to the church in Thessalonica, warning them against being lulled into a false sense of peace and security.

Thessalonica was part of the Roman Empire. It was not a large city, but it was a hub for business and travel. Its wealth was heavily tied to Roman beneficence, and it had the status of a free city, giving it some tax privileges and other benefits. The people of Thessalonica, including the religious leaders, wanted to keep that relationship strong. They regularly courted Roman favor through displays of political and religious patriotism. They mistook privilege and prosperity for peace and security.

"Stay awake and stay sober," Paul warns the fledgling church in Thessalonica. The followers of Christ were not to be intoxicated by privilege, prosperity, and patriotism. Nor were they supposed to seek peace and security by cozying up to political and civic authorities. Instead, their eyes were supposed to be focused on the imminent return of Christ. With apocalyptic hope, they were to wait and watch for the in-breaking of God's kin-dom. And they had to do this while resisting the pressure to cater to the culture of privilege, prosperity, and patriotism that surrounded them.

While the passage of two thousand years has tempered the expectation that Christ's return will happen in our lifetime, Christians today must still heed Paul's charge: *Stay woke, stay ready, and stay resistant.*

God of grace, help us stay awake and alert in a world that tries to lull us to sleep with promises of privilege and prosperity. Help us see signs of your kin-dom. Amen.

Grace is in short supply in our increasingly polarized world. "Choose a side!" the world demands. There is no room for deviation, no tolerance of complexity. Polarization encourages us to make snap judgments about each other, to quickly assign each other to "good" and "bad" categories, and to treat each other accordingly. Good people belong to this type of religious group, follow this set of beliefs, vote for this political party, and shop at these kinds of stores. Bad people . . . well, they are everybody else. It's a way of thinking that makes lots of enemies.

Life in Thessalonica was similar. Thessalonica's political and religious leaders were constantly trying to prove themselves good citizens, loyal to Rome. But this upstart group of Christ followers refused to participate. What's more, they were proselytizing others. The religious leaders wanted to expel them from the city. The lines of hostility solidified, each group condemning the other. Inevitably, the tension infiltrated the church itself as the church began looking for signs of dissent within its own ranks. Who were the true believers and who were the bad Christians? Who was woke and who was asleep?

But "Jesus died for us so that, whether we are awake or asleep, we will live together with him" (CEB). God's grace extends to the woke, the asleep, and the anti-woke! Our categorizations of people as good or bad is fruitless. What matters is whether we are committed to living together with one another and with Jesus, to facing our differences and disagreements with faithfulness, love, and the hope of salvation. Because being woke means nothing without grace.

God of everlasting love, you have called us to fellowship with one another across the lines of difference and diversity that you have intentionally seeded into the earth. Grant us the strength to resist polarization, the grace to sustain fellowship, and the wisdom to build each other up. Amen.

Awake, Alert, and Ready to Act   379

I raise my eyes to you—you who rule heaven" (CEB). Immediately I think of the climactic scene in Zora Neale Hurston's *Their Eyes Were Watching God.* Janie and her lover, Tea Cake, and their friends have regretfully decided to wait out a hurricane. In the early hours of the storm, they partied, intoxicated with feelings of invincibility. The confidence faded with the light. By night, they were huddled in darkness, feeling the storm's rage, powerless to do anything except to watch for God.

But that second verse? The hierarchical language of servants attending to their masters' and mistresses' hands "hit different" in a twenty-first century context that values equality and shared power. At best, it evokes the image of a kindly patriarch patting someone like a beloved pet. At worst, it evokes the cultural trauma of my enslaved ancestors fearfully watching the hands of their enslavers, ready to receive abuse. Those hands wielded oppressive power.

The psalmist writes on behalf of a people who know oppressive power. The oppressors, identified here only as "the self-confident" and "the proud," have the power to shame and mock the petitioners. Lacking both dignity and power of their own, the petitioners turn to the One who wields all power and who can be expected to exercise it on their behalf. Perhaps they simply want God to end the mockery. Maybe they want God to end the suffering that has merited the shame in the first place. We do not know. What we do know is that they await God's action, trusting God to be the merciful master and mistress that God is.

God of the oppressed, you have revealed yourself to be a liberator of the enslaved, a balm to the downtrodden, and a friend to the lonely. Help us to trust you to be that still. Free us from the crush of oppressive power. And teach us to wield power justly when we hold it. Amen.

Twenty years. It seems so short compared to nine hundred. Perhaps it even seems like an improvement after forty years of wilderness wandering. But twenty years is a long time to endure horrific oppression. An entire generation was born and raised in those circumstances, their worldviews and nervous systems shaped by cruelty.

I am writing this nearly two years into the COVID-19 pandemic, which brings its own sort of cruelty: being unable to visit, hug, and share a meal with loved ones; constantly assessing our surroundings for signs of danger; loss of jobs and income from the economic downturn; difficulty finding routine goods and services; unending death, grief, and loss; disruption to traditions of gathering, celebrating, and mourning. Even with vaccine availability, the loneliness and isolation of pandemic life is exhausting at best and life-threatening at worst. It hasn't even been two years. The Israelites suffered cruel oppression for twenty. I can only imagine the suffering.

As with COVID-19, the suffering the Israelites endured under King Jabin was partially of their own doing. Their evil unleashed the events leading to their conquest in much the same way that our abuse of creation and lack of care for one another have unleashed and worsened the virus. God didn't necessarily cause the suffering, but God allows human beings to deal with the logical and natural consequences of their actions.

But the nature of God is such that the people still cry out for God's intervention. They know that they made the mess, and they also know that they don't deserve this much suffering. They know that God, though disappointed with them, loves them and is with them still. So too, God is with us.

God of salvation, we have sinned against you and against creation. Forgive us. Deliver us from ourselves. Heal us and our relationship to the earth. Amen.

Awake, Alert, and Ready to Act

Sometimes in our suffering, we wait for God awake and alert to the possibilities that God will reveal. And God comes, issuing promises of deliverance. But deliverance does not always come the way we expect.

This is one of those lectionary passages that leaves us hanging. Reading further in Judges, we learn Barak was reluctant to heed Deborah's command and agreed to obey only if she accompanied him. He trusted her pastoral authority, but maybe he didn't trust himself to be the vessel of God's promises. Perhaps he had already heard God's command: "The path you're taking won't bring honor to you, because the LORD will hand over Sisera to a woman" (CEB). He expected Deborah to be that woman.

Deborah did indeed bring victory to Barak. He prevailed over Sisera's army with Deborah at his side. But Sisera himself? It turned out that God handed him over to a different woman, Jael. As Barak routed Sisera's forces, Sisera sought refuge from one who was a friend of King Jabin.

Jael is a stealth figure in this narrative, an unexpected heroine. Aligned with the king, she had no discernible reason to risk her life and her family's status by attacking the commander of his army, especially not on behalf of an oppressed people. Yet when opportunity came, she was ready. She was woke. She was alert. And she acted.

Scripture does not mention either woman again after Deborah sings her song praising Jael (see Judges 5). We do not know what becomes of them. But we know that they were ready to do God's bidding when the time came. And because of their decisive leadership, the twenty years of oppression ended. "And the land was peaceful for forty years" (Judg. 5:31b, CEB).

God of the unexpected, enable us to remain awake and alert to your possibility, and to act with bold assurance when it arises. Amen.

Awake, Alert, and Ready to Act

The kingdom of heaven is like a man who was leaving." It's a strange start to a parable. At this point in Matthew's Gospel, the disciples have been following Jesus for nearly three years. Doing so had required some leaving of their own. They left their families, homes, and work behind to follow Jesus because they thought he would point the way to God's heavenly kingdom. None of them, I'm sure, wanted to hear this "leaving" language.

But leaving was part of the divine plan from the beginning. Christ came knowing that he would love us and then leave us. He didn't leave us alone, of course. He gifted his followers with divine guidance (the Holy Spirit) and with sacred community (the church).

He also left us with sacred work. In the parable, it's safeguarding valuable coins. There are three servants here, each charged with protecting part of their master's treasure. Apparently, they aren't given much instruction and are left to figure it out on their own. They all have varying degrees of treasure. They also have varying degrees of risk tolerance. Two servants put the coins to work and get a return on their investment. The third opts to safeguard what little he has; he buries the treasure in a hole in the ground.

The kingdom of heaven is about the leaving; it is about what the followers of Christ do with the treasure that Jesus has given us while we await Christ's action in the world. It requires being awake to who God is, being alert to what God is doing in the world, and being ready to act even when we don't have precise instructions.

All three of the servants were well-intentioned, but two acted and one just kept waiting. Which are we?

God of action, help us to be awake and alert to what you are doing in the world, and to be ready to act in accordance with your will. Amen.

Awake, Alert, and Ready to Act

Three servants were entrusted with their master's riches. Two multiplied them, earning their master's approval. The third hid his away in a safe place and was thrown into the farthest darkness. It is an image that strikes anxiety into anyone who wants to be a faithful follower of Christ. It drives us to act, lest we be like the servant who simply waited.

But we must be more than ready to act. We must know how to act.

It would be tempting to read this text materially and conclude that the goal of discipleship is to increase our wealth so we can put it to use for the kingdom. But Jesus' riches were not material wealth. His riches were the gift of salvation, his commitment to justice and mercy, and his unending love. This passage, after all, is immediately followed by Matthew 25:31-46, where Jesus equates discipleship with feeding the hungry, welcoming the stranger, clothing the naked, caring for the sick, and visiting the incarcerated.

This, then, is how we must act. Christ did not come into the world to offer the gift of salvation just so that we could squirrel it away, sequestering ourselves in "safe" worship and theological spaces where people have our same degree of privilege and think like we do. Doing that is no different than burying our faith in a hole in the ground.

It is when we take risks with our faith by working with and on behalf of the marginalized that our faith is challenged in ways that stretch it and enable it to grow. If we don't, our faith does not just stagnate; it disappears. And we find ourselves in the farthest darkness, weeping and grinding our teeth.

God of the marginalized, help us take seriously your command to befriend and serve the least of these. Strengthen us to take risks with our faith so that it can grow. Amen.

Cultivating a Grateful Heart

NOVEMBER 20–26, 2023 • BRADLEY BUNN

SCRIPTURE OVERVIEW: The Bible uses metaphors meaningful in their time, and the image of a shepherd and sheep evokes protection, care, and safety. Through the prophet Ezekiel, God declares that all the scattered sheep will be joined together again. The weak and oppressed will receive special protection and justice from God. The psalmist says that the Israelites are the sheep of God's pasture. In the Gospel reading, Jesus describes the final judgment as separating the sheep (those who are his) from the goats (those who are not). The distinction is made in part based upon how they treated the weakest among them. Although the epistle does not use the imagery of sheep, it describes the promises of a glorious inheritance reserved for those in God's flock.

QUESTIONS AND SUGGESTIONS FOR REFLECTION

- Read Ezekiel 34:11-16, 20-24. What does it mean for you that God seeks you as an individual as well as part of your faith community?
- Read Psalm 100. In times of trial or pain, how do you gather with others to praise God?
- Read Ephesians 1:15-23. How do you express gratitude to God for your faith community?
- Read Matthew 25:31-46. How do you sit with unresolved questions of faith? How does asking questions of the Bible strengthen your faith? Are you comfortable not having answers to your questions?

Associate Minister at First Congregational Church in Mansfield, OH; Christian educator and visual artist with interests in youth ministry, sacramental theology, and leadership studies.

As I reflect on today's scripture, I wonder what kind of person the prophet Ezekiel must have been. Here was an official Temple priest who was ripped from his profession and taken to another country. Ezekiel and several thousand other Judeans were separated from the holy places and deprived of their ritual access to God. Their situation was dire, and they had to make sense of their new reality among the ravines of Babylon.

However, today's passage proclaims restoration and renewal. Ezekiel's message is that the Lord, like a shepherd, will find and protect the lost and scattered sheep no matter what! He will strengthen their resolve in their weakness. Ezekiel's earlier oracles of God's anger and judgment have evolved into divine proclamations of justice through the renewal of God's people.

I'm reminded that every Sunday morning, parishioners enter the many diverse holy spaces to experience the divine shepherd. People from all walks of life have various reasons for wanting to come to church. But I've come to understand that they all come to hear a "word"—whether through the liturgy, the music, or the sermon—that God is restoring and renewing them in grace, even when they feel everything is shifting beneath their feet. When we understand what God is up to, then we can approach life with a renewed interest and gratefulness for all God is doing in our lives.

God of our salvation, show your glory so that we may abide in your fulfilled hope. Amen.

The old adage "Sticks and stones may break my bones, but words will never hurt me" is simply not true. This idea that others' viewpoints and comments can't hurt us unless we let them is a dubious sentiment of a bygone era. Words can coerce, manipulate, and break our spirits. Conversely, words can also elevate, support, and encourage.

At the end of Ezekiel's ministry, he prophesies how God is going to judge the bullies. We can speculate that the bullies represent those in leadership and with privileged status who have forgotten their ethical duties to love their neighbors. In fact, they "shove with flank and shoulder, butting all the weak sheep with [their] horns until [they] have driven them away" (NIV). However, they not only use brute force; they also use words. The gentry are mocking those from the lower classes, telling them to just adapt and get over the whole exile thing. The bullies want Judah to succumb to a foreign land and culture, which also means worshiping foreign gods. This is where God enters the picture because God will restore Judah through a Davidic lineage.

Throughout our lives, people will try to convince us to betray our principles and better judgment for their own benefit. The powers of the world maintain their power by ensuring that the least and the lost have no hope. But we do have hope because we have a Good Shepherd who teaches us to live faithfully and show compassion, love, justice, and mercy. As we stand before God, we are called to live with grateful hearts.

God of redemption, whose liberating Spirit resides in the Son, remind us of our divine inheritance with you, so that we may know your infinite grace, wisdom, truth, and mercy. Amen.

Cultivating a Grateful Heart

From time to time, life pushes us toward cynicism. As the challenges take their toll, we question whether we can find peace. But we can counteract the wear and tear on our souls by practicing a spiritual discipline of gratitude—learning how to gather the spiritual nourishment that falls from heaven.

The starting place is engaging the world with awe and wonder. For example, it may be the way we watch the setting sun as it slowly sinks behind the trees. It could be a chance encounter with a dear friend we haven't seen in quite a long time. Whatever the event, engaging the world with wonder helps us slow down, pay attention, and give up the illusion of control in our daily lives.

Your response might be, "That sounds well and good, but my life is way too busy to stop and smell the roses." I can appreciate that sentiment, but I believe we can all experience seasons of gratitude—cycles or degrees of wonderment—in the spaces and in the places we live and work.

The psalmist reminds us that we are known by God: "It is he who made us, and we are his; we are his people, the sheep of his pasture" (NIV). If the divine shepherd knows our inmost being and is still proud to call us his sheep/children, then why wouldn't we be filled with joy and gratitude? Our heavenly Father accepts us completely and calls us to become the best versions of ourselves.

O Mighty God, forge something new within us so that we can become grateful people praising your name. Amen.

THANKSGIVING DAY (USA)

As I stare at a blank computer screen this morning, I'm reminded of the absence of words, sounds, smells, and images for some of us during the Thanksgiving and Christmas holidays. Although many will experience blessings of kids and grandkids around a majestic table with all the trimmings, others will have only the memories of holidays past. Today, I find myself among the latter.

My favorite memories center around my Meemaw, who was the matriarch of my family. Her contagious smile and loving arms always found their way to me as I entered her quaint, country kitchen. She was cooking all the time, and during the holidays there would be cakes, pies, and candies fashioned on top of one another with a shimmering light reflected from the massive amount of aluminum foil wrapping. As I would attempt to sample all her delicacies, she would shoo me away and say, "Bradley Edward! Get out of here!" in her most amused and affectionate voice. At least that's how I remember it. My Meemaw left this world a few years ago, but I'm thankful for those special memories we shared in her kitchen.

In today's scripture, Paul writes to the Corinthian church about the importance of becoming a "cheerful giver." Paul is emphasizing the need for sharing resources with the larger Christian community. His imagery of the one who sows and reaps parallels an ongoing dilemma for most of us today: How much is enough? This is, of course, thought about in terms of material wealth or its absence. But I suggest we think of sowing and reaping in the context of relationships. My grandmother sowed seeds of love and compassion in me. Then I reaped those precious rewards and now share her priceless story with others.

Almighty God, protector and sustainer, help us to be grateful for those who are a part of our story. Amen.

At the outset of the Thirty Years War, a French soldier by the name of Nicholas Herman had a profound encounter with God. After being wounded in battle, he entered a Carmelite monastery in Paris and became known affectionately as Brother Lawrence. During his time at the monastery, he noticed God's presence in the mundane, repetitive activities of life. For example, he came to the realization that communing with God could happen in the simple act of peeling potatoes. His work as a cook allowed him to pray and meditate on the goodness of God.

We too can experience the goodness of God through the mundane. God's wonderment is all around us. The psalmist reminds us, "The Lord is good and his love endures forever" (v. 5a, NIV). We give thanks for the opportunity to worship together; we give thanks for the fresh, brisk air of a wintry night; we give thanks for the health and safety of our loved ones. We experience God's goodness through God's love, and this love is truly praiseworthy. Because we know God's goodness through everyday moments of life, we become grateful to the One who calls us into the "courts of praise." We are invited to commune with a God who knows our heart's longing for joy and peace.

Too often we find ourselves compartmentalizing our lives. We categorize and subcategorize work, family, church. Instead of an interconnected flow to life, we're tempted to drudge through our work week toward "eventful" weekends. However, if we take the psalmist's words to heart, every day can be an eventful encounter with our good God.

Loving God, you are like the stars in the sky and the grains of sand. Your love lives even within the utterance of your name. We praise you with grateful hearts. Amen.

When I lived in Silver Spring, Maryland, I spent most of my free time hanging out at the National Mall in Washington, D.C. As a novice artist, I couldn't get enough of the paintings and sculptures that lined the massive hallways of the Smithsonian museums. There were times when I felt I had to pinch myself, as I would feverishly sketch a cast of Auguste Rodin's *Monument to Balzac*—a massive, expressive sculpture located in the Hirshhorn Sculpture Garden. The National Mall was a wonderful escape for me, and it planted the seeds for how I would eventually incorporate the arts into my ministry.

Today's scripture highlights Paul's prayer for the Ephesians to receive hope and power from the resurrection promise of Jesus Christ. For Paul, faith is about total transformation—it is the Christ residing in us who moves us toward final completion (sanctifying grace).

As I've matured as a Christian artist, I've realized how important it is to lean on God's understanding of creation: God creates order out of chaos (see Genesis 1:1-2). Paul picks up on this notion as well when he writes, "That power is the same as the mighty strength [God] exerted when he raised Christ from the dead and seated him at his right hand in the heavenly realms" (NIV). In other words, we are co-creators with Christ.

On the doorway of the studio at Wesley Theological Seminary in Washington, D.C., a sign says, "An artist is not a special kind of person, but every person is a special kind of artist."

We can give thanks to God for the opportunities to create a world filled with hopeful hues, majestic venues, and kingdom-building brushstrokes. We all are artists in God's eyes.

Master Artist, your heavenly kingdom reaches into the depths of our creativity. May we create this world anew with your guidance. Amen.

Cultivating a Grateful Heart

In today's passage, we read how the Son of Man will separate the righteous from the unrighteous like a shepherd separates sheep from goats. It's an apocalyptic passage that exposes the passivity of those who falsely believe they are righteous—goats who join the flock of sheep—but are uncharitable and do not show God's love.

In an episode of the late-1980s sitcom *Murphy Brown*, Murphy decides she wants to attend a church. But before she goes church-shopping, she asks some of her co-workers why they go to church. They give her several pat answers, but she really harps on one particular co-worker, anchorman Jim Dial. He is evasive throughout most of the episode; but he finally breaks down in exasperation and says, "I don't know why!" He goes on to share with her that he's waiting for something when he and his wife go to church, but he's not quite sure what that something is. Maybe it was the same quandary that many seekers of faith have experienced. That is, how does "going to church" and parroting religious words create a relationship with the living God?

In the Sermon on the Mount, Jesus told his listeners, "Not everyone who says to me, 'Lord, Lord,' will enter the kingdom of heaven, but only the one who does the will of my Father." Just so, in our Matthew reading, Jesus lays out what it means to be his follower. No matter how faithful we may think we are, when we fail to meet the opportunities God presents us every day—to offer acts of kindness and compassion to "the least of these," our faith is not real; we are only fooling ourselves. Acts of compassion may be simple kindnesses or significant sacrifices; but they are the only way to know God.

God of justice, mercy, and loving-kindness, assist us in our efforts to meet people's needs; help us as well to pay attention to our own. Open our eyes to see the opportunities in front of us. Amen.

Sensing God's Presence

NOVEMBER 27–DECEMBER 3, 2023 • WILLIE JAMES JENNINGS

SCRIPTURE OVERVIEW: The readings from the Hebrew scriptures have a common theme: The people have sinned and turned away from God, and now they cry out for God to forgive them. Even though they have created the separation from God, the authors are confident that God will restore them. These images of longing for God are appropriate as we begin the season of Advent. Paul opens First Corinthians reminding the Christians in Corinth that they have been richly blessed by God with spiritual gifts to sustain and strengthen them as they wait for the coming of Christ. Again this week, the Gospel reading refers to the return of Christ, a day known only to God.

QUESTIONS AND SUGGESTIONS FOR REFLECTION

- Read Isaiah 64:1-9. When have you treated God as a vending machine and held a grudge against God? What restored your faith or changed your perspective?
- Read Psalm 80:1-7, 17-19. When have you been frustrated by others' praises of God's blessings? When have you cried out to God, "Restore us"?
- Read 1 Corinthians 1:3-9. What spiritual gifts are you conscious of having? What might your faith community look like if everyone employed their spiritual gifts?
- Read Mark 13:24-37. What is your job in the household of God? How do you stay alert?

Associate Professor of Systematic Theology and Africana Studies, Yale Divinity School; ordained Baptist minister in New Haven, CT.

The prophet is looking for God who seems to be hidden. This sounds absurd, both the looking for God and the idea that God hides. But this is a common scene of faith and a common feeling that lives within our faith. How is it that we sometimes experience God as hiding from us individually or hiding from the peoples we identify with collectively? We come to this place of searching when we enter times and places of struggle. Struggles of mind or body or both turn our sensing inward to the point where our senses are technically available to us but forgotten by us. Two kinds of struggles mark the inward journey that silences our sensing.

The first struggle is encountering adversaries or adversarial conditions. Whether real or imagined, these threats can cause us to feel as though there is a great chasm between God and us. We are on one side constantly harassed by our adversaries, and God is on the other side seemingly uninterested in stopping those who are trying to do us harm. Yet God defies the distance and denies the separation between our well-being and the divine will for our lives. God is with us in our fears and with us when an adversary or adversity comes after us. God promises that our adversaries will never have the final victory.

The second struggle is knowing that we have done what is wrong in God's sight. We have sinned against God, against our neighbor, or against ourselves in some way, and we feel again a distance between our life and God's presence. Yet God claims us like a good parent or guardian reaching to hold their child. God takes us like a potter lovingly molding her clay toward the beauty it will show. God is present holding us, drawing us toward the visible elegance of a life joined to the divine life.

God, show me that you hold my life close, so my struggles will never convince me that I am separated from you. Amen.

Waiting for the Lord's help is holy work. Yet it is work that could easily make us despair if we don't remember what it means to wait on God. The psalmist shows us that waiting on God is not waiting for God to show up in our lives and in particular situations, as if God has gone missing or has wandered away from us. Waiting on the Lord is an active waiting, like waiting for someone you love and who loves you to say something in response to what you just said. It is waiting inside a conversation that is happening inside a life with God. The psalmist speaks of waiting within a long history of Israel's life with God, which means this is waiting that remembers the goodness of God and what God has done for them in the past, is seeking to hear God's voice in the present, and believes in a future with God.

Difficult times challenge each part of this sequence, especially when those difficult times mean that something has been lost, irrevocably damaged, or taken from us. The plea to God for restoration is always appropriate because it is made to the One who created us and who always wills the good for us even when we cannot sense it. God restores in ways, however, that draw us toward a future with God. It is a future no longer determined by sorrow and shame. That future as the psalmist names it is one where the Lord's face shines on us, always showing God's joyous love for us. Yet this waiting does not end; it forms our posture as those who wait daily on the goodness of God, eagerly continuing the conversation with God. We wait knowing that our lives of faith are engaged in actively trusting in God, who never forsakes us.

Gracious God, strengthen me through the work of waiting on you, knowing that you hear my call and will answer my prayers in due time. Attune my mind to enter our conversation so that I may hear your voice clearly today. Amen.

Sensing God's Presence

Loss can be a heavy burden. Whether it is unexpected and sudden or slowly and inevitably irreversible, our minds move to the desire for restoration. Yet desiring restoration can sometimes feel like insulting torture added to the loss itself because restoration seems like a fantasy, a reversal of time or a resetting of events or a dramatic, sudden change in our character or the character of others. Restoration is often a hope for a do-over or a return to just as it was before the loss. Israel cried out to God for restoration, and in this psalm that cry became the refrain of a song, its repetition signaling a good and righteous hope—*restore us*—that orients us toward the future and not the past.

God's grace takes us forward not backward. The restoration God gives is life after loss. It is life where the burden of that loss lessens daily in the light of life with God. God's face shines on us, meaning that God offers us a sense of the divine joy in our existence, the sheer delight God takes in each of us. This is divine restoration that draws us beyond regrets and the morbid rehearsals of what went wrong or what we did wrong or who is to blame, not to forget but to remember that a merciful God is with us now.

God invites us into a new kind of living that remembers in hope. To remember in hope means holding on to the losses—of loved ones, ways of living, opportunities, or abilities—in the promise that God who created us and sustains us will one day renew us and this world. We will see our loved ones again. We will know good life again, and that knowledge begins now. The salvation God offers us binds hope to loss and binds us to God.

Sustaining God, free me from the burden of loss. Guide my heart toward the hope of restoration in you so that I may live toward the new day that you have promised me through Jesus Christ, our source of hope and the giver of life. Amen.

Grace means divine presence. It means life with a giving God who never tires of offering us the inexhaustible riches of the divine life. In Jesus Christ, we learn that those riches are rooted in God's creating and sustaining Word. Yet the words of Jesus and the Word that is Jesus are not just instruction or guidance; they are a place in which to live with God. It is an enriching place that God invites us to enter and in which we take rest, allowing ourselves to live in the place where we are permeated by the presence of God.

God calls us to a practical mysticism where we daily center ourselves in the divine voice by yielding our voice in praise and thanksgiving to God. As we offer our voice to God in prayer and worship, God accompanies us in our speaking, thinking, listening, and learning. This is grace—ever expanding and generous—where God fills us with the divine life and with fresh strength.

Grace also means strength. God strengthens us through the Word. Relentlessly. This is the reality of life with God where we learn that we are in constant need of renewal and refreshing, and God never tires of meeting our need. Being exhausted carries its own particular struggle, especially when that exhaustion greets us at the beginning of a day. Whether the source of our exhaustion is a person, a situation, or an occupation, it can easily cause us to lose sight of the new strength God offers us.

Yet this is strength with direction. God always seeks to point us toward the waters of life that are in God and around us, inviting us to angle our day and arrange our lives to tap into refreshment. The strength for living that God gives is also the strength for living right. It is the strength to follow the will of God in our journey, which is always a journey in grace.

Thank you, God, for your word and your Word that sustain me. Guide me into the sources of refreshment all around me, and show me the path of righteousness. Amen.

Sensing God's Presence 397

No person of faith is ever alone. Our faith points to a greater reality that surrounds us. We have communion with God through Jesus Christ. God has brought us through the Spirit into a wide space of life together with our loving Savior and with those who have gone before us in faith. We are encircled by that great cloud of witnesses as well as those disciples of Jesus who are around us now.

Loneliness, however, can conceal this reality and slowly over time cause us to imagine that we live on a deserted island, either because of our personality or as punishment or both. We can sometimes think that deep friendships are in short supply, and we do not have enough to obtain or sustain the ones we want or need. Yet this text reminds us that God gives us gifts in community and for creating community.

You are such a gift. Realizing this is the first part of the antidote to loneliness. The second part is always reaching out in person or in prayer to others who understand their life is in Jesus Christ. You are a gift for community that is only revealed in community. God formed us for creating community, and when we yield to the Spirit, we can sense the voice of God calling us into communion and life together.

Reaching out is a step toward healing where we invite the Spirit to open the doors of our perception to see that we have in us the power to connect. That power, flowing from God's faithful and loving presence, will always demolish the lie that we are destined to be alone. Our destiny is already a reality—we are part of a holy community that is even now calling to us.

Holy Spirit, refresh in me the power to connect with others for the sake of the saving life you have made real in this world and in me through Jesus Christ. Amen.

Ｗe are in God's time. God's own life encircles our beginning and our ending, permeating our present with the reality of eternity. Now we have life eternal. Yet we still hear the ticking of clocks, and we sense the movement of life, the change of seasons, and the changes in our bodies. We are creatures of time. It is this wonderful paradox that, if misunderstood, can cause us to lose ourselves in time.

To be lost in time is to be consumed by the anxieties of time. We are often burdened by the past, and so we either obsess over it or ignore it and become trapped in the past. We are often overwhelmed by the present, and the need to get things done or the frustration of falling behind schedule drives us to despair or fills us with anxiety. We often fear the future, wondering how long our lives will extend into it. So we build structures that focus obsessively on protecting us from potential dangers, and we build monuments and legacies that ensure that we will not be forgotten even when our bodies have turned to dust.

God, however, invites us to understand time differently. Time is our partner as we walk with God. Time is not our ruler or our guide or that which brings meaning to our lives. Only God can guide us in time and through time in ways that keep time from becoming a burden. This text speaks of a Savior who is marking time and will return to us and therefore calls us to mark time with him. We live and work by the rhythm of divine return, which means we live and work in the hope and joy of our redemption. We live in the redeeming reality of God, and each day our actions announce our expectation that the Son of God will return.

Merciful God, grant me a greater sense of my time held in your hands. Attune my senses to your presence in each moment, guiding me in all that I do. Should I lose myself in the worries of time, remind me that you hold the future. Amen.

Sensing God's Presence   399

FIRST SUNDAY OF ADVENT

Nothing is permanent, and it is much easier to know this truth than to feel it. No one wants to feel the impermanence of life because that means feeling loss or experiencing collapse or watching something crumble that you thought would continue. Even when we can explain why someone did not survive or something did not last, it does not take away the sense of vulnerability that comes with feeling the end.

This condition of impermanence is part of what it means to be a creature created by God. Yet God wishes to guide us, moving with us on this collapsing and unstable ground. On this path it is easy to become overwhelmed by the impermanence of it all. We sometimes allow the instability around us and in us to affect how we engage the world. We might treat things and people as fleeting and withhold deep levels of commitment from them, or we could obsessively try to create something we hope will be permanent, like an institution or a family legacy.

God's path leads us away from despair or stoic acceptance of impermanence and toward life eternal. The first signs of life eternal for us are God's words. Those words show us that God is not only speaking, guiding, and instructing us, but that God is present with us and to us through the Holy Spirit. God's words are permanent, and this is not primarily a statement about the character of divine speech but about the depth of God's promise to us. God invites us to take hold of God's words and allow them to attune our hearts and minds to a lasting peace and a lasting joy, even when things are collapsing and crumbling all around us. God's word stabilizes us in an unstable world.

Gracious God, let your words take deep root in me today so my life has the stability only you can give, and my daily path has the peace and joy of an eternity that is already mine. Amen.

The One Who Changes Everything

DECEMBER 4–10, 2023 • JONATHAN C. WALLACE

SCRIPTURE OVERVIEW: Hopeful anticipation characterizes this week's texts. God's people have come to terms with their inability to save themselves. Isaiah 40 states that Jerusalem has "served her term" in bondage to sin; a new era is about to dawn. Psalm 85 continues the theme of old sins forgiven, emphasizing an urgent need for some fresh outbreak of God's initiatives. Harmonious and responsible relationships are to dominate the hearts of the people. Thoughts of righteousness and peace also pervade the passage from Second Peter. Yet the focus is clearly on Christ's Second Advent. His coming will be sudden and unannounced; the new creation will then appear. The Gospel text focuses on the earthly ministry of Jesus as John the baptizer comes to sensitize all hearts to the advent of the One promised long ago.

QUESTIONS AND SUGGESTIONS FOR REFLECTION

- Read Isaiah 40:1-11. God's word of comfort brings challenge as well. How are you preparing the way of the Lord?
- Read Psalm 85:1-2, 8-13. What glimpses of heaven in your daily life give you confidence in God's steadfast love?
- Read 2 Peter 3:8-15a. How are you using this time of Advent waiting to move toward more faithful living?
- Read Mark 1:1-8. What is the new thing that John the Baptizer could teach you? How will you get ready for the coming of the Christ child?

Pastor of First Presbyterian Church (PCUSA), Foley, AL.

At this time every year, my kids love to go into the attic and bring down our family's nativity scene—a hand-knitted, child-friendly set of yarn figures my mother bought from a talented friend years before my kids were born. The fact that they are now all young adults has not dampened their enthusiasm in taking out and playing with these delightful and educational toys.

Every year I watch them as they unwrap each character: The baby Jesus, Mary and Joseph, the shepherds, the wise men, and all the animals. They then move the figures around until they get the scene just right. Yet every year as I look at this gentle scene, I am struck not so much by who is there as by who is missing. The fact is, I have never seen a Nativity scene, or any Christmas-themed scene, with John the Baptist in it. Not even once!

That's not how Mark sees it. The oldest Gospel does not begin with a manger. There are no stars, no shepherds, no wise men bearing gifts. It doesn't even begin in Bethlehem but in the desert, with a voice proclaiming that God is up to something new. John, echoing the voice of another wilderness prophet from centuries earlier, proclaims that God is on the move. It is time to get ready—not with decorations for our homes and offices but with a change of heart, a change of lifestyle, a change of life orientation.

Mark begins quickly and gets right to the point. He has little time for holiday niceties. As much as we treasure our scenes of heavenly peace, we run the risk of missing the point of Mark's message to us if we tarry there too long. We would do well to heed the Baptist's advice and clean up our lives a bit. After all, not just anyone is coming but the One who will change everything!

God of Advent expectation, may I not miss the point of your coming among us. Amen.

We haven't heard John the Baptist's physical voice in two thousand years, yet in my more irreverent moods I imagine him sounding like one of those colorful parrots that some people keep as pets. One of the more fascinating characteristics of these birds is that they can actually speak. That talent is also one of their more annoying traits because they repeat the same words over and over again.

I've caught myself wondering from time to time if John knew any words other than *repent*. His message arrives right on time during the Advent season, reminding us of things we'd rather not think about during this festive season. But we don't want an honest telling of what God is up to, what is at stake, what it will cost, or how at risk we really are in the wake of this message. Yet in his time, John pierces through the uncertainty and suffering with a message that God has begun a new day. Things are going to change, and the one who comes after John will be the one who will make it all happen. This one, Jesus, will transform lives. The world as we know it will pass away. John tries to get our attention. *What* is coming and *who* is coming will make all things new and offer us a chance at the life God intended for us in the first place.

Maybe we are the parrots. *We* are the ones who keep repeating the same words, singing the same songs, and putting up the same decorations. *We* are the ones who appear to be stuck.

John presents no problem here. *We* are the problem. John brings the antidote. He reminds us that what we await is nothing less than justice being served, the poor being lifted up, and the rough places of inequity, unfairness, and selfishness being smoothed out. We want the same old thing. John is desperately trying to teach us something new.

O God, make me receptive to the newness you bring in this season to my life. Amen.

The One Who Changes Everything　　　403

What better indicator of trouble in a relationship than the "silent treatment"? At least when we argue, we engage one another. But when we go silent—either because we don't care enough to confront the problems or because we are too angry, too hurt, or too tired to engage any further—it signals an ill-at-ease relationship. What will the other person say when he or she speaks to us again? Will there be words of hope, forgiveness, or apology?

In today's passage, God has been giving the people of Israel the silent treatment. In the first thirty-nine chapters, God lays out an overwhelming case against the people, charging them with indifference at best and downright rejection of God at worst. As a result of their infidelity to God, they lose the land and are carried off into exile. Then God goes silent. About 150 years pass between the end of chapter 39 and the first verses of chapter 40. Will the people ever hear from God again? If so, what will God say after all this time?

The first two verses of chapter 40, no doubt, contain the best news possible. After over a century of silence, God finally speaks. God speaks comfort, forgiveness, hope. The tone of the conversation totally changes. Despite all that has happened, God is willing to speak, tenderly, to the people at last. Bitterness, anger, hurt, and grief do not last. Comfort, hope, and forgiveness emerge as the conversation begins again.

What about us? Do we feel that God is giving us the silent treatment? Or is it we who are withholding our conversational intimacy with God? God speaks tenderly to God's people, offering forgiveness and hope. If it's been a long time since you've spoken to God, what will you say? If it's been a long time since you've heard God's voice, what do you think God is trying to say to you?

God, I long to hear your voice. Speak to me this day. Amen.

Have you ever read the ending of a book before you read the rest of it? Have you ever watched the last fifteen minutes of a film before seeing the rest of it? I confess to having done both. I do feel a bit like a cheater. However, when we know how a story will end, we read it from a different perspective. We can probe into and enjoy the subtleties and the nuances of the characters and the plot. Or maybe we can simply take comfort in knowing, for better or for worse, how it all works out.

The Second Letter of Peter is a small document near the back of the Bible that gets little attention. Yet, at this time of year when we focus on waiting for the fulfillment of God's promises, it offers good pastoral advice for us all. Peter reminds his troubled and confused congregation of an important fact: They already know the end of the story. God is not slow in fulfilling promises but proceeds at God's own pace. Unlike us, God is patient. The return of our Lord will come suddenly and without warning, but it will come. Because they know that God's plan will be fulfilled at the end of time, the rest of the story that is unfolding now makes a little more sense. Peter reminds them that God is in control of the future. Because that is true, they can face the difficulties that lie ahead in confidence and hope. They can busy themselves with being the people God created them to be in the first place, regardless of what the world may think of them at the moment.

The future resides in God's hands, which frees us to deal with today. There is no shortage of work to be done, and no shortage of love and good news to give. We have hope to share, a faith to proclaim, and compassion to spread. That will keep us busy as we await the time when righteousness truly is at home!

God of creation, may I stay busy doing your work of proclamation and compassion. I await your righteousness. Amen.

The One Who Changes Everything

This time of year feels a lot like those long drives many of us take as a part of our family vacations. I've finally packed everything, herded the kids into the car, and gotten on the road. I relax and begin to enjoy the trip. That sense of peace does not last long, however. From the back of the car come the words that no parent wants to hear, "Are we there yet?"

Waiting is never easy, especially if you feel your very life might depend on what comes next. The community reading this epistle might fit into that category. They've heard the story. They've left their previous lives to come into community around the story of Jesus and his teachings. They've changed everything in anticipation of his return. The months turn into years, the years into decades. Where is he? When is he coming? Some have returned to their old lives.

The writer of Second Peter takes a more patient approach to his congregation than I did with my kids, but the message remains the same. The world will come to an end, and Christ will return when God decides—period. God's sense of time and perspective differs from ours, yet God is immensely patient. God wants no one left behind.

But since we cannot know God's timing, we can put the time we have to good use. We can live our lives in anticipation of history's fulfillment. We can do good, and do it well. We can let our actions and words reflect the hope that we have been given by the life, death, and resurrection of Jesus.

We have plenty left to do before the big day. Perhaps we should quit wondering where Jesus is and keep the light of love and welcome on in our hearts until he arrives. He'll get here when he gets here.

Jesus, my light of love and welcome is on. I await your salvation. Amen.

Despite the attempts of our culture to make this season a time of instant gratification in the here and now, I believe that the Advent and Christmas seasons, at their core, are a time to remember. In our families, we gather around the tree and hang ornaments that we made ourselves as children or that we bought to mark special occasions. Sometimes we bring out the photo albums and let the ghost of Christmas past have its way with us. We laugh at what we once looked like and remember those who can no longer be in our pictures in the present. What we most often do is tell stories. We do not want to forget those important times. We don't let those around us forget them either! We need those memories. We need them to remind us of who we are. We need them to strengthen the bonds of family, friendship, and community.

Most of all, we need them to remind us of what is important. That is what the singer of Psalm 85 does as he lifts his voice in worship. Before anything else is uttered, before any description of the situation is broached, the psalmist sings of what God has done for the people of Israel in the past. The psalmist reminds the people of their liberation at God's hand, of God's forgiveness, and God's unwillingness to have anger and bitterness be the last word. In order to face the present, the psalmist first calls the people to remember.

In Advent we remember the past hopes that were fulfilled and the promise made to Mary, Joseph, the shepherds, and the wise men. But we also live in the "not yet" of God's ultimate fulfillment. As the disappointments inevitably come, let us not succumb to spiritual amnesia. Above all, this season may we remember what God has done for us . . . and will do for us!

I recall your work on my behalf, O God. You have extended your graciousness to me, and I am grateful. Amen.

The One Who Changes Everything   407

SECOND SUNDAY OF ADVENT

The Advent and Christmas seasons bring many images to our minds. We think of gentle scenes of snow or of bright stars in the sky. Some prefer to envision a crude crib and the tiny life nestled into it. Others see, and perhaps even believe in, the possibility of "peace on earth, goodwill to all people."

Psalm 85 gives us none of those things. However, Psalm 85 paints a picture; a vision; an artist's rendering, if you will, of what the kingdom of God looks like. It is a song of promise, and a reminder of what God has done for us in the past. Because of that past, we can rest confident in the future.

And what does that future look like? Verse 10 offers an image. There, the psalmist imagines the steadfast love and the faithfulness of God coming together with the people. They don't come to shake hands or to bow respectfully to one another. They come together and kiss. We can imagine the passionate kiss of lovers or the kiss of greeting of family and friends. With apologies to the movie *Casablanca*, a kiss is *not* just a kiss. A kiss is a tender, affectionate, vulnerable, and passionate expression of friendship, love, and peace. Perhaps that is why Judas's betrayal is so emotionally wrenching for us. To be betrayed with a kiss is the ultimate indignity.

But here, the vision of the future is of two people greeting each other with the most disarming expression of friendship. This peace is not simply the absence of violence. It is the presence of genuine affection and welcome.

It's not exactly greeting card material or something we will see in any Christmas play. But this image gives us a good idea of what God has in mind for us.

Jesus Christ, you come among us with disarming friendship and peace. We welcome you. Amen.

Cultivating Hope

DECEMBER 11–17, 2023 • CAROL T. CAVIN-DILLON

SCRIPTURE OVERVIEW: Isaiah speaks of the day in which God's Anointed One (Messiah) will bring good news to the poor and hope to the oppressed. Jesus will later read this passage and declare it to be about himself (Luke 4), so we read Isaiah's prophecy during Advent. The psalmist rejoices that God has restored the fortunes of the people. They have come through a period of difficulty, but God has brought them into a place of joy. Throughout Advent, we also look forward to such rejoicing. Paul encourages the Thessalonians to pray continually with gratitude and rejoicing, and the God of peace will sustain them. In the Gospel reading, John the Baptist repeats the theme from last week—that he is merely the messenger to prepare the way for the Lord.

QUESTIONS AND SUGGESTIONS FOR REFLECTION

• Read Isaiah 61:1-4, 8-11. God is coming. How do Isaiah's words of praise and justice inspire you to act?

• Read Psalm 126. How do you celebrate the justice that you have seen come to fruition while hoping for future justice? How does your anticipation of the fullness of justice affect your faith?

• Read 1 Thessalonians 5:16-24. How can you return to the basics of faith during Advent?

• Read John 1:6-8, 19-28. How is this Advent season both familiar and new for you? How might simple announcements of Jesus' coming change your experience of the season?

Senior Pastor of West End United Methodist Church, Nashville, TN.

Today we hear the voice of the prophet Isaiah speaking a word of hope to the people of Israel, who have been devastated by the armies of Babylon. They are poor, powerless, and hurting, yet the prophet speaks of a God of justice who comes with liberation and favor. God, it seems, is on the side of the powerless.

When I hear these words of the prophet, I wonder, *What does this mean for me?* I am not oppressed. I am comfortable. Well fed. Free. I have choices and power. Is the coming of the God of justice good news for me?

Before I can get to "yes," perhaps I must first be convicted by these words and allow them to break me open. Am I mindful of the brokenheartedness of others? Does the oppression in the world break my heart?

If my heart is in tune with God's heart, the answer will be yes. Of course, there are many forms of oppression, and no one in this life is free of suffering. We are all together in one common humanity that can unite us if we realize that our liberation is bound up with everyone else's. If you are not free, I am not free.

So part of this good news is that, as the people of God, we get to share in God's liberating work! Whether we are powerful or powerless, we are called to be God's people and announce God's love for all. We get to help build a world where no one is oppressed, where all are fed, where power is shared, and where no one is lost. Now that's good news!

O God who sees the suffering of the oppressed, give us eyes to see and hearts to care. Thank you for setting us free. Help us do the same for others, in your holy name. Amen.

In verse 11 of today's text, the prophet uses the image of a garden to offer a word of hope to the people of Israel who had suffered through decades of exile in Babylon. Though they might have felt that God had forsaken them, the prophet proclaims that God will restore them to the Land of Promise and will bring forth new life among them.

So much of the growth in a garden happens underground, when it looks like nothing is going on at all. The earth works its wonders unseen. In the same way, God's wondrous work is sometimes hidden from us. Whether we can see evidence of it or not, God is always at work in the soil of our lives, bringing forth life in places that look forsaken.

My husband and I have a small garden in our backyard. We initially tried to grow tomatoes, peppers, and lettuce, but eventually we gave up. We blamed the deer and rabbits; we blamed the heat; but deep down we knew the problem: We just didn't pay enough attention to the garden.

Just as a garden requires tending, God's work in us needs attention. We cannot expect to bear spiritual fruit if we do not spend time turning over the soil of God's word and cultivating spiritual practices.

There is no doubt that God is the source of the growth happening beneath the surface. But God invites us to do our part to tend to it. Although I still hope one day to grow the world's most gorgeous tomato, I long even more to grow in God's love by paying attention to God's presence under the surface of every day.

Loving God, you are working even now in our lives and in our world. Help us pay attention and tend the garden of our hearts that we may bear the fruit of your love. Amen.

Cultivating Hope

In our scripture reading for today, the psalmist remembers a moment when the people of God were filled with laughter because God had restored them to the Promised Land after years of exile. They were laughing with gratitude and joy. There's something about laughter that is healing and even holy.

Can you think of a time when you laughed with gratitude and joy? Has God's goodness ever brought grateful laughter to your heart? If so, take a moment to call that memory to mind. If you can't recall a time of such joy, imagine yourself surrounded by the light of God, laughing with gratitude and joy.

It's important to remember these moments and hold on to them so that we can return to them when life gets hard. If we can recount how God has helped us in the good times, we can more deeply trust God in the difficult times.

That's what the writer of Psalm 126 does. In the first three verses he recalls how the people rejoiced in God's deliverance. Then he asks God once again for help. Times, it seems, are not as good as they once were. Some scholars suggest that Israel was facing a drought that threatened the harvest. They needed God's deliverance once again. They remembered the provision of God in the past, and they believed that their tears would once again be turned into joy.

No matter what season you find yourself in—one of joy or struggle—know that God is with you and is able once again to bring you laughter and joy.

O God, thank you for being with us in all things. Help us call to mind those moments when you brought us laughter. Help us to trust you in harder times, knowing that you love us and are leading us toward you. Amen.

Today's psalm offers us another image of planting. Verses 5 and 6 describe the people of God going out into the field with their seeds, weeping as they sow. Why are they weeping? Maybe they have lost hope. Maybe they look at the parched ground and believe that all is lost. Maybe they cannot envision a way out of the drought.

Their eyes are blurred by tears—all they see is dry, parched ground—but they plant anyway. Perhaps they have some hope left. Though they weep as they work, they do the work. Then the psalmist speaks. Where the people's hope wavers, he steps up and offers a vision of hope. In verse 6, his prayer turns from pleading to certainty: The people "shall come home with shouts of joy."

Many of us know what it's like to be in a "parched place," to face a situation with very little hope of getting through it. This psalm encourages us to follow the example of the Israelites and sow seeds anyway—to take what steps we can, even through tears, to move forward in faith.

But thanks to the psalmist, there's more to the story. The psalm invites us to grab on to a bigger hope. When we can't find much hope within ourselves, the psalmist can carry our hope for us and remind us of God's love and care.

We don't know how everything turned out for the Israelites that year. We don't always know how things will turn out in our own lives. But we can hold on to the assurance of Psalm 126 that God will be with us in all things.

God of hope, thank you for the promise of your presence with us. Though our hope may waver at times, help us be faithful to take the next right step. Help us trust that you will provide what we need. Amen.

Cultivating Hope

There are some challenging instructions in this letter from Paul to the Thessalonians: Rejoice always, pray without ceasing, give thanks in all circumstances. If Paul is telling us that we should always be happy, praying, and feeling grateful for everything that happens to us, then we all fall far short. We are human beings after all, and life is hard.

Part of being human is experiencing a wide range of emotions. Any good therapist will tell us that feelings are neither good nor bad. They just are. What we are invited to do is notice them and make loving choices about how we act on them. As a pastor, I have learned never to judge people's feelings. Allowing someone to express anger, to cry through grief, or to shiver with anxiety without judging them can help them heal.

So where does that leave us in the conversation with Paul? Is Paul telling us that we just need to grit our teeth and pretend to be happy all the time? Are we meant to be grateful when tragedy strikes? Do these teachings of Paul lead us to live in denial? No. Remember, Paul says that we are to be grateful to God *in* all circumstances, not *for* them. We can be sad and grateful at the same time. Could it be also that gratitude to God is a source of our healing?

Paul issues an invitation to an abiding trust in God, deeper than anything life throws our way. God is always with us. No matter what we are going through or feeling, we are held by God. We don't have to fake it. We can be real with God and with each other, knowing that underneath every circumstance is an unconditional love that will not let us go.

Gracious God, thank you for always loving us. Thank you for the gift of emotions that can guide us and teach us. Help us trust that underneath all the waves of emotion and all the circumstances of life, your abiding presence is with us. We will never stop being grateful. Amen.

The Gospel of John opens with the soaring proclamation "In the beginning was the Word." The writer takes us all the way back to that moment before time, before the stars and the planets were ordered, when God simply was. Imagine the vastness of space, the swirling dust of the universe, and the fellowship of the Trinity dancing in love together.

Then we get to verse 6: "There was a man." Suddenly, we are taken from the eternal dance of the Trinity before time into a specific moment in history. We zoom through the galaxies to planet Earth until we see one man, whose name was John.

The transition from verses 1 through 5 to verse 6 is jarring. We go from the expansive universe to the Jordan River, from the cosmic to the earthly, from eternity to a particular moment, where we find one man in dusty sandals crying out in the wilderness.

These few verses tell us a lot about our God, who is God of the universe but chooses to use everyday people like John the Baptist to testify to the "light that is coming into the world."

God called John the Baptist to testify to a particular people in a particular moment of history.

Just as God called John the Baptist, so God calls you and me. Our mission is the same as John's: to point to the light of a God who loves us all unconditionally. How are you called to point to that light?

The story of God moves from "In the beginning was the Word" to "There was a person sent from God whose name was _____." What would it mean to fill in the blank with your name?

God of the universe, we marvel that you want to be in relationship with us. Help us use the gifts you have given us to point others to your love. Amen.

THIRD SUNDAY OF ADVENT

In our reading today we find John the Baptist being questioned by religious leaders. It seems as if all the powers that be have joined together to find out what John is up to. You can tell by the way they interrogate him that they did not make the long trip from Jerusalem because they wanted to hear a word from God. They are on a mission to put John in his place.

They ask John, "Who are you?" in several different ways. They want to know if he's claiming to be the Messiah, to be Elijah, or to be a prophet. To all of these questions, John answers no. He doesn't fit into any of their boxes. He simply says that he is "the voice crying out in the wilderness," standing far outside the structures of their institutions. He's just a voice preparing the way for the One who is coming after him.

His answers don't satisfy them, so they begin to question his authority. Behind their question—"Why are you baptizing?"—is the question, "Who do you think you are?" Again, John evades their questions and simply points to the One who is coming. He cannot be managed or silenced by them.

Often the coming of God into the world does more to disrupt the status quo than it does to reinforce it—and that is true in our hearts as well as our institutions. As we prepare to welcome Christ, let us get ready for him to disrupt our complacency. Let us be open to the life–upending arrival of the Messiah.

O Holy One, come into our hearts and into our world once again. Break us open and move among us as you will. Keep us from trying to manage you. Lead us out of old patterns into new ways of loving and living. Amen.

Waiting in Hope

DECEMBER 18–24, 2023 • RICHARD L. MORGAN

SCRIPTURE OVERVIEW: In the fourth week of Advent, we focus on prophecies of the arrival of the Messiah. Isaiah foretells the coming of the Prince of Peace who will reign on the throne of David forever. In the first reading from Luke, Mary rejoices after her visit to Elizabeth, for she understands that her child will play a key role in God's redemptive work. Paul reminds Titus that our great God and Savior, Jesus Christ, has brought salvation to all. The second reading from Luke might more logically have come first this week, for it describes how Mary reveals the importance of her child in her song of rejoicing.

QUESTIONS AND SUGGESTIONS FOR REFLECTION

- Read Isaiah 9:2-7. What title for Jesus stands out to you today? How does that inform your discipleship?
- Read Luke 1:46-55. Consider how you magnify the Lord. How do you pass on your faith to future generations?
- Read Titus 2:11-14. Why would today's reading jump right to waiting for Jesus' return? What does this say about his birth?
- Read Luke 1:26-38. In this season of giving and receiving, how do you remember that God is the giver of all good gifts? How do you return your God-given gifts to God?

Author, chaplain, pastor (PCUSA), and professor; most recently served as a volunteer chaplain at Redstone Highlands, the senior living community where he resided near Pittsburgh, PA; died at the age of 93 during the production of this book.

Advent is that season of the Christian year when we look backward with gratitude for the birth of Christ and forward with hope as we await the second coming of Christ. It is a time of preparation and patient waiting before celebrating the joy to the world that comes with Christmas.

In his letter to Titus, the apostle Paul wrote, "The grace of God has appeared, bringing salvation to all." This salvation is in three tenses: past, present, and future. It looks back to the saving work of Christ in the past, urges believers to live transformed lives in the present, and looks forward to the promise of Christ's return in glory.

Advent is not only waiting to celebrate the birth of Christ but also being ready for that same Christ's return in glory. As the forty days between Easter and the Ascension ended, the disciples wondered when Jesus would return. Heartbroken that he was leaving them, it was natural that they wanted to know when their Lord would come back. Jesus told them that only the Father had the authority to determine those dates and times, and it was not for them (or us) to know (see Acts 1:7). Living Christlike in the present was far more important than speculation about the future.

As we sing the seventh-century hymn "O come, O come Emmanuel," our prayer is not only that Christ be born in us but that we constantly hold on to the hope of Christ's return. Let us do the work of Christ with deeds of kindness and mercy so others may see Christ living in us. May our ministry to "the least of these" be a witness to what Advent means.

In this Advent season, let us get beyond giving and receiving presents to offer our presence to others in need.

During the Advent season, my late wife, Alice Ann, and I had a custom of visiting a person in our parish who lived alone. Mary, a single woman, lived a solitary life in her apartment. She had been in poor health for years and was confined to a wheelchair. She relied on her only brother for financial assistance and home health.

We visited her often and knew she sat by the window, hoping members of the church would visit her. Although several members passed by her apartment, they rarely stopped to visit. Their neglect reminded me of a story of a Sunday school class studying the story of the Good Samaritan. The teacher asked the class why the priest and Levite passed by on the other side, never stopping to help the man in need. A little girl replied, "Because they saw he had already been robbed." Mary had been robbed of good health and had little means or service to offer the church. So, she was forgotten as if she were of little value.

When we entered her apartment, Mary smiled and seemed glad someone had come to visit. She told us, "Life is hard, but I have no complaints. The Lord is with me and will never forsake me. I patiently spend precious moments in prayer and listen to what he asks of me, and then I obey without hesitation."

In a real way, Mary mirrored the obedient faith of the virgin Mary. When the angel Gabriel brought the astounding news that she would bear a son who would be called the Son of God, she replied, "Here am I, the servant of the Lord; let it be with me according to your word" (Luke 1:38).

God of the neglected, give us eyes to see those whom others have passed by. Then stir our hearts and direct our steps to them. May our help go beyond words to action. Amen.

When I taught psychology at a community college, I always took students during Advent to an Operation Santa Claus mission at a state mental hospital. Part of our experience was to tour wards, singing Christmas carols. We finished singing at one locked ward, and the attendant unlocked the door so we could leave.

We entered another ward and began to sing. I suddenly noticed we had a new choir member on the back row. A patient had walked out with us, and with a deep bass voice was singing, "God Rest Ye, Merry Gentlemen." The attendant saw that a patient was missing and quickly ushered him back behind locked doors. But for a moment, the man was free to sing with all his heart.

Every psalm seems to open with an explosion. At times the first verse is an affirmation of the grandeur and majesty of God. Other psalms begin with a cry of lament. Psalm 96 begins with a mighty call, "O sing unto the LORD a new song." The psalmist reminds worshipers, "Honor and majesty are before him, strength and beauty are in his sanctuary." In a way, our choir made the halls of that mental hospital a sanctuary, with voices lifted in song. Those Christmas carols were a reminder that the good news of Christmas began with the music of angelic voices on the hills of Bethlehem.

Since I was a counselor, a social worker told me in confidence that the man who joined our choir suffered from depression. He had battled this "noonday demon" for years, but thanks to therapy and medicine, was getting better. It may be that when the man joined our choir, it was a step forward to freedom and the beginning of a "new song" for him.

O God, may the singing of Advent and Christmas music bring joy and light to those who live in darkness. In the name of the One who has come and will come again—Jesus, the Christ. Amen.

It was Christmas Eve on a ward of a large hospital. My sister, Mary Ann, was a nurse and always volunteered to work on this night. She was single and wanted other nurses on her ward to be with their families. It was quiet on the ward. The only sounds were the moans and groans of some of the patients.

Mary Ann had bonded with a little boy who was dying of leukemia. Near midnight Mary Ann heard someone singing, "Jingle Bells, Jingle Bells, Jingle all the Way." She soon discovered it was the little boy. His weakened voice drifted down the halls of the ward until many of the sick patients began singing "Jingle Bells." Their singing transformed a place of suffering into a place of joy.

The prophet Isaiah had foretold that the Messiah would come as a child. It would be a child who would deliver the people from bondage and suffering. In a real way, that little boy became a Christ-gift to those sick people. His contagious joy rekindled a spirit of joy and hope when all seemed lost.

The story from the hospital ward was reminiscent of other songs at midnight. It was midnight when Paul and Silas sang hymns from that Philippian jail as the prisoners listened to them (see Acts 16:25). The little boy died in a few weeks, but his song was a strong reminder that the Christchild would suffer and die on the cross, as he took all the pain of the world and turned it into a glorious song of salvation.

Teach us, O God, to be able to sing in the worst of circumstances and to trust your care when life is against us. Amen.

Brenden, a Celtic monk, appeared before the king in Inverness and challenged him to become a Christian. The king replied, "And if I become a Christian, what difference would that make?" Brenden told him, "Sire, if you become Christ's man, you will behold wonder upon wonder and every wonder true!" Among the names the prophet Isaiah gave to the coming messiah, the first was *Wonderful*.

Consider the wonder of what and how it happened at the Advent of Jesus. God stepped into this world as a human being. His birth was not heralded with the fanfare of trumpets, nor was he born in the comfort of a warm home. He came silently with a mother's lullaby, and his birth took place in a stable in God's backyard.

Consider what this meant. King David's heartfelt desire was to build a temple to house God's glory (see 2 Samuel 7). It did not happen in his time but awaited God's time. Nor did it happen as David wished, but in God's way. God's way was not to dwell in houses made by hands but to become incarnate in Jesus, his son.

Consider what followed. Christ brought a new beginning for humankind, a kingdom not of this world but one where the last shall be first and love embraces all. And through this ever-present Christ, human beings can realize God's Spirit living in them.

O God of light, help us pause to experience the wonder of Advent. Move us beyond the hustle and bustle of the season to find the Christ-child breaking into our lives. Amen.

During Advent I always made sure to visit the homebound in my congregation. It was near Christmas when I went to visit Mrs. Sharman and her family. Lizzie lived in a small company house owned by the tannery where her husband, Morris, used to work. Now he was homebound and was strapped to his bed because of mental illness. When I entered the house, Morris was crying and shrieking in anguish.

Lizzie's only child, Donnie, sat at the kitchen table. Donnie had leukemia, and his life would soon end. For me, it seemed a hopeless situation. So I was surprised to see Lizzie hanging popcorn on an evergreen tree she had cut down from the nearby woods. There was no panic on her face, only a glow I will never forget.

How could this woman be so happy, surrounded by so much suffering and the imminent death of her son? I helped her hang some popcorn on the tree and, after a prayer for the family, departed. As I drove down the road to my home, I realized Lizzie's strength came from God (see Romans 6:25).

Some years later, I revisited this church and learned that all members of that family had died. But the memory of Lizzie's faith remains forever enshrined in my soul. Her faith mirrors the faith of the virgin Mary. At first, Mary felt the news that she would bear a child called the Son of God was unbelievable (Luke 1:35, AP). Then Mary's faith enabled her to say, "Here am I Lord, the servant of the Lord; let it be with me according to your word" (Luke 1:38). Mary and Lizzie both witness to the truth that God lifts up the lowly and gives them strength.

Gracious God, thank you for all whose faith is a witness that you are their strength. Amen.

Waiting in Hope

FOURTH SUNDAY OF ADVENT AND CHRISTMAS EVE

It was Christmas Eve, and we gathered for worship in Memory Care behind locked doors. I read the Christmas story from Luke, and we sang the familiar Christmas carols. Most of the residents were in wheelchairs, and some of them were asleep. Although denied short-term memory, some of them likely remembered Christmas Eve services from their past.

One of the residents there was Serena, who sat quietly at the back of the room. Before Alzheimer's disease had impaired her mind, she had told me some of her stories. Her home was in Czechoslovakia, and she had lived through both German and Russian occupations. Serena told me that she kept the key to the village church and opened the doors for worship. She remembered how some of her Jewish friends disappeared, never to be seen again. She dearly loved her husband, who had rescued her and brought her as an immigrant to America.

Serena had been sitting quietly, staring in space. We always ended the service singing "Silent Night." My wife began softly playing "Silent Night," when we heard a voice from the back of the room. It was Serena singing, *"Stille Nacht! Heilige Nacht! Alles schläft; ensam wacht."* We paused as her voice filled the room. Serena was a victim of a disease that robbed her of her mind but not her soul. She was back in her village church on Christmas Eve.

This experience became what the Celts call a thin place, where the veil between heaven and earth is lifted for a moment, and one glimpses the Holy. We remembered that first Christmas Eve and the song of the angels, "Glory to God in the highest heaven, and on earth peace among those whom he favors."

O God of all, we give thanks for that first silent night. May the Spirit of the Christchild walk among and within us, granting a Bethlehem in our hearts. Amen.

To Be

DECEMBER 25–31, 2023 • CHERISNA JEAN-MARIE

SCRIPTURE OVERVIEW: As we celebrate the birth of our Savior, we do so with cries of praise to God. Isaiah delights and rejoices in God, who will bring reconciliation to all nations. Psalm 148 declares that all of creation praises the Lord, for creation knows who formed and sustains it. Paul explains to the Galatians that God sent Jesus to redeem us, and as a result we may now call out to God as God's children. In the Gospel reading, Luke sets the story of Jesus within the history of the Israelites. Both Simeon and Anna are devout people, filled with the Holy Spirit. They have been praying for God to send the Redeemer, and God gives them insight to recognize him as Jesus. Praise be to God for this indescribable gift!

QUESTIONS AND SUGGESTIONS FOR REFLECTION

- Read Isaiah 52:7-10. How are you spreading the message of peace in Christ? From whom have you heard that message?
- Read Psalm 148. Pause and consider the joy of God's coming salvation for the whole world.
- Read Galatians 4:4-7. Consider your identity as a child of God through Christ. What joy does this identity bring you?
- Read Luke 2:22-40. How can you, like Anna, joyously proclaim the freedom and redemption Christ brings all of humanity?

Ordained minister in the Christian Church (Disciples of Christ); lives in Nashville, TN.

CHRISTMAS DAY

It took me a while to understand that the true essence of praise is to be my authentic self. Coming from a charismatic church tradition, I was taught that praising God happens on Sunday mornings with musical instruments, choirs, and dancers. So I never understood how to translate praising in church into praising in daily life without a song or a dance. Praise was something I did. Praise was something I did at a certain time. Praise was something I did at a certain time for a particular reason. It became a performance and duty to fulfill my Christian, good church-girl obligations.

Boy, was I wrong! Psalm 148 is a beautiful reminder that praise is not a duty or obligation to be fulfilled at a particular time. Praise is not something we do; praise is who we are. To be our authentic selves is to praise.

Unfortunately, many of us wear a mask (not the good kind that prevent the spread of disease). We often don't know who we are because the mask has become how we define ourselves and others based on social constructs like race, gender, and sexual orientation. We are so blinded and deafened by hate and ignorance that we are unable to see the human or divine spark within ourselves or others. We are so lost in wanting to be right that we can't be who God wants us to be.

What would change in your life if, as a form of praise, you committed to a spiritual discipline of showing up as your true self? What could it mean for the people you are in community with to be conscious of acknowledging their human spark in every encounter? True praise begins with finding and living our true humanity. And humanity is colorful, just as God intended.

Dear Creator, remind us of the beauty in your creation, and call us back to our authentic self so that we praise you! Amen.

My biological parents were respected community leaders in the Haitian community where I grew up in New Jersey. They would often tell me that bearing their name came with a certain type of privilege and responsibility. Who they were in the community was often associated with who I was as their child.

So it is with our spiritual Parent. God sent the Son so that all might become children of God. We are associated by name and deed with a God that breathes into us the breath of life. And by the Spirit of Jesus we utter the word *Abba*—Father. We benefit from and have a huge responsibility in our relationship with God in the world.

As children of God, we are siblings in Christ. And it is through our relationships that God is made real to others who may not yet know God. Sometimes God shows up in a person whose life reflects God's activities in the world. So it is most often through us, God's children, that God is made known in the world. Love is made real when God's children love. Peace is possible when God's children live in peace. Justice is realized when God's children seek justice on behalf of those who are downtrodden.

Love, peace, and justice are possible if we actively pursue them for ourselves and our neighbors. This is how we bear the name of God in our hearts. This is what connects us to the divine in our humanity. May we all utter the name Abba in word and in deed so that we live to create a world where the beloved community becomes more than just a dream.

Dear God, teach us to be active participants of your works in the world through your name—for your name bears witness to the hope we seek. Amen.

Beautiful are the feet of those who announce peace. . . . Beautiful are the feet of those who bring good news and announce salvation." In my community, the many feet of those I see and hear announcing the word of God are not often described as beautiful. Most media coverage calls them thugs or trouble-makers. These are the young leaders who cry out *No justice, no peace* when another Black person is gunned down by police. *No justice, no peace* when elected officials act immorally. *No justice, no peace* when women are paid less than men for the same work. *No justice, no peace* when another transgender woman is brutally assaulted. *No justice, no peace* is the word of God. *No justice, no peace* is good news. *No justice, no peace* is a proclamation uttered by God.

We live in a world where peace is understood as the absence of disturbance. But in reality, true peace may require disturbance and come only after the norms that rob people of justice are destabilized. Peace is when justice is accessible to every person regardless of race, gender, sexual orientation, age, or self-identi-fication. Peace is a human right that comes only when justice is realized. I am grateful for the divine courage and work of those in my community who disturb systems and people in power to stand with the oppressed, even if that means troubling the comfort of false peace. I am encouraged by the many people who lead protests, rallies, sit-ins, and other forms of resistance to pro-claim the word of God in action.

Justice and peace are possible—even probable—when you and I take up *our* cross and proclaim by our sacrificial living this word from God: *No justice, no peace.*

Dear God, in the days to come, remind us that peace is possible when we live out your word by resisting injustice. Amen.

As a clergywoman, my vocational path has been colorful. I have served in many ways, many places, and with different people. One of the most profound roles I served was as a hospital chaplain in Atlanta. It was especially impactful because of the intentionality that chaplains hold when serving in a hospital.

On my first day as a chaplain, my supervisor told me to be mindful of how I walked into a patient's room because I became God's word in the flesh to someone experiencing a bad day. My body represented the word of God for the one who might feel hopeless. I was both testifying to the light and embodying the transformation that comes from that enlightenment. That continues to resonate for me as I walk in the world attempting to embody hope as a representation of God in the flesh.

The world is filled with hopelessness. Yet I am also reminded of the hope I have in my faith and the many ways I get to participate in igniting hope in others.

I want to invite you to be intentional about becoming someone's hope today. How does God's word in the flesh—your flesh—speak hope to people around you? How do you help those who are sick, lost, or in need? How do you embody hope for the immigrant at the border or in your town? How are you giving hope to someone one experiencing racism? How are you helping those who are suffering from the fear, hatred, and resentment they are carrying? How are we walking together in the world as God's word in the flesh? The world needs representations of God manifested every day in every way.

God, help us to take your light into the darkest places and situations, knowing that the darkness will not overcome us. Amen.

Babies come from God. Children are gifts from the Holy One that can remind us of life, love, hope, possibilities, and a future. I am reminded of special moments in the life of the church when we dedicate, lay hands on, and pray for and with families who bring their children to be blessed by their community of faith. So it is in the text today, a specific tradition that reminds us how precious children are to God.

Baby dedication Sundays are some of my favorite moments in the church. The moment is holy and it belongs to God, the children, their families, and us as a people—people who tell the children with words, actions, and rituals that they are special, have a purpose, and can dream dreams. These kinds of traditions remind us of the sacred task we share to help raise, influence, and speak life to children in our village. What a holy task from God to be part of a community that is committed to raising children together!

I am inspired by the African proverb that says that it takes a village to raise a child. Beloved, I believe we all play a role in raising the children in our community. Simeon believed his destiny was tied to that of baby Jesus, and Anna, a widowed prophet, was able to see the promises of God in Jesus.

The world would be very different for the children in our lives if we were able to see them the way Simeon and Anna saw Jesus: No matter their circumstances or where they come from, their very existence is vital for our future.

Dear God, turn our hearts toward the children, and help us never forget that they are precious in your sight and hold the future in their hands. Amen.

This has been a difficult season to be happy. Considering the many uproars in our nation, communities, churches—and even our homes if we are honest—it's been a time of turmoil and grief, a time when I have questioned the presence of God. *Where are you?* I ask. *Do you even care?* It's been a tough season to offer gratitude or to praise God with words.

I often associate praising God with good things and moments—joys, answered prayers, good health reports, and the like. Praising God has often been about all the ways I am happy and fulfilled. Then the year 2020 made finding joy difficult. To be honest, it's been rough finding time or motivation to say "thank you." I've been grieving. Yet in the midst of my grief I am learning something deeper about being grateful. I am learning something important about praising God. Beyond the happy moments, praising God is an identity, a posture, a relational act of service. It's a way of life.

To praise God is to be . . . To be *authentic*, to be *still*, to be *present*. I have learned in this season of grief and turmoil that my relationship with God and how I respond to what is happening to me are all connected to who I understand myself to be. I am a child of God. My faith has been my anchor, the solid foundation by which I stand amid the whirlwind of life's circumstances. That is why I can praise God in spite of the sadness and grief all around me.

I invite you to acknowledge all that has happened and the many losses from the last several years. Take a breath. Lean in and know that in spite of it all, God is still in control.

Dear Lord, amid devastation, loss, disappointment, and hurt, put a new song in our hearts that will draw us closer to you in praise. Amen.

To Be

First Sunday after Christmas

Today's text is a fitting reading for the first Sunday after Christmas because it is one of the earliest statements we have about who Jesus is. It is Christology in the making. In particular, the first part says that Jesus is greater than the prophets, and the second part says he is greater than the angels. The prophets told us about God and spoke for God, and the angels serve God. But in Jesus Christ we meet that same God face to face. We see the depth of God's love through Jesus' identity: Jesus, appointed heir of all things, Jesus, the reflection of God's glory, Jesus, the imprint of God's very being.

Do you feel the excitement in the depths of God's love for us? We have access to God directly because we have access to Jesus. Higher than the angels, located at the beginning of Creation, Jesus is God. Creator of life. Alpha and Omega. The One who sits at the right hand of the Majesty on high has come to us. Jesus is God, and God has become human in Jesus.

This text gives me chills in a good way! I get excited about who Jesus is because I am reminded that even in our humanity we have access to divinity. In the days past and in the days to come, we are anchored in this truth: God in Jesus remains the same. There are different days and different seasons. Perhaps there are even different people surrounding us. Yet God remains the same. I want to invite you to sit still for a little while today and take in this truth: *You have access to God in Jesus.* In our best selves and even at our worst, we have access. May this truth bring you courage to reflect faith, hope, and love.

Dear God, thank you for giving yourself to us in Jesus! Amen.

The Revised Common Lectionary* for 2023
Year A—Advent / Christmas Year B
(Disciplines Edition)

January 1
NEW YEAR'S DAY
Ecclesiastes 3:1-13
Psalm 8
Revelation 21:1-6a
Matthew 25:31-46

> **January 6**
> EPIPHANY
> *(may be used on January 1)*
> Isaiah 60:1-6
> Psalm 72:1-7, 10-14
> Ephesians 3:1-12
> Matthew 2:1-12

January 2–8
BAPTISM OF THE LORD
Isaiah 42:1-9
Psalm 29
Acts 10:34-43
Matthew 3:13-17

January 9–15
Isaiah 49:1-7
Psalm 40:1-11
1 Corinthians 1:1-9
John 1:29-42

January 16–22
Isaiah 9:1-4
Psalm 27:1, 4-9
1 Corinthians 1:10-18
Matthew 4:12-23

January 23–29
Micah 6:1-8
Psalm 15
1 Corinthians 1:18-31
Matthew 5:1-12

January 30–February 5
Isaiah 58:1-9a (9b-12)
Psalm 112:1-9 (10)
1 Corinthians 2:1-12 (13-16)
Matthew 5:13-20

February 6–12
Deuteronomy 30:15-20
Psalm 119:1-8
1 Corinthians 3:1-9
Matthew 5:21-37

February 13–19
THE TRANSFIGURATION
Exodus 24:12-18
Psalm 2
2 Peter 1:16-21
Matthew 17:1-9

February 20–26
First Sunday in Lent
Genesis 2:15-17; 3:1-7
Psalm 32
Romans 5:12-19
Matthew 4:1-11

February 22
Ash Wednesday
Joel 2:1-2, 12-17
Psalm 51:1-17
2 Corinthians 5:20b–6:10
Matthew 6:1-6, 16-21

February 27–March 5
Second Sunday in Lent
Genesis 12:1-4a
Psalm 121
Romans 4:1-5, 13-17
John 3:1-17

March 6–12
Third Sunday in Lent
Exodus 17:1-7
Psalm 95
Romans 5:1-11
John 4:5-42

March 13–19
Fourth Sunday in Lent
1 Samuel 16:1-13
Psalm 23
Ephesians 5:8-14
John 9:1-41

March 20–26
Fifth Sunday in Lent
Ezekiel 37:1-14
Psalm 130
Romans 8:6-11
John 11:1-45

March 27–April 2
Palm/Passion Sunday

Liturgy of the Palms
Psalm 118:1-2, 19-29
Matthew 21:1-11

Liturgy of the Passion
Isaiah 50:4-9a
Psalm 31:9-16
Philippians 2:5-11
Matthew 26:14–27:66

April 3–9
Holy Week

Monday, April 3
Isaiah 42:1-9
Psalm 36:5-11
Hebrews 9:11-15
John 12:1-11

Tuesday, April 4
Isaiah 49:1-7
Psalm 71:1-14
1 Corinthians 1:18-31
John 12:20-36

Wednesday, April 5
Isaiah 50:4-9a
Psalm 70
Hebrews 12:1-3
John 13:21-32

Maundy Thursday, April 6
Exodus 12:1-14
Psalm 116:1-2, 12-19
1 Corinthians 11:23-26
John 13:1-17, 31b-35

Good Friday, April 7
Isaiah 52:13–53:12
Psalm 22
Hebrews 10:16-25
John 18:1–19:42

Holy Saturday, April 8
Job 14:1-14
Psalm 31:1-4, 15-16
1 Peter 4:1-8
Matthew 27:57-66

Easter Day, April 9
Acts 10:34-43
Psalm 118:1-2, 14-24
Colossians 3:1-4
John 20:1-18

April 10–16
Acts 2:14a, 22-32
Psalm 16
1 Peter 1:3-9
John 20:19-31

April 17–23
Acts 2:14a, 36-41
Psalm 116:1-4, 12-19
1 Peter 1:17-23
Luke 24:13-35

April 24–30
Acts 2:42-47
Psalm 23
1 Peter 2:19-25
John 10:1-10

May 1–7
Acts 7:55-60
Psalm 31:1-5, 15-16
1 Peter 2:2-10
John 14:1-14

May 8–14
Acts 17:22-31
Psalm 66:8-20
1 Peter 3:13-22
John 14:15-21

May 15–21
Acts 1:6-14
Psalm 68:1-10, 32-35
1 Peter 4:12-14; 5:6-11
John 17:1-11

May 18
ASCENSION DAY
(may be used on May 21)
Acts 1:1-11
Psalm 47
Ephesians 1:15-23
Luke 24:44-53

May 22–28
PENTECOST
Acts 2:1-21
Psalm 104:24-34, 35b
1 Corinthians 12:3b-13
John 20:19-23

May 29–June 4
TRINITY SUNDAY
Genesis 1:1–2:4a
Psalm 8
2 Corinthians 13:11-13
Matthew 28:16-20

June 5–11
Genesis 12:1-9
Psalm 33:1-12
Romans 4:13-25
Matthew 9:9-13, 18-26

June 12–18
Genesis 18:1-15; 21:1-7
Psalm 116:1-2, 12-19
Romans 5:1-8
Matthew 9:35–10:23

June 19–25
Genesis 21:8-21
Psalm 86:1-10, 16-17
Romans 6:1b-11
Matthew 10:24-39

June 26–July 2
Genesis 22:1-14
Psalm 13
Romans 6:12-23
Matthew 10:40-42

July 3–9
Genesis 24:34-38, 42-49,
  58-67
Psalm 45:10-17
Romans 7:15-25a
Matthew 11:16-19, 25-30

July 10–16
Genesis 25:19-34
Psalm 119:105-112
Romans 8:1-11
Matthew 13:1-9, 18-23

July 17–23
Genesis 28:10-19a
Psalm 139:1-12, 23-24
Romans 8:12-25
Matthew 13:24-30, 36-43

July 24–30
Genesis 29:15-28
Psalm 105:1-11, 45b
Romans 8:26-39
Matthew 13:31-33, 44-52

July 31–August 6
Genesis 32:22-31
Psalm 17:1-7, 15
Romans 9:1-5
Matthew 14:13-21

August 7–13
Genesis 37:1-4, 12-28
Psalm 105:1-6, 16-22, 45b
Romans 10:5-15
Matthew 14:22-33

August 14–20
Genesis 45:1-15
Psalm 133
Romans 11:1-2a, 29-32
Matthew 15:10-28

August 21–27
Exodus 1:8–2:10
Psalm 124
Romans 12:1-8
Matthew 16:13-20

August 28–September 3
Exodus 3:1-15
Psalm 105:1-6, 23-26, 45b
Romans 12:9-21
Matthew 16:21-28

September 4–10
Exodus 12:1-14
Psalm 149
Romans 13:8-14
Matthew 18:15-20

September 11–17
Exodus 14:19-31
Psalm 114
Romans 14:1-12
Matthew 18:21-35

September 18–24
Exodus 16:2-15
Psalm 105:1-6, 37-45
Philippians 1:21-30
Matthew 20:1-16

September 25–October 1
Exodus 17:1-7
Psalm 78:1-4, 12-16
Philippians 2:1-13
Matthew 21:23-32

October 2–8
Exodus 20:1-4, 7-9, 12-20
Psalm 19
Philippians 3:4b-14
Matthew 21:33-46

October 9–15
Exodus 32:1-14
Psalm 106:1-6, 19-23
Philippians 4:1-9
Matthew 22:1-14

> **October 9**
> THANKSGIVING DAY, CANADA
> Deuteronomy 8:7-18
> Psalm 65
> 2 Corinthians 9:6-15
> Luke 17:11-19

October 16–22
Exodus 33:12-23
Psalm 99
1 Thessalonians 1:1-10
Matthew 22:15-22

October 23–29
Deuteronomy 34:1-12
Psalm 90:1-6, 13-17
1 Thessalonians 2:1-8
Matthew 22:34-46

October 30–November 5
Joshua 3:7-17
Psalm 107:1-7, 33-37
1 Thessalonians 2:9-13
Matthew 23:1-12

> **November 1**
> ALL SAINTS DAY
> *(may be used on November 5)*
> Revelation 7:9-17
> Psalm 34:1-10, 22
> 1 John 3:1-3
> Matthew 5:1-12

November 6–12
Joshua 24:1-3a, 14-25
Psalm 78:1-7
1 Thessalonians 4:13-18
Matthew 25:1-13

November 13–19
Judges 4:1-7
Psalm 123
1 Thessalonians 5:1-11
Matthew 25:14-30

November 20–26
Ezekiel 34:11-16, 20-24
Psalm 100
Ephesians 1:15-23
Matthew 25:31-46

> **November 23**
> THANKSGIVING DAY, USA
> Deuteronomy 8:7-18
> Psalm 65
> 2 Corinthians 9:6-15
> Luke 17:11-19

November 27–December 3
FIRST SUNDAY OF ADVENT
Isaiah 64:1-9
Psalm 80:1-7, 17-19
1 Corinthians 1:3-9
Mark 13:24-37

December 4–10
SECOND SUNDAY OF ADVENT
Isaiah 40:1-11
Psalm 85:1-2, 8-13
2 Peter 3:8-15a
Mark 1:1-8

December 11–17
THIRD SUNDAY OF ADVENT
Isaiah 61:1-4, 8-11
Psalm 126
1 Thessalonians 5:16-24
John 1:6-8, 19-28

December 18–24
FOURTH SUNDAY OF ADVENT
2 Sam 7:1-11, 16
Luke 1:46b-55
Romans 16:25-27
Luke 1:26-38

December 24
CHRISTMAS EVE
Isaiah 9:2-7
Psalm 96
Titus 2:11-14
Luke 2:1-20

December 25–31
FIRST SUNDAY AFTER
CHRISTMAS
Isaiah 61:10–62:3
Psalm 148
Galatians 4:4-7
Luke 2:22-40

December 25
CHRISTMAS DAY
Isaiah 52:7-10
Psalm 98
Hebrews 1:1-12
John 1:1-14

December 31
WATCH NIGHT/NEW YEAR
Ecclesiastes 3:1-13
Psalm 8
Revelation 21:1-6a
Matthew 25:31-46

A Guide to Daily Prayer

These prayers imply worship time with a group; feel free to adapt the plural pronouns for personal use.

MORNING PRAYER

In the morning, LORD, you hear my voice;
>in the morning I lay my requests before you
>and wait expectantly.
>
>—Psalm 5:3

Gathering and Silence

Call to Praise and Prayer
>God said, "Let there be light," and there was light.
>God saw that the light was good.

Psalm 63:1-5
>God, my God, you I crave;
>>my soul thirsts for you,
>>my body aches for you
>>like a dry and weary land.
>
>Let me gaze on you in your temple:
>>a vision of strength and glory.
>
>Your love is better than life;
>>my speech is full of praise.
>
>I give you a lifetime of worship,
>>my hands raised in your name.
>
>I feast at a rich table,
>>my lips singing of your glory.

Prayer of Thanksgiving

We praise you with joy, loving God, for your grace is better than life itself. You have sustained us through the darkness, and you bless us with life in this new day. In the shadow of your wings we sing for joy and bless your holy name. Amen.

Scripture Reading

Silence

Prayers of the People

The Lord's Prayer (ecumenical text)

Our Father in heaven,
    hallowed be your name,
    your kingdom come,
    your will be done,
    on earth as in heaven.
Give us today our daily bread.
Forgive us our sins as we forgive
    those who sin against us.
Save us from the time of trial,
    and deliver us from evil.
For the kingdom, the power, and the glory
    are yours, now and forever. Amen.

Blessing

May the light of your mercy shine brightly on all who walk in your presence today, O Lord.

I will extol the LORD at all times;
God's praise will always be on my lips.

—Psalm 34:1

Gathering and Silence

Call to Praise and Prayer

O LORD, my Savior, teach me your ways.
My hope is in you all day long.

Prayer of Thanksgiving

God of mercy, we acknowledge this midday pause of refreshment as one of your many generous gifts. Look kindly upon our work this day; may it be made perfect in your time. May our purpose and prayers be pleasing to you. This we ask through Christ our Lord. Amen.

Scripture Reading

Silence

Prayers of the People

The Lord's Prayer (ecumenical text)
Our Father in heaven,
hallowed be your name,
your kingdom come,
your will be done,
on earth as in heaven.

Give us today our daily bread.
Forgive us our sins as we forgive
   those who sin against us.
Save us from the time of trial,
   and deliver us from evil.
For the kingdom, the power, and the glory
   are yours, now and forever. Amen.

Blessing

Strong is the love embracing us, faithful the Lord from morning to night.

Truly my soul finds rest in God;
   my salvation comes from God.
                    —Psalm 62:1

Gathering and Silence

Call to Praise and Prayer

From the rising of the sun to its setting,
let the name of the LORD be praised.

Psalm 134

Bless the LORD,
      all who serve in God's house,
      who stand watch
      throughout the night.

Lift up your hands
      in the holy place
      and bless the LORD.

And may God,
the maker of earth and sky,
bless you from Zion.

Prayer of Thanksgiving

Sovereign God, you have been our help during
the day, and you promise to be with us at night.
Receive this prayer as a sign of our trust in you.
Save us from all evil, keep us from all harm, and

guide us in your way. We belong to you, Lord. Protect us by the power of your name. In Jesus Christ we pray. Amen.

Scripture Reading

Silence

Prayers of the People

The Lord's Prayer (ecumenical text)
> Our Father in heaven,
>> hallowed be your name,
>> your kingdom come,
>> your will be done,
>> on earth as in heaven.
> Give us today our daily bread.
> Forgive us our sins as we forgive
>> those who sin against us.
> Save us from the time of trial,
>> and deliver us from evil.
> For the kingdom, the power, and the glory
>> are yours, now and forever. Amen.

Blessing

> May your unfailing love rest upon us, O LORD,
> even as we hope in you.

This Guide to Daily Prayer was compiled from scripture and other resources by Rueben P. Job and then adapted by the Pathways Center for Spiritual Leadership while under the direction of Marjorie J. Thompson.

CPSIA information can be obtained
at www.ICGtesting.com
Printed in the USA
BVHW060731300722
643243BV00003BA/3